Law and Religion in a Global Context

Volume 1

Series editor

Frank S. Ravitch, USA

Law and Religion in a Global Context will focus on law and religion issues from a global perspective at a time when that field is of increasing importance and relevance around the world. Designed to be broad, the scope allows for books on the relationship between religion and government as well as on religious law. Focus will be placed on comparative law issues, but also on issues within single countries. Representative areas of focus will be:

- the relationship between government and religion ranging from *laïcité* to theocracy
- religious freedom in pluralistic societies
- the relationship between religious freedom and other freedoms such as freedom of speech and sexual freedom
- regulation of religion by government
- original contributions on religious law

The series seeks to highlight up and coming voices in the field alongside those of established scholars. We encourage scholars from a wide range of geographic perspectives to apply. Purely doctrinal analysis of law and religion is not preferred. Nor is analysis of religious law issues without any original contribution or insights. The only exception to this rule might be books on legal doctrine from a region that has been under analyzed in English language literature.

More information about this series at http://www.springer.com/series/15625

Jessica Giles · Andrea Pin
Frank S. Ravitch
Editors

Law, Religion and Tradition

Springer

Editors
Jessica Giles
Law School
The Open University
Milton Keynes, UK

Frank S. Ravitch
Michigan State University College of Law
East Lansing, MI, USA

Andrea Pin
Department of Public, International
and Community Law
University of Padova (UNIPD)
Padua, Italy

Law and Religion in a Global Context
ISBN 978-3-030-07242-1 ISBN 978-3-319-96749-3 (eBook)
https://doi.org/10.1007/978-3-319-96749-3

This Springer imprint is published by the registered company Springer Nature Switzerland AG
The registered company address is: Gewerbestrasse 11, 6330 Cham, Switzerland

To the much-loved next generation to whom I entrust my cherished traditions: Maria, James, Ellen, Matthew, Greta, Emile and Alex

Jessica Giles

Thanks to the planters, to the waterers, and to the one who has given growth to my life

Andrea Pin

To Chika, Elysha, Ariana, Carl and Arline, and to Alan Silverstein and the late Gershon Schwartz who made sure that I understood the importance of tradition in both connecting to the past and adapting to the future

Frank S. Ravitch

Foreword

Europe has traditionally been labelled as the "old continent" and the birthplace of many ideas and concepts that have shaped history. It is, however, to America that European scholars active in the field of law and religion have needed to travel, in particular, to engage in discourse by participating in the American Academy of Religion annual conferences. For some time, a similar European platform was missing. In December 2016, a new network and system of academic cooperation was created—the European Academy of Religion (EuARe). As a direct participant at the EuARe *ex nihilo* conference in 2017, I was able to contribute and learn at this gathering of hundreds of representatives of universities, faculties, journals and individual scholars from Europe and beyond. This took place in the oldest European and Italian University of Bologna. I am convinced that the EuARe presents promising and important potential for scientific research and relevant knowledge on different aspects of contemporary religions and their impact on history, law and society. Meetings of the EuARe are now organized annually, and academic exchanges occur throughout the year.

This book belongs to the first fruits of the initial EuARe conference. It aims to show the dynamics, contradictions and relations in the current law and religion agenda. Besides the issues connected with religious freedom, the role of the secular state, gender and equality, judicial cases and history, we can find interesting argumentation on tradition and traditionalism to counteract the plentiful existing discourse on secularism.

Freedom of religion or belief is not a minor issue. In and of itself important, it also represents freedom of thought and conscience. It is an essential value, expansive universal right and civilizing principle. Therefore, we need to seek to find ways to strengthen the implementation and arguments for its defence and promotion. This book *Law, Religion and Tradition* edited by Jessica Giles, Frank Ravitch and Andrea Pin is of great value for scholars, students and engaged citizens in this constructive quest and noble effort.

Brussels
July 2018

Ján Figel'
Special Envoy for Promotion Freedom of Religion or Belief outside the European Union
European Commission

Acknowledgements

We are most grateful to colleagues who joined us at the European Academy of Religion ex nihilo conference in Bologna in June 2017. They contributed to the reflections on the topic of tradition. They were Professor Javier Martinez-Torron, Professor Mark Hill, Associate Professor Gila Stopler and Pasquale Annicchino. Reflecting on tradition has engaged some of us on a personal journey; indeed it seems impossible to debate the topic without personal reflection on the influence of tradition on our own lives. For others, it has opened up new and exciting vistas of interdisciplinary study and instilled in us a hope for the resolution of some apparently intransigent problems either at a national or international level. We are all deeply grateful to the many whom we have encountered who have cherished freedom and tradition so much that they have not given away one for the other. We would like to dedicate this book to our children and the younger generations whom we hope will see in us the ability to cherish both freedom and tradition and be encouraged to take the tradition we hand on to them.

Introduction

The relationship between law and religion has rarely been smooth or easy. This is no secret. At least since the time when Peter and the Apostles made the bold affirmation, “We must obey God rather than men”, the conflicts between the two have never left us.

The contemporary perception of the very nature and structure of both law and religion seems to be the seedbed for such conflicts. Law can be seen as a tool to protect human rights and develop a better society, to enable society to flourish while freeing it from long-standing prejudices and false perceptions about human beings, the society they live within, and the political orders that they inhabit. The values that law often channels are progressive, anti-hierarchical, equalitarian and evolutionary—if not revolutionary. Part of their political attractiveness and intrinsic worthiness consists in their capacity to innovate the social order. In an age of acceleration,[1] law challenges customs; it questions social assumptions; it redirects common sense.

There is little question that such a picture of law and contemporary legal philosophy hardly squares with religion. Religions are multi-generational endeavours. They embrace past, present and future, under some axiomatic assumptions. Their beliefs extend through time. Their opinions bind generations. There is a sense of time consistency that runs against the value of rupture that law appears to cherish instead. Religions want the future to reflect the past while law, according to the picture painted above, aims to break away from it. Religious structures are often hierarchical. They usually consist in multi-layered bodies, each of which has its own prerogatives, rights, and obligations. That there may sometimes be a conflict between law and religion comes as little or no surprise.

But this description captures only a portion of the whole picture. An important part of the conflict might be born out of the contemporary legal mindset, rather than out of the real structure and mechanisms that characterize religions. The narrative

[1] Borrowing from the title of Prandini (2013) 731.

that is associated with contemporary *nomos*[2] may emphasize the challenges that religion poses to legal values, even if religions do not necessarily understand themselves this way. If law is synonymous with progress, development, (r)evolution, equality, freedom and individual autonomy, *then* religion easily appears to associate with inertia, stability, hierarchy, inequality and submission. In other words, since contemporary mentality conceives law this way, it can feed a perception of religion that is distant from the self-perception of believers or of religious thinking altogether.

In the average scenario, the tension between law and religion inevitably deflagrates for at least two reasons. On one hand, religion and law can conflict from a political point of view. Religions normally aim to embrace the whole spectrum of human activities. They often wish to affect also how people live together, including secular law. Through processes of secularization, religions intentionally withdraw from, or were chased out of, the political and legal sphere. But, even where religions actually relinquished the legal terrain to give way to secular political institutions, they can still affect how law-makers—be they autocrats or democratically elected bodies—think and shape secular laws. Religion can still play a political role in a secular state through the democratic process. This is where secularization has ramified at least into two: some countries have allowed religions to remain public moral players, whereas others have challenged their role in the name of secularism, or of the secularization of public morality.[3]

On the other hand, conflicts between religion and law can translate into specific legal or judicial controversies. Religious freedom claims and modern individual freedom claims are connected in contemporary societies, especially in the West. Whether reproductive rights, marriage rights, assisted suicide, education or other claims are called into question, it is very likely that their enjoyment at some point will clash with religious freedom rights.

The primary focus of this book is not how to solve the conflicts between law and religions. As I explained at the beginning of this introduction, such conflicts never leave us: they are here to stay. And yet, there seems to be room to better understand their deep connections on a global scale. Through its various contributions, this volume identifies and explores one of the reasons for which the tension between religion and law seem to be so difficult to handle. By using some national experiments and reflecting on the overarching theories on religion, history and law, this book takes on a special angle to explore the relationship between law and religion.

The belief that underpins this whole book is that law and religion have at least one value in common that could make each understand the other more than they normally do. That is tradition. As a concept, both law and religion address and cherish tradition. Tradition can be many things. It can express the ambition that a value, a structure or an intellectual framework may last over time, instead of fading away. It can identify the mechanisms through which a political or legal system—be

[2]To some extent, there seems to be a reversal of the process that develops the *nomos* out of social narratives that include religions of the kind that is described in Cover (1983–1984) 5.

[3]The literature in this field is legion. However, this topic is dealt with in depth by Perry (2010).

it religious or secular—preserves itself or evolves through time. It can single out the core values of an intellectual journey, or the binding force that it casts on future generations.

Recovering the role of tradition is not easy in a time that seems to undervalue the role of the past in the name of human reason. In Anthony Kronman's words, "Given the immense prestige that reason now enjoys in every department of political life and the extent to which a philosophical point of view incapable of seeing any intrinsic moral meaning in the distinction between past and present has penetrated our political attitudes generally, it is hardly to be expected that modern philosophers of law would in their accounts of precedent endorse the traditionalist idea that the past possesses an authority of its own".[4]

In contrast, this work explores the assumption that law and religion are hardly conceivable without a sensible appreciation of tradition, and they are surely irreconcilable without it (this latter observation permeates Zachary Calo's as well as Giada Ragone and Luca Vanoni's chapters). Recovering tradition may mean recovering some of the reasons for which religious people fiercely resist what they perceive to be an external pressure to change; but it may also convey the reasons for which any right's claim is such a powerful call to postmodern human beings for whom the language of rights is their mother tongue (as Frank Ravitch shows in his chapter). It may help explain why some areas of the world perceive the circulation of rights and freedoms as a new form of cultural and legal colonization, as well as shedding light on the public morality of an adult society (Muhammad Ahsan Qureshi and Marziyeh Bakhshizadeh's pieces are both illuminating in this respect). The contrary may also hold true. Reluctance in embracing new rights can find an easy justification in tradition. Resistance to demands of freedom may find a useful hideout in tradition (as Hugh McFaul illustrates in his piece). Finally, neither law nor religion can exist without some sense of stability and certainty, which the concept of tradition certainly embeds (Ryszard Bobrowicz's chapter is instructive also in this respect). In a nutshell, the concept of tradition is a rich well, which conceals as well as reveals the value of law and religion in contemporary societies (as Jessica Giles demonstrates).

A short story is worth telling because it demonstrates the importance of the topic of tradition to the scholarly debate about law and religion. Near the end of the Vatican II, the Catholic Church's Fathers drafted the Declaration *Dignitatis Humanae*, making bold affirmations about the role, importance and scope of religious freedom for the Church. They embarked on a daring process of change. They struggled among themselves and fought not just to affirm and defend religious freedom, but even to explain why and how they were innovating the Catholic doctrine of freedom. Within the circles that endorsed this change, some stressed the continuity between *Dignitatis Humanae* and the Church's previous doctrines on the same subject. Others emphasized that the Declaration was a sea change, which no one could underplay by considering it a small adjustment. In other words, even the Church Fathers who agreed upon religious freedom disagreed on how to square it

[4] Kronman (1990) 1046.

with the tradition of the Church. Thus, after considering the possibility of reconciling *Dignitatis Humanae* with the prior Catholic doctrine on religious freedom through a detailed explanation, they surrendered and decided that this task would fall on the shoulders of theologians and historians.[5]

This short story does not only elucidate why tradition is important and why it is up to scholars to tackle it. It also teaches that traditions are not a monolithic component of the systems they have contributed in engineering, in terms of methodology as well as content. With *Dignitatis Humanae*, the Vatican II adopted a new doctrine of religious freedom, although it was unclear how it connected with the pre-existing doctrine.

Similarly, this book cannot provide the ultimate answer on the proper understanding of tradition and of its role in shaping both religion and law. If there was a disagreement among the Catholic Church's Fathers, there will certainly be disagreement among the scholars of different disciplines, proveniences and faiths, who have contributed to this volume. But giving voice to as many readings of tradition as possible means making justice of the human striving to explain why something is so dear and so intimately connected with one's life, past and belief.

This book concedes that there is a clear tension between law and religion, but it adds that much of the conceptual clash between the two stems from an intellectual framework that understands two social phenomena as inherently conflictual, while forgetting that they have deep common roots. It is hard to find a more provocative, yet illuminating, observation about the importance of tradition for any society than in an ironic passage from the Great English thinker Gilbert Keith Chesterton. In a time of widespread belief in modernity and in its success, he tellingly defended tradition by making it the "democracy of the dead:"

> I have never been able to understand where people got the idea that democracy was in some way opposed to tradition. It is obvious that tradition is only democracy extended through time. It is trusting to a consensus of common human voices rather than to some isolated or arbitrary record. The man who quotes some German historian against the tradition of the Catholic Church, for instance, is strictly appealing to aristocracy. He is appealing to the superiority of one expert against the awful authority of a mob. It is quite easy to see why a legend is treated, and ought to be treated, more respectfully than a book of history. The legend is generally made by the majority of people in the village, who are sane. The book is generally written by the one man in the village who is mad. Those who urge against tradition that men in the past were ignorant may go and urge it at the Carlton Club, along with the statement that voters in the slums are ignorant. If we attach great importance to the opinion of ordinary men in great unanimity when we are dealing with daily matters, there is no reason why we should disregard it when we are dealing with history or fable. Tradition may be defined as an extension of the franchise. Tradition means giving votes to the most obscure of all classes, our ancestors. It is the democracy of the dead. Tradition refuses to submit to the small and arrogant oligarchy of those who merely happen to be walking about. All democrats object to men being disqualified by the accident of birth; tradition objects to their being disqualified by the accident of death. Democracy tells us not to neglect a good man's opinion, even if he is our groom; tradition asks us not to neglect a good man's opinion, even if he is our father. I, at any rate, cannot separate the two ideas of

[5] See Hellin (2008).

> democracy and tradition; it seems evident to me that they are the same idea. We will have the dead at our councils. The ancient Greeks voted by stones; these shall vote by tombstones. It is all quite regular and official, for most tombstones, like most ballot papers, are marked with a cross.[6]

Reframing the relationship between law and religion in the light of tradition does not simply resurrect the role of tradition in legal, political and moral matters. It helps re-assessing the role of law and religion for human societies, while emphasizing the importance of mutual practical accommodation between contemporary needs and traditional practices, customs and beliefs. Tradition is not the mere "social glue"[7] with which both are imbued; tradition embeds the human need to transform cultural, social and political debates into a cross-generational conversation,[8] which tests the past instead of either ignoring or worshipping it.

Padua, Italy Andrea Pin

References

Chesterton GK (2009) Orthodoxy. Moody Publishers, Chicago
Cover RM (1983–1984) The Supreme Court, 1982 Term—Foreword: Narrative and Nomos, Harv L Rev 97(5)
Hellin F (2008) Declaratio de libertate religiosae Dignitatis humanae, EDUSC, Rome
Kronman AT (1990) Precedent and tradition. Yale L J 99:1029
Pelikan J (1984) The vindication of tradition, Yale University Press, New Haven-London
Perry MJ (2010) The political morality of liberal democracy. Cambridge University Press, New York
Prandini R (2013) The future of societal constitutionalism in the age of acceleration. Ind J Global Legal Stud 20:731

[6]Chesterton (2009) 74.
[7]Pelikan (1984) 6.
[8]Id. 81.

Contents

From the Secularisation Theory to the Pluralistic Approach: Reconciling Religious Traditions and Modernity in Italian Case-Law

Luca Pietro Vanoni and Giada Ragone

Abstract One of the fields where the clash between the ambition toward secularism and the need to enhance cultural traditions mostly emerges is the debate on the presence of religions in the pluralist public space. From a Constitutional point of view, Courts and judges are often asked to solve conflicts involving religious claims, trying to maintain simultaneously respect for religious identities, religious freedom and the principle of equality of every belief before the state. The difficulty of this task arises clearly within the extensive case law on religious symbols and ceremonial prayers in Europe, but also in the USA. In order to address this challenge, constitutional judges often try to extract from a certain definition of "secular state" a particular legal standard and use it as the legal tool useful to reconcile, once and for all, all the cases concerning religions in public spaces. In a nutshell, neutrality as a legal standard implies two main goals: strict and strong separation between state and church; and freedom from religion (instead of freedom of religions). This idea of neutrality has received many criticisms: as some political thinkers pointed out, neutrality is incoherent because any determinate politics must necessarily rely upon and promote some contestable scheme of values. Another legal standard is often used by judges: the so-called "historical argument". It comes from a different conception of the secular state, and it is raised up in opposition to a strong idea of assertive secularism and strict neutrality. According to this argument, judges must take into account the cultural and religious traditions of their systems as far as they are strongly rooted in the institutional (or even constitutional) history of their Nations. The historical argument has the merit of reconciling the secular state with its cultural heritage. Nonetheless, the use of the historical argument alone is both weak and formalistic:

Albeit the unitary conception of the Chapter, Luca Pietro Vanoni drafted sections 1, 2, 3 and 4; Giada Ragone drafted sections 5 and 6 (including paragraphs 6.1, 6.2, 6.3). Section VII was drafted together.

L. P. Vanoni (✉) · G. Ragone
Department of Italian and Supranational Public Law, University of Milan, Milan, Italy
e-mail: luca.vanoni@unimi.it

G. Ragone
e-mail: giada.ragone@unimi.it

J. Giles et al. (eds.), *Law, Religion and Tradition*, Law and Religion in a Global Context 1, https://doi.org/10.1007/978-3-319-96749-3_1

above all, practical jurists cannot solve hard conflicts just resorting to "what has always been done". After having shown why the two legal standards mostly used by courts are not convincing enough, our chapter points to a third way to realize the ambition toward a secular state, on the one hand, and to enhance religious traditions according to their true meanings, on the other. This third solution is based on three main premises: (a) the idea of finding a unique abstract legal standard, capable of resolving every case, is a utopia; (b) the place of religion in the public space does not involve a binary relation (state vs. church), but rather it is a complex triangular relational principle (that involves state, religion, and civil society); (c) the goal of the courts is not to enforce a certain idea of the secular state or *laicità*, but to facilitate pluralism and religious peace. In the final part of the chapter we try to verify, within the most recent Italian case law on religious rituals in State schools (i.e. pastoral visitations and bishops' benedictions), whether and when this third approach—which considers *laicità* a tool, not a goal—has succeeded.

1 Religious Traditions and the Challenge of the Secular Principle

One of the most complex challenges of modern constitutional democracies concerns the relationship between cultural and legal traditions and the moral and political duty to be "secular". The secular, indeed, "has become a central modern category—theological/philosophical, legal-political, and cultural-anthropological—to construct, codify, grasp, and experience a realm or reality differentiated from 'the religious'".[1] As Charles Taylor pointed out, "it is generally agreed that modern democracies have to be 'secular'. There is perhaps a problem, a certain ethnocentricity, involved in this term. But even in the Western context the term is not limpid and may in fact be misleading. What in fact does it mean?"[2] According to Taylor, a secular regime involves a certain separation between state and church, but also "more than this"; especially in our pluralistic postmodern societies, the secular principle "requires that there be some kind of neutrality, or 'principled distance', to use Rajeev Bhargava's term".[3] But, again, "neutrality" and "principled distance" are very blurred terms, and there is not a strong consensus on what they really mean.

As is well-known, the separation between state and church or between politics and religions is not a novel issue, and "the interaction between the state and religious institutions goes back to the emergence of the state as a distinct legal or constitutional construct".[4] For that reason (and many others), the issues concerning the secular principle have evolved in Western democracies in different forms and legal models, strictly related to the historical, economic, social, religious and moral developments

[1] Casanova (2009), p. 1049.
[2] See Taylor (2010), p. 23.
[3] Ibid.
[4] Venter (2015), p. 9.

of every country and society. We do not want here to explore the legal, cultural, and historical differences in the meaning of the secular principle in Western countries.[5] Nonetheless, we can explicate two general and very broad approaches to the term "secular" that are useful to explain the tricky relationship between religious tradition and secular law in our modern (and post-secular) age.

Some think that the term "secular" implies a strong impenetrable separation between politics and religion, and an absolute strict neutrality of the public space (this is the secularist position). The core of this theory is that religion must be confined to the private sphere because it "is either an irrational force or a non-rational form of discourse that should be banished from the democratic public sphere".[6] This conception of secularism rose from the historical clash between the absolute states of the 16th century and the rise of the Enlightenment's political thought, and from the idea that the traditional role of religion in shaping the cultural tradition of the European societies was "a leftover of the past defeated by the Reason of the West" and "an ancient idea that has to be relegated in the pre-legal, if not in the personal conscience".[7] Starting from this secularist approach, secularization produces the following paradox: "in the name of freedom, individual autonomy, tolerance, and cultural pluralism, religious people—Christian, Jewish, and Muslims—are being asked to keep their religious belief, identities, and norms 'private' so they do not disturb the project of modern, secular, enlightened Europe".[8]

From a constitutional point of view, the clearest example of this secularist approach is the French principle of *läicité*, established by the *Loi concernant la séparation des Églises et de l'État* in 1905 and later codified in art. 2 of the French Constitution. According to this principle, government must be neutral towards religions and has the duty to actively remove every religious reference, connection, or symbol from the public space. In its most extreme applications, it undertakes a certain political idea of modern democracies that directly clashes with the religious freedom of believers. As Flores D'arcais contended after the Charlie Hebdo terrorist attack in Paris, "religion is compatible with democracy only if it accepts the exile of God from citizen's public field, and only if it's willing to acknowledge the first commandment of the Republican Sovereignty: Thou shalt not take the name of the Lord thy God in public spaces".[9]

[5]See Taylor (2009), p. 1147: "the history of this term 'secular' in the West is complex and ambiguous. It starts off as a term in a dyad, which distinguishes two dimensions of existence, identifying them by the kind of time essential to each. But then building on the clear immanent/transcendent distinction, it mutates into a term in another dyad, where 'secular' refers to what pertains to a self-sufficient immanent sphere, and its contrasting term (often identified as 'religious') relates to the transcendent realm. This can then undergo a further mutation, via a denial of this transcendent level, into a dyad in which one term refers to the real (the secular), and the other to what is merely invented (the religious); or where 'secular' refers to the institutions we really require to live in 'this world,' and 'religious' or 'ecclesial' to optional extras that often disturb the course of this-worldly life".

[6]Casanova (2009), p. 1052.

[7]Zagrebelsky (2011), p. 18.

[8]Casanova (2006), pp. 66–67.

[9]Flores D'Arcais (2015).

This idea of secularism has a strong and oppositive impact on cultural heritage and traditions, as clearly shown several years ago by the European battle for the inclusion of a reference to Europe's Judeo-Christian roots in the European Constitution.[10] In sum, especially in Europe, "any public recognition of the Christian heritage or of the living religious traditions of contemporary Europeans would make liberal political coexistence and pluralist toleration in a united Europe nearly impossible" because some "dominant discourse in Europe prefers to hold on to the idea of single secular modernity, emerging out of the Enlightenment".[11]

The secularist approach of the privatization of religion was used for several years to explain modernity. But it is probably not useful anymore to understand the very complexity of our postmodern (and post-secular) societies. As Peter Berger pointed out, "the theory that modernity brings about a decline of religion (…) has to be discarded" for two main reasons. First "most of the sociologists of religion now agree that this theory has been empirically shown to be false". Second, the theory "fails spectacularly in explaining the difference between the United States and the Europe".[12]

The first reason is strictly related to the so-called *Revanche de Dieu*,[13] and with the phenomenon of the "deprivatization" of religions; as clearly shown by the studies of Josè Casanova, religious traditions all over the world are refusing to accept the marginal and privatized role that some theories of secularization have reserved to them.[14] The second reason provides a new perspective into the inquiry of the proper meaning of the secular principle, that, according to Peter Berger, needs to be investigated in light of US secularization. The United States, indeed, embraces a particular conception of the secular state that, at the same time, strongly recognizes the religious and transcendental heritages of the nation (expressed by the famous motto "one Nation under God") and a concrete "wall of separation between church and state", established by the First Amendment of the Constitution.[15] In this light, the

---

[10]See Weiler (2007), pp. 143–150.

[11]Casanova (2006), p. 66.

[12]Berger et al. (2008), p. 10.

[13]Title of a famous book of Kepel (1991).

[14]Casanova (2000).

[15]The history of the American religious clauses is a very complex one. During at least the last seventy years, Supreme Justices endorse a lot of different meaning of these clauses and developed at least three separate tests for determining whether a law violates either clauses. The First Amendment of US Constitution enact the separation between state and church, and this provision was often linked to the Jefferson's metaphor of the "wall of separation". The metaphor was used by Justice Black in the seminal decision *Everson v. Board of Education* (1947), stating that "in the words of Thomas Jefferson, the [First Amendment] clause against the establishment of religion by law was intended to erect 'a wall of separation between church and state' (…). That wall must be kept high and impregnable. We could not approve the slighted breach". Beside the fact that Jefferson's phrase slightly differs in significant respect from the Constitutional clause (see Dreisbach 2002) it "has profoundly influenced church-state law, policy, and discourse" (ibid. p. 3) and, more important, "the judiciary has embraced the metaphor, adopting it not only as an organizing theme of church-state analysis, but also as a virtual rule of constitutional law" (see Whaley and Dreisbach 1999), p. 628. Nonetheless, this metaphor was questioned over the years by scholars and Justices: in 1971 Justice

First Amendment paradoxically served to reinforce a strong link between religion and the nation; as Dwight D. Eisenhower said: "Our Government makes no sense unless it is founded on a deeply held religious belief—and I don't care what it is!".[16]

This second approach to the secular principle is perhaps useful to reconcile the clash between tradition and modernity in the secularization process. This is particularly important from a political point of view because, as Charles Taylor pointed out, "for people to act together, to deliberate in order to form a common will on which they will act, requires a high degree of common commitment, a sense of common identification. A society of this kind presupposes trust, the basic trust that members and constituent groups have to have, the confidence that they are really part of the process, that they will be listened to and their views taken account of by the others. Without this mutual commitment, this trust will be fatally eroded".[17]

But reconciling tradition with modernity is also important from a constitutional point of view: as Mary Ann Glendon pointed out, "after all rights emerge from cultures; rights cannot be sustained without cultural underpinnings; and rights, to be effective, must become part of each people's way of life".[18] Starting from this perspective, according to Andrea Pin, "national religious and cultural traditions have recently come to play a new role in shaping the contemporary identity of the states: they have been considered in their connections with modern human rights, rather than as opposed to them".[19]

Burger suggested that the line of separation "far from being a wall is a blurred, indistinct and variable barrier depending on the circumstances of a particular relationship". See *Lemon v. Kurtzman*, 403 U.S. 614 (1971). Later on, Chief Justice Rehnquist pointed out in *Wallace v. Jaffree*, 472 U.S. 38, 107 (1985) that «[it] is a metaphor based on bad history, a metaphor which has proved useless as a guide to judging. It should be frankly and explicitly abandoned». In sum, particularly starting from the eighties, the *Everson*'s wall theme has failing to provide clear solutions to the difficult questions facing the Court, and some commentators started arguing that the wall was eroded by some opinions of the US Supreme court, and "it came tumbling down". See Levinson (1984), p. 707. To conclude, "an examination of Jefferson's celebrated wall, constructed two centuries ago, casts light not only on the past, but also on the future place of religion in American public life. Today, the Supreme Court's conception of that wall stands as a defining image of the prudential and constitutional role of religion in the public arena. Serious consideration must be given to whether that wall accurately represents constitutional principles and usefully contributes to American democracy and to a civil society". See Dreisbach (2006) available at https://www.heritage.org/political-process/report/the-mythical-wall-separation-how-misused-metaphor-changed-church-state-law.

[16]See Berger et al. (2008), pp. 42–43.

[17]Taylor (2010), p. 30.

[18]Glendon (2008), p. 926.

[19]Pin (2014b), p. 432.

2 The Constitutional Clash Between Secularism and Traditions: The Principle of Neutrality

One of the fields where the clash between the ambition toward secularism and the need to enhance cultural traditions mostly emerge is the debate on the presence of religions in the public space. Courts and judges are often asked to solve conflicts involving religious claims, trying to maintain respect for religious identities, religious freedom and the principle of equality of every belief before the state simultaneously. The difficulty of this task arises clearly within the extensive case law on religious symbols and ceremonial prayers, both in Europe and in the USA.[20] This is one of the biggest challenges that the constitutional courts have to address in our days: as Justice Rehnquist pointed out, all Establishment Clause challenges

> present us with the difficulty of respecting both faces. Our institutions presuppose a Supreme Being, yet these institutions must not press religious observances upon their citizens. One face looks to the past in acknowledgment of our Nation's heritage, while the other looks to the present in demanding a separation between church and state. Reconciling these two faces requires that we neither abdicate our responsibility to maintain a division between church and state nor evince a hostility to religion by disabling the government from in some ways recognizing our religious heritage.[21]

In order to address this challenge, constitutional judges often try to extract from a certain definition of "secular state" a particular legal standard and use it as the legal tool useful to reconcile, once and for all, all the cases concerning religions in public spaces. The most-used legal standard is the so-called principle of "strict neutrality", which finds varied implementations. As will be discussed later in the paper, there are of course different conceptions of "neutrality".[22] Anyway, the core of this legal standard comes from Rawls' definition of neutrality: "as a practical political matter no general moral conception can provide a public recognized basis for a conception of justice in the modern democratic state".[23] Starting from this perspective, neutrality as a legal standard implies two main goals: strict and strong separation between state and church; and freedom *from* religion (instead of freedom *of* religions).

The neutrality principle has been used by constitutional judges in both the United States and Europe. In America, the US Supreme Court first referred to this principle in the seminal case *Everson v. Board of education* stating that:

[20] For an analysis of ECHR and US jurisprudence in cases concerning religious symbols, see Tega (2008), Calo (2014).

[21] See Van Orden v. Perry 545 U.S. 677 (2005) (Chief Justice Rehnquist concurring opinion).

[22] The neutrality principle was highly discussed and debated in America such as in European scholarships. As will be discussed later in this paper, it embraced different meaning not only in different jurisdictions, but also in the same US Supreme Court and ECtHR case law. For an overview about the polymeric meaning of neutrality, see (among others) Smith (2014), Ravitch (2007).

[23] Rawls (1985), p. 205. The philosophical idea of neutrality is one of the most studied principles of our time. See (for example) Rawls (1971), Nozick (1974), Ackerman (1980), Dworkin (1985), Larmore (1987).

> [the First] Amendment requires the state to be a *neutral* in its relations with groups of religious believers and nonbelievers; it does not require the state to be their adversary. State power is no more to be used so as to handicap religions than it is to favor them.[24]

According to Ledewitz, this statement summarized the "promise of neutrality"[25] that—at least for some years—oriented the US Supreme Court's decisions on the First Amendment. In order to keep this promise, Supreme Court justices elaborated some judicial tests (and particularly the *Lemon test*) that incorporate the duty of the State to ensure a position of neutrality in the relationship between man and religion.[26] But, as we will see, none of these tests really helped the justices to keep the neutrality promise they made.

Neutrality also has been a relevant principle in the ECtHR's decisions. Despite the fact that art. 9 of the Convention does not mention it, European judges have used neutrality "as a hermeneutical device to enforce religious freedom although the Convention doesn't command that the states be neutral in order to protect religious freedom".[27] European judges started using neutrality as a principle stemming from the general theory of institutional separation between state and churches, and from the State's lack of jurisdiction on the Churches' affairs and doctrines.[28] But neutrality rapidly spread across ECtHR jurisprudence, and became a relevant legal tool also in cases concerning the relationship between democracy and religions,[29] or the display of religious symbols and veils in the public space. Notably in case-law concerning religious displays, European judges mainly apply the principle of neutrality to legitimate state restrictions on religious practices established by countries such as France and Turkey in which the secularist approach was (and still is) a hallmark of their constitutional framework. This brings some confusion in the meaning of the term "neutrality" (sometimes used by judges as synonymous with "secularism"): as pointed out by Martinez Torron, "justifying the French and Turkish restriction to religious display, ECtHR seems to embrace a *laique* policy that considered less problematic a public space" in which "religions are absent or, at least, invisible".[30]

The idea of neutrality has received much criticism from a theoretical and philosophical point of view. As some political thinkers pointed out, neutrality is "incoherent because any determinate politics must necessarily rely upon and promote some contestable scheme of values".[31] Despite the indisputable charm of the terminology, "the quest of neutrality is an attempt to grasp an illusion" because "theories of religious freedom are always offered from the viewpoint of one of the competing

---

[24]Everson v. Board of Education, 330 U.S. 18 (1947).

[25]Ledewitz (2011), p. 39.

[26]See e.g. *Abington School District v. Schempp*, 374 U.S. 217 (1963): "in the relationship between man and religion, the State is firmly committed to a position of neutrality".

[27]Pin (2014a), p. 605.

[28]See, for example, *Hasan e Chaush v. Bulgaria Eur. Ct. H.R. 78 (2000).*

[29]See *Refah Partisi v. Turkey, Eur. Ct. H.R. (2003).*

[30]Martinez-Torron (2012), p. 81.

[31]See, e.g., Galston (1991), pp. 92–94.

positions that generate the need for such theory; there is no neutral vantage point that can permit the theorist or judge to transcend these competing points".[32]

But the idea of neutrality was also inconsistent from a constitutional point of view.[33] In the USA as in Europe, indeed, the enforcement of neutrality as a judicial tool was not helpful in solving the conflicts caused by the separation between state and church and did not really implement religious freedom on either continent for two main reasons. First, it brings confusion into the interpretation of constitutional religion clauses. Second, it does not address the challenge of reconnecting cultural tradition within modern secular democracies.

First, neutrality as a legal standard has multiple meanings not only in different jurisdictions, but even within the same court's case law. In order to better understand the judicial use of neutrality in America, some scholars divide formal neutrality from substantive neutrality.[34] According to Movsesian, the US Supreme Court addressed at least three different conceptions of neutrality that promote different values and were used by judges to solve the cases in disparate ways.[35] But despite the theories or classifications of the different meanings of neutrality addressed by judges, the US Supreme Court never clarified the proper meaning of this principle, and "in several cases justices in the majority and dissenting opinions claimed to be relying on the same or similar principle of neutrality, yet they reached the opposite conclusions".[36] This is probably why even the most famous test created by the Court in order to solve all the Establishment Clause cases (the *Lemon* test) does not really achieve its goal, and quickly became "so elastic in its application that it means everything and nothing".[37] And, from a general point of view, it explains the failure of the "neutrality promises" made by *Everson*: as Justice Breyer summarized, indeed:

> Where the Establishment Clause is at issue, tests designed to measure 'neutrality' alone are insufficient, both because it is sometimes difficult to determine when a legal rule is 'neutral,' and because [as Justices Goldberg and Harlan pointed out] 'untutored devotion to the concept of neutrality can lead to invocation or approval of results which partake not simply of that

---

[32] Smith (1995), pp. 96–97.

[33] The incoherence of neutrality was raised also from a constitutional point of view. See Koppelman (2004), pp. 635–636: "The charge of incoherence was raised against the idea of neutrality in the Supreme Court's religion jurisprudence. This objection focused on a deep tension in the Court's position, between the idea that religious conscientious objectors ought to be accommodated and the idea that government should be neutral between religion and nonreligion." See also Ravitch (2007).

[34] See e.g. Laycock (1990), pp. 993–1005.

[35] As clearly shown by Movsesian (2013b), p. 510 ff.

[36] Ravitch (2007), p. 13.

[37] Laycock (1986), p. 450. As sarcastically pointed out by Justice Scalia's concurring opinion in *Lamb's Chapel v. Ctr. Moriches Union Free Sch. Dist.*, 508 U.S. (1993) "like some ghoul in a late-night horror movie that repeatedly sits up in its grave and shuffles abroad after being repeatedly killed and buried, Lemon stalks our Establishment Clause jurisprudence once again, frightening the little children and school attorneys of Center Moriches Union Free School District (…) The secret of the Lemon test's survival, I think, is that it is so easy to kill. It is there to scare us (and our audience) when we wish it to do so, but we can command it to return to the tomb at will. (…) Such a docile and useful monster is worth keeping around, at least in a somnolent state; one never knows when one might need him".

> noninterference and noninvolvement with the religious which the Constitution commands, but of a brooding and pervasive devotion to the secular and a passive, or even active, hostility to the religious.' *Schempp*, 374 U.S., at 306 (concurring opinion).[38]

Similarly, the puzzled meaning of neutrality created even more confusion in ECtHR case law. This is unsurprising because the European framework is much more fragmented than the American one, and it is composed of the very variegated cultural and legal traditions of the Member States. This is especially true in the law and religion field: even if they share the very broad goal of religious freedom, the European countries embrace very different conceptions of secularism, secularity or *laïcité* that strongly impact the constitutional models adopted by each country. On one hand, the European Convention was born to protect "the marvelous richness of diversity"[39] of the Member States enforcing the subsidiarity principle; on the other hand, art. 9 claims to protect pluralism in all the continent. These two interests (pluralism and subsidiarity) sometimes clashed "when the handling of religious matters in certain member state impedes the flourishing of pluralism".[40] The mixed signals communicated to Member States on the interpretation of art. 9 was well-captured by an article published by the *Economist* in 2005:

> A Danish supermarket fired a cashier for wearing the headscarf on the grounds that in might get stuck in the till. The German state of Baden-Wurttemberg prohibits the wearing of headscarves by teachers, not students. France bans the garment altogether from state schools, citing Article 9 of European Convention of Human Rights. A British court cites the same articles to uphold a schoolgirl's right to wear the much bulkier covering known as jilbab.[41]

Perhaps the ECtHR's judicial use of an unequivocal term such as neutrality created even more confusion. First, as Pin pointed out, "neutrality is not a shared value throughout Europe, and (…) especially Orthodox legal culture is not at ease with it".[42] Second, as clearly showed by the two decisions made by the European judges in Italian crucifix case law (*Lautsi v. Italy*), neutrality as a legal standard sometimes leads to opposite outcomes, and it "was used both to censor and to legitimize official religious symbols in the name of human rights".[43]

The second reason for the failure of judicial neutrality is strictly connected with the role played by cultural and religious traditions in secular democracies. As we mentioned before, according to Rawls' definition neutrality entails that "no general moral conception can provide a public recognized basis for a conception of justice".

---

[38] *Van Orden v. Perry, 545 U.S. 699 (2005).*

[39] Mahoney (1998), p. 2 ff.

[40] Berger et al. (2008), p. 80.

[41] Reported by Berger et al. (2008), p. 81.

[42] Pin (2014a), p. 616.

[43] Pin (2014a), p. 614: "the Lautsi case is extremely relevant in this respect. The first decision, which was released by a section of the ECtHR (Lautsi I), decided that the presence of the crucifix in Italian public classrooms was inconsistent with the state's duty of neutrality; the final decision, which was made by the ECtHR's Grand Chamber (Lautsi II), decided that state neutrality allows the display of official religious symbols. Interestingly, the two decisions diverge in their outcomes, but both use neutrality to scrutinize the relevant Italian legislation".

On other hand, the moral conceptions of law were (and maybe still are) the cornerstone of the different traditions of constitutional systems; and that is probably the reason why, according to Böckenförde, "[t]he liberal secularized state lives by prerequisites which it cannot guarantee itself".[44] In sum, starting from this perspective, the judicial use of strict neutrality as a legal standard addresses the clash between secularism and cultural traditions by dismissing the latter from public life.

From a constitutional point of view, this use of neutrality produces a paradoxical effect on the side of traditional heritage in the USA as in Europe. This is especially true in America, where religious tradition played an important historical role in shaping the constitutional and cultural framework of the Nation; as Justice O'Connor pointed out:

> certain ceremonial references to God and religion in our Nation are the inevitable consequence of the religious history that gave birth to our founding principles of liberty. It would be ironic if this Court were to wield our constitutional commitment to religious freedom so as to sever our ties to the traditions developed to honor it.[45]

As we noticed before, European countries don't share a common system of religious and cultural traditions. For that reason, especially when neutrality is confused with secularism, it cannot be enforced in all the continent without diminishing some cultural and legal heritages in favour of others: as notice by Judge Powers in her concurring opinion in the *Lautsi* case,

> Neutrality requires a pluralist approach on the part of the State, not a secularist one. It encourages respect for all world views rather than a preference for one. To my mind, the Chamber Judgment was striking in its failure to recognize that secularism was, in itself, one ideology among others. A preference for secularism over alternative world views—whether religious, philosophical or otherwise—is not a neutral option.[46]

In sum, neutrality as legal standard was not helpful to address the clash between modernity and cultural heritage in our democracies. Perhaps, as Ravitch pointed out, the quest for neutrality as a legal standard is similar to the tooth fairy tale: "like the tooth fairy, neutrality is just a myth, but like children who want the tooth fairy to visit, we want it to be real, or at least for something to stand in for it to make us believe it is real".[47]

3 A Second Approach to the Problem: The Use of History as Legal Standard

These criticisms cannot be levelled against a second legal standard used by judges: the so-called "historical argument". It comes from a different conception of the

[44] Böckenförde (1976), p. 60.

[45] See *Elk Grove Unified School Dist. v. Newdow* 542 U.S. 1 (2004) (Justice O' Connor concurring opinion).

[46] *Lautsi v. Italy, App. No. 30814/06 Eur. Ct. H.R.* Powers dissenting opinion (2011).

[47] Ravitch (2007), p. 18.

secular state, and it is raised up in opposition to a strong idea of assertive secularism and strict neutrality. According to this argument, judges must take into account the cultural and religious traditions of their systems as far as they are strongly rooted in the institutional (or even constitutional) history of their Nations.

This kind of argument has been widely used in the Western word and especially by the Supreme Court of the United States in order to support the constitutionality of the so-called "American ceremonial deism".[48] Historical argument was easily adopted by US Supreme Court justices when it concerned specific legal traditions explicitly endorsed by the Framers during the starting years of the Federal Government. For example, in *Marsh v. Chamber* the US Supreme Court upheld the constitutionality of the Nebraska legislature's practice of beginning its sessions with a prayer led by a state-paid chaplain, arguing that similar practices could be traced to the First Continental Congress and to the First Congress that framed the Bill of Rights and so are deeply embedded in the history and tradition of the country. In the majority opinion, Justice Berger explicitly rejected the *Lemon* test and rested the Court's opinion on historical argument:

> While historical patterns, standing alone, cannot justify contemporary violations of constitutional guarantees, historical evidence in the context of this case sheds light not only on what the drafters of the First Amendment intended the Establishment Clause to mean, but also on how they thought that Clause applied to the chaplaincy practice authorized by the First Congress. In applying the First Amendment to the states through the Fourteenth Amendment, it would be incongruous to interpret the Clause as imposing more stringent First Amendment limits on the states than the draftsmen imposed on the Federal Government. In light of the history, there can be no doubt that the practice of opening legislative sessions with prayer has become part of the fabric of our society. To invoke divine guidance on a public body entrusted with making the laws is not, in these circumstances, a violation of the Establishment Clause; it is simply a tolerable acknowledgment of beliefs widely held among the people of this country.[49]

Sometimes, the historical approach to Establishment Clause was helpful to legitimate some religious heritages (such as the use of the phrases "under God" or "in God we trust") that were not explicitly linked with a cultural practice supported by the Framers, but have become over the years part of the institutional life of the Nation. Relying on this approach, for example, Chief Justice Rehnquist would have upheld the constitutionality of the Pledge of Allegiance arguing that, even if it was not part of the original Pledge's version,[50] the challenged phrase "under God" was a patriotic

---

[48]This argument was strongly used by the Chief Justice William Rehnquist in order to declare the compatibility of some American traditions (such as the phrase "under God" of the Pledge of Allegiance) with the Establishment Clause. As pointed out by Ledewitz (2011), p. 33, "Chief Justice Rehnquist relied primarily on the presence in American history 'of patriotic invocations of God and official acknowledgments of religion's role in our Nation's history'. From numerous examples, such as the national motto 'in God We Trust' and opening of the United States Supreme Court sessions with the language 'God Save the United States and this honorable Court', Chief Justice Rehnquist concluded that 'our national culture allows public recognition of our Nation's religious history and character'". This argument was mostly used by conservative Justices of the Supreme Court.

[49]*Marsh v. Chamber*, 463 U.S. 783 (1983) Syllabus.

[50]Congress first officially adopted the original version Pledge of Allegiance (made by the Baptist minister Fraces J. Bellamy in 1892) in 1942, during World War II, to encourage patriotism. In 1951,

invocation deeply rooted in American history that could be traced to George Washington's first inauguration speech, or in the Gettysburg Address made by Lincoln in 1863. According to Rehnquist's concurring opinion:

> The phrase 'under God' is in no sense a prayer, nor an endorsement of any religion, but a simple recognition of the fact noted in H. R. Rep. No. 1693, at 2: 'From the time of our earliest history our peoples and our institutions have reflected the traditional concept that our Nation was founded on a fundamental belief in God.' Reciting the Pledge, or listening to others recite it, is a patriotic exercise, not a religious one; participants promise fidelity to our flag and our Nation, not to any particular God, faith, or church.[51]

As Ledewitz pointed out, "Chief Justice Rehnquist relied primarily on the presence in American history 'of patriotic invocations of God and official acknowledgments of religion's role in our Nation's history'".[52] But other Justices explicitly endorse this argument in opposition to the strict neutrality one, arguing that:

> To forbid any government focus upon this aspect of our history is to display what Justice Goldberg called 'untutored devotion to the concept of neutrality,' *Abington Township*, 374 U.S., at 306 (concurring opinion), that would commit the Court (and the Nation) to a revisionist agenda of secularization.[53]

In Europe, the historical argument didn't have the same impact as in the USA. As we noticed before, European countries do not share a common legal and cultural tradition on law and religion issues, and one of the main goals of the Convention is to achieve the proper balance between unity and diversity. In this perspective, ECtHR judges cannot extrapolate a legal argument from a European common historical background, but they have to deal with the very different histories and traditions that shaped the Member States' legal frameworks. Nonetheless, cultural traditions also play a special role in ECtHR jurisprudence. First European judges must take into account the different legal traditions rooted in the constitutional framework of each Member State in order to properly solve the different controversies; as noticed by the ECtHR,

> Where questions concerning the relationship between State and religions are at stake, on which opinion in a democratic society may reasonably differ widely, the role of the national decision-making body must be given special importance (…). This will notably be the case when it comes to regulating the wearing of religious symbols in educational institutions, especially (as the comparative-law materials illustrate – see paragraphs 55-65 above) in view of the diversity of the approaches taken by national authorities on the issue. It is not possible to discern throughout Europe a uniform conception of the significance of religion in society (…), and the meaning or impact of the public expression of a religious belief will differ according to time and context. Rules in this sphere will consequently vary from one

---

the Knights of Columbus, a Catholic fraternal organization, first began the practice of saying "one nation under God" as a part of the Pledge. They encouraged many others including Congress to follow the same practice. In 1954, Congress passed and President Eisenhower signed an amendment adding the words "under God" to the Pledge.

[51] *Elk Grove Unified School District v. Newdow*, 542 U.S. 19 (2004) Chief Justice Rehnquist concurring opinion.

[52] Ledewitz (2011), p. 33.

[53] *McCreary country v. ACLU*, 545 U.S. 844 (2005), Scalia dissenting opinion.

> country to another according to *national traditions* and the requirements imposed by the need to protect the rights and freedoms of others and to maintain public order.[54]

Second, in order to deal with the historical and cultural differences among Member States, the ECtHR elaborated the margin of appreciation doctrine, reserving to the Member States a degree of latitude in respect of the manner in which they discharge their obligations under the Convention. Relying on the very different cultural and legal approaches of the Member States, the margin of appreciation doctrine basically justifies the ECtHR's self-restraint every time that (a) there is not a general European consensus and (b) the different solutions adopted by Member States are deeply rooted in their history and tradition. Throughout the years, this doctrine has played a pivotal role in art. 9 (and art. 2-P1) decisions,[55] and European judges recognized a wide discretion for the Member State. This led to different (and sometimes opposite) conclusions in the case-law concerning the use of religious symbols in public spaces: because of the margin of appreciation, indeed, European judges upheld the legitimation of French *laïcité* and the ban of headscarves in schools and public spaces,[56] but also the Italian *laicità* and the presence of crucifixes in Italian classrooms.[57]

Even if it played a different role in Europe and the US,[58] the historical argument can be generally described as a wide umbrella under which cultural traditions—such as religious ceremonies and habits—can find protection when they are eligible to be considered historical customs deeply rooted in societies. From this perspective, it has the merit of reconciling the secular state with its cultural heritage. Nonetheless, the use of the historical argument alone is both weak and formalistic: first, practical jurists cannot solve hard conflicts just resorting to "what has always been done".[59] Second, it has the following—paradoxical-effect: a religious tradition can find a place in the public space only if its meaning is no longer "religious" but strictly "secular". This opens up the Pandora's box of the interpretation of symbols and traditions: when can a crucifix or a tablet of the Ten Commandments or a religious invocation be described as "secular" or as "religious"? How many years must a religious symbol stay in the public space in order to be considered part of the national historical tradition?

One example taken from US jurisprudence could be helpful to better understand the weakness of the historical argument alone. On 27th June of 2005, the US Supreme Court decided two apparently similar cases presenting two different solutions. The first case, *McCreary Country v. ACLU*,[60] resolved a conflict arising from the efforts

---

[54]See, *Leyla Sahin v. Turkey*, cit., par. 109.

[55]See (e.g.) Lugato (2013). Available at SSRN: https://ssrn.com/abstract=2182377.

[56]See (among others) *Dogru v. France*, Corte Edu, 4 December 2008; *Ebrahimian v. France*, 26 November 2015.

[57]*Lautsi v. Italy, App. No. 30814/06 Eur. Ct. H.R.*

[58]While in the US historical argument worked horizontally in opposition to a strong idea of assertive secularism and strict neutrality, in Europe it worked vertically, justifying all the different conceptions of secularity adopted by the Member States.

[59]From this point of view, the historical argument presents some similarities with the theory of original intent developed by Justice A. Scalia.

[60]*McCreary County v. American Civil Liberties Union of Ky*. 545 U.S. 844 (2005).

of two Kentucky counties to erect public displays including the Ten Commandments in their county courthouses. The second case, *Van Orden v. Perry*,[61] involved a six-foot-tall monument inscribed with the Ten Commandments placed at the Texas State Capitol, near the front of the Supreme Court of Texas' building. Both cases presented the similar constitutional question on the Establishment Clause.[62] Yet, despite all the similarities, "two sharply divided opinions" struck down the Decalogue display in Kentucky but left the other one in Texas standing, sending a conflicting message regarding the historical argument.[63]

In *McCreary* the majority opinion argued that, even if it was linked to the historical and legal traditions of the Nation, the Ten Commandments display was a religious symbol because it clearly embraced a religious message. As Justice Souter pointed out:

> This is not to deny that the Commandments have had influence on civil or secular law; a major text of a majority religion is bound to be felt. The point is simply that the original text viewed in its entirety is an unmistakably religious statement dealing with religious obligations and with morality subject to religious sanction. When the government initiates an effort to place this statement alone in public view, a religious object is unmistakable.[64]

On the other hand, in *Van Orden* Justice Rehnquist—writing for the plurality—emphasized the role played by the Decalogue in the Nation's heritage, showed as well by hundreds of other religious displays erect in or near government buildings all over the nation such as the religious statue of Moses placed on the frieze in the Supreme Court's building. According to Rehnquist, therefore:

> Of course, the Ten Commandments are religious–they were so viewed at their inception and so remain. The monument, therefore, has religious significance. According to Judeo-Christian belief, the Ten Commandments were given to Moses by God on Mt. Sinai. But Moses was a lawgiver as well as a religious leader. And the Ten Commandments have an undeniable historical meaning, as the foregoing examples demonstrate. Simply having religious content or promoting a message consistent with a religious doctrine does not run afoul of the Establishment Clause.[65]

---

[61] *Van Orden v. Perry* 545 US 677 (2005).

[62] The constitutional questions raised by the appellant in the two cases were very similar: Do Ten Commandments displays in public schools and in courthouses violate the First Amendment's establishment clause, which prohibits government from passing laws "respecting an establishment of religion?" (McCreary). Does a Ten Commandments monument on the grounds of a state capitol building violate the First Amendment's establishment clause, which barred the government from passing laws "respecting an establishment of religion?" (Van Orden). For that reason, as noticed by Morrison (2007) "many observers viewed these cases as offering the Court an opportunity to clarify its analytical approach, not only in the realm of Ten Commandments cases, but also to the Establishment Clause generally".

[63] Witte and Nichols (2011), pp. 229–230.

[64] McCreary County v. ACLU of Kentucky, 545 U.S. 869 (2005).

[65] Van Orden v. Perry, 545 U.S. 688 (2005).

In sum, the twin decisions on the Ten Commandments showed the weakness of the historical argument and the difficulty of clearly defining when a public display can be described as "secular" or as religious.[66]

4 A Possible Solution? the Pluralistic Approach

As we have attempted to explain, the two legal standards mostly used by courts present some benefits, but in the end are not convincing enough. On one side, neutrality can address a certain separation between politics and religion, and endorse the principle of equality or equidistance of the state before religions. But too often constitutional judges used neutrality in order to eradicate religious tradition from national and cultural heritage, and it has mostly become the legal transplant of a secularist approach that implies the privatization of any religion.

On the other side, the historical argument has the merit of reconciling the secular state with its heritage, taking into account the religious traditions when these were rooted in the history and the constitutional framework of the country. Nonetheless, the use of this argument alone is not capable of fixing all the religious conflicts in modern democracies. In particular, the historical argument looks at the past and freezes time, and it is perhaps too rigid to deal with the religious traditions of newcomers and with the immigration processes that are re-shaping our democracies.

The reason why both these arguments are unable to deal with the current issues facing our democracies most likely relates to the origins of the arguments. Both legal arguments were born from the so-called "secularization theory" that was based on the idea that modernity necessarily brings about a decline of religion. As noted earlier, although for many years the "secularization theory" was the paradigm for the study of religion in the modern era, that theory proved to be worthless in the post-secular age because it "can no longer be maintained in the face of empirical evidence".[67]

---

[66]To be clear, it's important to explain that the twin cases on the Ten Commandments were quite different as matter of context and facts. On one hand, In *McCreary* the Ten Commandments display was ordered by legislative's body of the Countries, and it was accompanied by a pastor of a local church, that endorsed the religious meaning of the display testifying to the certainty of the existence of God. On the other hand, in *Van Orden* the Ten Commandments monument was donated more than 40 years before the case by a secular organization (the Fraternal Order of Eagle) and it stands in a large park nearby a lot of other monuments or historical markers designed to illustrate the "ideals" of those who settled in Texas and in US. It's quite understandable that, especially because of the Kentucky officials' behavior, in *McCreary* the Court concluded that "the reasonable observer could only think that the Counties meant to emphasize and celebrate the Commandments' religious message" *Mccreary County V. ACLU* 545 U.S. 844 (2005). But this argument is not suitable within the Texas case, where "the physical setting of the monument, moreover, suggests little or nothing of the sacred" and the 40 years of continuing display of the monument "suggests that the public visiting the capitol grounds has considered the religious aspect of the tablets' message as part of what is a broader moral and historical message reflective of a cultural heritage" (*Van Orden v. Perry* 545 U.S. 677 (2005) (Breyer concurring).

[67]Berger (2014), p. IX.

The failure of the secularization theory itself may indeed be considered the deep reason for the failure of neutrality and the historical argument. Assuming the idea of incompatibility between modernity and religion, these arguments are trying to resolve conflicts between law and religion in a bi-dimensional perspective (religion or tradition vs. neutrality or modernity) that is however unable to properly understand the multi-dimensional complexity of our societies.

In his most recent work, Berger embraces this perspective and proposes to replace the secularization theory with a new paradigm based on "the many implications of the phenomenon of pluralism".[68] The core of Prof. Berger's theory is that this new paradigm "should be able to deal with two pluralisms—the co-existence of different religions and the co-existence of religious and secular discourse".[69] From a constitutional point of view, this approach breaks down the dichotomy of the secularisation theory between religion and modernity, and pushes the Courts (and also the legislators and all other institutional actors) to look at the concrete objectivity of every single case in order to find the right balance between different positions.[70]

According to this perspective, our aim is to point to a third way to realize the ambition toward a secular state, on the one hand, and to enhance religious traditions according to their true meanings, on the other, in the context of a pluralist, post-secular, age. This third solution is based on three main premises: (a) the idea of finding a unique abstract legal standard capable of resolving every case is just a utopian dream; (b) the place of religion in the public space does not involve a binary relation (state vs. church), but rather it is a complex triangular relational principle (that involves State, Religion, and Civil Society); (c) the main aim of the courts tasked to decide on conflicts involving religious claims should be that of protecting individuals from the concrete harm of their religious (and non-religious) rights: the goal of the courts is not to enforce a certain idea of the secular state or *laïcité*, but to ensure pluralism and religious peace.

Since pluralism implies the simultaneous presence of multiple *Weltanschauungen* in the public sphere, judges are not asked to enforce an absolute and abstract idea of secularism, but a concrete and practical religious peace. In the following pages, we will try to implement these theoretical premises within a practical case study. We choose to test the pluralistic theory and the third way approach within the Italian case-law, focusing on some of the most recent issues involving the presence of religious traditions in state schools.

---

[68]Ivi, p. X.

[69]Ivi, p. IX.

[70]Similary Venter (2015), p. 237: "the complexity of interface between law and religion has escalated and continues to do so as religious pluralism spreads across the globe"; for that reason, the A. suggest "that the notion of state/legal neutrality towards religion within the context of liberal constitutionalism should be replaced with *objectivity*, applied in the context of *constitutionalism*, understood as a standard for just exercise of the authority of the state as it has crystallized over centuries of human experience with the allocation and limitation of public authority".

5 The Historical Roots of the Italian Constitutional Peculiarity

Because of its peculiar political and diplomatic history with the Catholic Church, Italy has an odd church-state relationship. It is worth remembering that the Roman Catholic Pope started exerting his temporal power on regions positioned within the Italian borders in the 8th century, after the Carolingian Donations.[71] The Papal State lasted throughout modern history, until the end of 19th century when, a year after the s.c. Breach of Porta Pia, the Parliament of the Italian Reign enacted the "Law of Guarantees" (May 13th 1871), that deprived the Pope of his lands and of his sovereignty over them. After the fall of the Papal State, the principle that inspired the relationship between state and church in Italy was Cavour's proposal for "a free church in a free state".[72] This lasted until the signature of Lateran Treaty of 1929,[73] a pact between the Pope and the Italian government according to which the papacy recognized the Italian state, while Italy, in return, recognized papal sovereignty over Vatican City.

The Lateran Treaty was confirmed by the Republican Constitution of 1948, and hints of the Italian Catholic history are still deeply rooted at the core of the constitutional system.[74] The first evidence of this can be found in Articles 7 and 8 of the Constitution. The former focuses on the relationships between the State and the Catholic Church only. It reads:

> The State and the Catholic Church are independent and sovereign, each within its own sphere. Their relations are regulated by the Lateran pacts. Amendments to such Pacts which are accepted by both parties shall not require the procurement of constitutional amendments.[75]

In case of amendments not accepted by the Catholic Church, therefore, the State must resort to the protective procedure of constitutional amendment. Differently, according to Article 8, the relationship between the State and all the other religions are regulated by the ordinary law:

> All religious denominations are equally free before the law. Denominations other than Catholicism have the right to self-organisation according to their own statutes, provided these do not conflict with Italian law. Their relations with the State are regulated by law, based on agreements with their respective representatives.[76]

The abovementioned Articles permit us to say that the Italian Constitution does not affirm a *tout-court* equality of all the religions before the law: indeed, the Catholic Church has a unique legal status. Nonetheless, if we read them in combination with

---

[71] For more details and sources see, among the others, Noble (1984), Partner (1972).

[72] See Del Giudice (1947).

[73] The Lateran Treaty was amended many years later with the "Villa Madama" Agreement of 1984.

[74] For a detailed study on the Catholic roots within the Italian Constitution and the Framers' debate, see Pin (2011), p. 110 ff.

[75] Art. 7, Italian Constitution.

[76] Art. 8, Italian Constitution.

Articles 3 and 19 of the constitutional charter, we can affirm that all religions are equally free and all the citizens have a right to religious freedom, without distinction of belief:

> All citizens have equal social dignity and are equal before the law, without distinction of [...] religion.[77]
>
> Anyone is entitled to freely profess their religious belief in any form, individually or with others, and to promote them and celebrate rites in public or in private, provided they are not offensive to public morality.[78]

Another peculiarity of the Italian Constitution, due to its religious roots, is that it does not contain any sort of "establishment clause". Article 7 says that church and state are both "independent and sovereign, each within its own sphere", but "it is obviously excessive to conclude that this idea of 'distinction' fully shaped the idea of *laicità*",[79] the word classically used to indicate the non-establishment principle and the separation between church and state in Italy. Some members of the Constitutional Assembly rejected the explicit reference to this principle "because it sounded hostile to religion due to its French pedigree".[80] Giorgio La Pira, a father of our Constitution, said that since the human being has an innate religious orientation, which inevitably must be expressed in religious communities, a secular state ("*Stato laico*"[81] in his words) cannot exist.[82] More generally, the Framers imagined a constitutional system where the "collaboration between church and state, both in Article 7 for the relationship with the Catholic Church and in Article 8 for the relationships with other religions", was pivotal and an explicit establishment clause was not necessary. As pointed out by Andrea Pin,[83] the choice of the Constitutional Assembly echoed the content of Leo XIII's encyclical letter *Immortale Dei* (November 1st 1885). The pope's letter, on the one hand, recognized that between the ecclesiastical power and the civil one "there is [...] an orbit traced out within which the action of each is brought into play by its own native right".[84] But, on the other hand, it affirmed that "God, [...] who is the author of these two powers, has marked out the course of each in right correlation to the other".[85]

The principle of *laicità*, unspoken by the Constitutional Assembly, was explicitly affirmed many years later by the Constitutional Court. But, still, the one introduced by the Court's decision no. 203/1989 was a brand-new idea of *laicità* that mirrors the Italian peculiarity. According to the judgment, this principle stems from articles

---

[77] Art. 3.1, *Principle of equality*, Italian Constitution.

[78] Art. 19, *Freedom of Religion*, Italian Constitution.

[79] Pin (2011), p. 114.

[80] Pin (2011), p. 116.

[81] See *La Costituzione della Repubblica nei lavori preparatori dell'Assemblea costituente*, edited by Segretariato generale della Camera dei Deputati, Rome, 1970, vol. 1, p. 323.

[82] See Ninatti (2008).

[83] See Footnote 79.

[84] See par. 13. The letter is available here: http://www.papalencyclicals.net/leo13/l13sta.htm.

[85] *Ibidem*.

2, 3, 7, 8, 19 and 20 of the Constitution,[86] and it can be described as the sum of some fundamental constitutional values, among which are religious freedom, the non-discrimination principle and religious pluralism.[87] It is worth mentioning that, in the Court's opinion, the supreme principle of *laicità* "does not imply indifference to religions, but the State guarantee for the protection of freedom of religion, under the religious and cultural pluralism".[88] The case at the origin of the judgment regarded the teaching of the Catholic religion in public schools and, under the light of the *laicità* principle, the constitutional compatibility of this traditional practice was affirmed. In the Court's opinion, indeed, as long as the teaching is optional, there cannot be found real discrimination towards pupils who are not Catholic[89] and, consequently, no impingement of the *laicità* principle could be recognized.

As we can see, this idea of *laicità* cannot be associated with strict neutrality and its hostility toward religions in public space: the principle described by constitutional judgment no. 203/1989 preserves a space for religion in the public sphere. However, it has been observed[90] that afterwards, within the Italian case-law (constitutional and otherwise), the idea of *laicità* has found various definitions, and it is not possible to identify a univocal significance of this term. The effort to transform *laicità* into an abstract and general judicial standard failed. And that should not be surprising, as the same happened even within jurisdictions where a secular principle is explicit in the Constitution.[91] Depending on the cases, the objects of the disputes and the fields, the Italian Courts have defined *laicità* as a synonym of equidistance among faiths, but also impartiality, not indifference, and even neutrality.[92] This last term has been used in the Constitutional judgment no. 235/1997, where the Court affirmed that different treatments among different faiths are allowed as long as

> equal freedom and the recognition of the total needs of each faith are assured, in compliance with the neutrality of the State in religious matters.[93]

The heterogeneity of the *laicità* principle within Italian jurisprudence will be later discussed more deeply in relation to pastoral visitations and Catholic benedictions in public schools. Before that, it is worth remembering that the Italian peculiarity, a

---

[86] Article 2 reads: "The Republic recognises and guarantees the inviolable rights of the person, both as an individual and in the social groups where human personality is expressed. The Republic expects that the fundamental duties of political, economic and social solidarity be fulfilled". Article 20: "No special limitation or tax burden may be imposed on the establishment, legal capacity or activities of any organisation on the ground of its religious nature or its religious or confessional aims".

[87] See par. nr. 3 and 4 of the decision (available here: http://www.giurcost.org/decisioni/1989/0203s-89.html).

[88] Par. 4.

[89] Par 8 and 9.

[90] See, among the other, See Vanoni (2013), p. 20 ff.

[91] In relation to the U.S. case, see Vanoni (2016), p. 122 ff.

[92] See Pin (2010), p. 159.

[93] See par. 4 of the *Considerando in Diritto*. Judgment available here: www.giurcost.org/decisioni/1997/0235s-97.html.

tendency toward a *favor religionis* and its rooted Catholic history, does not emerge uniquely in the Constitutional Charter or in the judicial genesis of the *laicità* principle. The weight of the religious traditions is still undeniable in many aspects of the public life of the citizens: religious feast days, processions in honour of the towns' patron saints, benediction of public buildings and so on.[94] And one of the first public spaces where this traditional heritage and secularism clash is school.

6 Religion and Public Schools: Dismissal or Recovery?

It is not by chance that the first constitutional judgment to mention the *laicità* principle considered the teaching of the Catholic religion in state schools. And some of the trickiest cases decided afterwards by the Italian courts concerning that principle again involved the presence of religion in public schools. Everyone knows the political and legal battle about the crucifix in Italian classrooms.[95] And actually there is extensive case law concerning the display of this religious/cultural symbol in Italy.[96] The most debated of the cases, the *Lautsi* case, is well-known all over the world as it has been discussed two times before the European Court of Human Rights.[97] For sure, the case law on the public display of crucifixes and other religious symbols in public schools[98] is one of the best case studies to observe—in action—both the use of strict neutrality and the historical arguments by the Italian judges. Let us take as examples these two judgments delivered, respectively, on the 23rd October 2003 by the Court of first instance of L'Aquila and the 22nd March 2005 by the Administrative Court of Veneto (i.e. the domestic judgment of first instance of the *Lautsi* saga). In both cases the judges addressed the question whether the display of the crucifix in a classroom was legitimate or not. In the former, the Court denied the legitimacy of this practice, because:

> the presence of the crucifix [...] shows the clear will of the state – we are in a state school – to put the Catholic worship at the centre of the Universe, as an absolute truth, without any respect for the role played by the other religious and social experiences within the historical process of the human development.[99]

Consequently, in the Court's opinion, the *laicità* principle—that was explicitly related to neutrality—was violated:

---

[94]See Chizzoniti (2006), pp. 79–100.

[95]In Italy, the presence of the crucifix in classrooms was firstly established during the end of the XIX century—almost simultaneously with the fall of the Papal States, by a regulation which implemented the s.c. Casati Law of 1859. Afterwards it was echoed under the fascist regime by decrees nr. 965/1924 and 1927/1928. See Vanoni (2017), pp. 268–269.

[96]See Vanoni (2013), p. 45 ff.

[97]The first decision was delivered as a chamber judgment on November 3, 2009. After the Italian government appeal, the second decision was released by the Grand Chamber on March 18, 2011.

[98]On this topic, see among the others Bin et al. (2004), Weiler (2010), Annichino (2010), Temperman (2012), Movsesian (2013a), p. 510 ff., Gedicks and Annichino (2014), p. 102 ff.

[99]Trib. Aquila, ord. 23 October 2003.

> As not only the pupils' religious freedom is put at risk, but also the neutrality of a state institution, it is not possible to consider that the *laicità* principle has been achieved.[100]

A totally different approach was followed two years later by the Administrative Court of Veneto. Here the judges attributed an historical meaning to the crucifix, which was not considered just a religious symbol. In the Court's opinion, "the crucifix is a symbol of that religious doctrine and culture that created the soil out of which human rights could grow, at least in Italy, and perhaps beyond".[101] As the decision reads:

> The rules governing the display of the crucifix in classrooms date from 1859, an historical context characterized by an intense contrast between the Pope and the unitary state […]. Evidently, at that time the display of the Christian symbol was considered, together with the display of the portrait of the King and the flag, as a call to the uniting values of the nation. Finally, the display of the crucifix in schools lasted so long, even after the fascist era, that it has been defined as a custom, in the legal sense of the word.[102]

As noted by Brett Scharffs, in the Court's argument, "to prohibit the crucifix is not only to forget or reject that history, but it is a kind of arrogant patricide—the children, who enjoy the human rights bequeathed by the parent, banishing, exiling, or ejecting that parent in the very name of the rights they enjoy".[103] A similar argument was followed by the domestic court of second instance, the Council of State, in 2006. On this occasion, the display of crucifix was considered as a symbol of the:

> religious origin of values as tolerance, reciprocal respect, promotion of the human person, proclamation of human rights, respect for human liberty, autonomy of the moral conscience before the public authority, human solidarity, and refusal of every discrimination, all values that characterize the Italian society.[104]

These brief examples demonstrate well that the presence of religion in public schools has been intensively debated within the Italian case-law. In the following pages, we want to bring attention to a case more recent than the crucifix one, which also involves the place of religion in state schools and which shows that the legal protection of our cultural traditions is still a live issue: the celebration of pastoral visitations and Catholic benedictions in public schools. Below, we will analyse some judicial decisions that followed the strict neutrality approach, some that resorted to the historical arguments, and finally also two judgments solved according to the pluralistic approach.

---

[100] *Ibidem.*

[101] See Scharffs (2017), p. 5.

[102] Tar Veneto, sez. III, sent. 22 March 2005, no. 1110 (Par. 5.5).

[103] Idem.

[104] See the decision no. 556 delivered by the Council of State on January 13th 2006.

6.1 *The Pastoral Visitation and the Use of the Historical Argument*

According to the Italian legal framework,[105] the autonomy of the educational institutions (protected by the Constitution at Article 117) permits them to schedule cultural events inside the school, both during classes and outside of lesson time. It is not infrequent that, among the other cultural events, the schools organize encounters with religious—especially Catholic—ministers. In some cases, this habit has raised legal questions: does the presence of a religious minister in a public school violate the separation between state and church? Does the presence of a Catholic minister constitute a discrimination based on religion for the pupils that are not Catholic?

With a judgment delivered 6th April 2010, the Council of State addressed those questions resorting to the historical argument and establishing that the visitation of a bishop in a state school does not have a discriminatory effect. Indeed, in the Court's opinion:

> the scheduled visitation cannot be defined as a worship activity, nor as an activity aimed at the care of souls [...], rather it has the value of a cultural testimony aimed at highlighting the contents of the Catholic religion that are worth knowing.[106]

Consequently, the bishop's visitation does not violate the *laicità* principle, and atheists or believers of other religions cannot complain of illegal discrimination. Describing the pastoral visitation as "cultural testimony", the Council "secularized" a very ancient religious ritual of the Catholic Church and allowed its presence in the public school only because it is a part of the cultural and historical tradition in Italy. In order to do so, the administrative judges had to exclude from the judgment the proper definition and meaning of the pastoral visitation, that—according to the Canon Codex—does constitute a religious event.[107] This verdict has been confirmed by the President of the Republic who, within an extraordinary appeal, rejected the complaints. He wrote:

> It is true that the pastoral visitation took place during lesson time; but it did not consist in a liturgical act (Eucharist, blessing, and so on), rather in a testimony of religious and cultural values [... that are] coherent with the principles of tolerance and respect for freedoms, individual and collective, protected by our democratic Constitutional charter and by our legal system.[108]

The arguments used by the President of the Republic and by the Council of State on this occasion are not so far from the ones used by the domestic courts in the *Lautsi* case analysed above, which affirmed that the crucifix can be displayed in public schools as the cultural traditions rooted in this symbol enforce the legal

[105] See D.lgs 416/1974, D.lgs 297/1994 and DPR 275/1999.

[106] See Council of State, VI Section, 6th April 2010, available here: http://irc.vicenza.chiesacattolica.it/documenti/professione/angolo_giuridico/altri_documenti/sentenza_6aprile2010.pdf.

[107] See Canons no. 396-398 of the Codex iuris canonici.

[108] See President Giorgio Napolitano's decision delivered on May 6th 2011, available here: http://www.culturacattolica.it/cm-files/2011/12/15/7377.pdf.

tradition of the Italian Constitution. All these decisions show well the paradox of the use of the historical argument within the Italian case-law: religious traditions can be "recovered" as long as they are not considered "religious", but instead as "cultural testimony" coherent with the values and the principles protected by our constitutional framework.

6.2 *The Catholic Easter Benediction Case: Strict Neutrality*

The second case we want to focus on has as its subject the Catholic Easter Benediction in a public school.[109] The main difference between this case and the previous one is that, in this case, the presence of the minister in the school is irrefutably to perform a religious ritual. Starting from this undisputed element, the administrative judges of first instance and those of the appeal decided the case in two opposite ways.

The Administrative Court of Emilia Romagna (9th February 2016) stated that the resolution of the school that allows the Easter Benediction—even if after classes and in the presence of only the pupils whose parents decide to attend that event with their sons[110]—is unconstitutional because it violates the constitutional principle of *laicità*. According to the statement:

> although the use of the school rooms is scheduled after classes, [… in these places] there is not space for religious rituals – that are by their nature reserved to the private sphere of the citizens. […] The insuperable borderline [… is traced] by the circumstance that the activity is or not an act of worship.[111]

The administrative judges used here the strict neutrality argument: i.e. the *laicità* principle imposes a strict separation between church and state, therefore a religious ritual (such as the Easter Benediction) cannot cross the walls of public schools (even if scheduled as extracurricular events) and have to be confined into the believers' private sphere.

6.3 *… and the Pluralistic Approach*

That verdict was appealed to the Council of State, which came to the opposite result. In his judgment, the Council does not deny that the benediction is an act of worship:

---

[109]About this case, see Di Iorio (2017), Cavana (2017), Muselli and Ceffa (2017), p. 51 ff.

[110]In compliance with Article 311.2 of D.lgs 297/1994 that affirms: "Per dare reale efficacia all'attuazione del diritto di avvalersi o di non avvalersi di insegnamenti religiosi, si provvede a che l'insegnamento religioso ed ogni eventuale pratica religiosa, nelle classi in cui sono presenti alunni che hanno dichiarato di non avvalersene, non abbiano luogo in occasione dell'insegnamento di altre materie, né secondo orari che abbiano per i detti alunni effetti comunque discriminanti".

[111]See Emilia Romagna Administrative Court (TAR), Bologna, Section I, 9th February 2016, decision no. 166.

As it is well-known, the Easter benediction is a religious ritual. [...] The aim of this ritual, for those who believe in the intimate meaning of this practice and welcome it, is the remembrance of the presence of God in every place.[112]

Nonetheless, in this concrete case, the Court says that the *laicità* principle was not violated. The judges affirm that, taking into consideration the particular elements of the case, the benediction was not imposed on all the pupils, but it was reserved for the ones who decided to attend it with their parents after classes. This means that it would be hard (if not impossible) to find someone who was concretely discriminated against or whose religious freedom was harmed because of the Benediction. In the Council's words:

It is legitimate asking to celebrate [the benediction] into the school, at the presence of those who want and after the school time; and this would not absolutely hurt the religious (or not religious) thought or feeling of anybody.[113]

It is worth noting that the Council of State ignored the applicants' claim that the Easter Benediction, even if optional, infringed the *laicità* principle because it shows an endorsement of a state institution (the school) of one specific religion. The Court's silence on this point clarifies that the goal of the Court is not to enforce a certain idea of the secular state (where religion cannot be professed in public), but to ensure pluralism and religious peace, taking into consideration that the public space is not owned by the state but by the members of society. Finally, the judgment states that, according to an elementary principle of non-discrimination, the religious nature of a tradition cannot be, itself, the only reason for forbidding it. There should be other concrete evidence that the habit jeopardises the maintenance of pluralism and religious peace. This latter argument has an interesting precedent in the Italian administrative case law. In decision no. 677/2005, the Administrative Court of Umbria declared the legitimacy of a Catholic Benediction in a public school as it was optional and brief. The concrete elements of the circumstance permitted the court to affirm that no one was concretely discriminated against, and that the Benediction did not take up an excessive part of the pupils' free time.

7 Conclusion

The approach followed by the Council of State in the Easter Benediction case takes into account the three main goals we used to describe the "third way approach" or "pluralistic approach". First, the judges did not try to solve the case by resorting to an abstract legal standard, but they started by analyzing it from a concrete point

[112]See Council of State, 27 March 2017, decision no. 1388.

[113]Ibid.

of view. Second, they considered the case taking into account civil society as well, and particularly the desire of a part of the school community to receive the Easter Benediction. Third, the judges embraced a legal approach that investigates the concrete real harm of the religious rights of the pupils in that particular case: the Court does not affirm the general rule that a Catholic benediction in a school is always in accordance with the *laicità* principle; it says that a religious event celebrated after classes and only in the presence of those who desire it is legitimate. In conclusion, the pluralistic approach does not provide an undisputable definition of *laicità*, capable of resolving—once and for all—all the problems raised in the (post-)secular age. Nonetheless it could provide the courts useful tools to solve—case by case—those conflicts raised in our multicultural society by the presence of religions in public spaces.

In the case of law and religion, the principle that should enlighten the decisions by the courts is not a certain idea of neutrality or secularity nor the historical argument alone. As we noted above, these two legal arguments stem from the secularization theory and are based on the dogma that religions and modernity are in opposition. In our post-secular societies, the new paradigm is the pluralistic theory, that stems from the need to endorse in fact religious peace among diversity.

As the principles of pluralism and religious peace are very general goals, they cannot be achieved through an abstract law. Rather they have to be pursued and lived within the concrete circumstances of ordinary life.

This idea indirectly echoes the considerations made by the ECHR in *Serif v. Greece*, 1999:

> "Although (…) it is possible that tension is created in situations where a religious or any other community becomes divided, this is one of the unavoidable consequences of pluralism", and "the role of the authorities in such circumstances is not to remove the cause of tension by eliminating pluralism, but to ensure that the competing groups tolerate each other".[114]

In conclusion, in cases regarding the presence of religion in the public space, "careful analysis of context is crucial. Different legal regimes, the products of different cultures and histories", will naturally adopt different responses and, "even within a single regime, a variety of responses may be appropriate, depending on place, speaker, and other circumstances. In this area, as in so many others in law and religion, a rigid, categorical approach seems unwise".[115] As Taylor pointed out, "one of our basic difficulties in dealing with these problems is that we have the wrong model, which has a continuing hold on our minds. We think that secularism [or *laicità*] has to do with the relation of the state and religion, whereas in fact it has to do with the (correct) response of the democratic state to diversity".[116]

---

[114]Par. 53.

[115]Movsesian (2013b), p. 6.

[116]Taylor (2010), p. 25.

References

Ackerman B (1980) Social justice in the liberal state. Yale University Press, New Haven

Annichino P (2010) Is the glass half empty or half full? Lautsi v Italy before the European Court of Human Rights. www.statoechiese.it. May 2010, pp 1–19

Berger P (2014) The many altars of modernity: toward a paradigm for religion in a pluralist age. Walter de Gruyter, Boston and Berlin

Berger P, Davie G, Fokas E (2008) Religious America, secular Europe? A theme and variation. Ashgate Pubblishing, Oxon-New York

Bin R, Brunelli A, Pugiotto A, Veronesi P (eds) (2004) La laicità crocifissa? Il nodo costituzionale dei simboli religiosi nei luoghi pubblici. Giappichelli, Turin

Böckenförde W (1976) Staat, Gesellschaft. Freiheit

Calo ZR (2014) Constructing the secular: law and religion jurisprudence in Europe and United States. In: EUI working paper, RSCAS 2014/94, 2014

Casanova J (2000) Oltre la secolarizzazione: le religioni alla riconquista della sfera pubblica. il Mulino, Bologna

Casanova J (2006) Religion, European secular identities, and European integration. In: Byrnes T, Katzenstein P (eds) Religion in expanding Europe. Cambridge University Press, Cambridge, pp 65–93

Casanova J (2009) The secular and secularisms. Soc Res 76(4):1049–1066

Cavana P (2017) Libertà religiosa e scuola pubblica. La piccola querelle delle benedizioni pasquali. www.statoechiese.it. n. 2/2017

Chizzoniti AGM (2006) Cerimonie, ordine delle precedente, festività civili e religiose. Casi particolari di uso pubblico di simbologia religiosa. In: Parisi M (ed) Crocifisso, velo e turbante. Simboli e comportamenti religiosi nella società plurale. Conference proceedings, ESI, Naples, 2006, pp 79–100

Del Giudice V (1947) La questione romana e i rapporti tra Stato e Chiesa fino alla conciliazione: con considerazioni sui Patti Lateranensi e sull'art. 7 della Costituzione Repubblicana. Edizioni dell'Ateneo, Rome

Di Iorio T (2017) Oltre il muro dell'intolleranza. Luci e ombre della benedizione nella scuola tra libertà religiosa e laicità dello Stato. www.statoechiese.it. n. 24/2017

Dreisbach DL (2002) Thomas Jefferson and the wall of separation between church and state. New York University Press, New York

Dreisbach DL (2006) The mythical "Wall of Separation": how a misused metaphor changed church–state law, policy, and discourse. In: First principles series report 6, The Heritage Foundation, 23 June 2006

Dworkin R (1985) "Liberalism", in a matter of principle. Harvard University Press, Cambridge, MA

Flores D'Arcais P (2015) La democrazia deve chiedere l'esilio di Dio. In: La Repubblica—on line, 9-3-2015

Galston WA (1991) Liberal purposes: goods, virtues, and diversity in the liberal state. Cambridge University Press, Cambridge

Gedicks FM, Annichino P (2014) Cross, crucifix, culture: an approach to the constitutional meaning of confessional symbols. Fir Am Law Rev 13:71–139

Glendon MA (2008) Justice and human rights: reflections on the address of Pope Benedict to the UN. Eur J Int Law 19(5):925–930

Kepel G (1991) La Revanche de Dieu. Paris

Koppelman A (2004) The fluidity of neutrality. Rev Politics 66(4):633–648

Larmore CE (1987) Patterns of moral complexity. Cambridge University Press, Cambridge

Laycock D (1986) A survey of religious liberty in the United States. Ohio State Law J 47:409–459

Laycock D (1990) Formal, substantive, and desegregated neutrality toward religion. DePaul Law Rev 39:993–1018

Ledewitz B (2011) Church, state, and the crisis in American Secularism. Indiana University Press, Bloogmington, IN
Levinson RB (1984) Separation of church and state: and the wall came tumbling down. Valparaiso Univ Law Rev 18:707–739
Lugato M (2013) The margin of appreciation and freedom of religion: between treaty interpretation and subsidiarity. J Catholic Legal Stud 52
Mahoney P (1998) Marvellous richness of diversity or invidious cultural relativism? Hum Rights Law J 1 36
Martinez-Torron J (2012) La (non) protezione della identità religiosa dell'individuo nella giurisprudenza della Corte di Strasburgo. In: Mazzola R (ed) Diritto e religione in Europa. Rapporto sulla giurisprudenza della Corte europea dei diritti dell'uomo in materia di libertà religiosa. Il Mulino, Bologna, pp 55–87
Morrison MJ (2007) The Van Orden and Mccreary County cases: closing the gaps remaining between the established lines of ten commandments jurisprudence. Wash Lee J Civ Rights Soc Just 13:436–462
Movsesian M (2013a) Crosses and culture: state-sponsored religious displays in the U.S. and Europe. In: Ferrari S, Cristofori R (eds) III religion in public spaces. Routledge, London, pp 509–521
Movsesian M (2013b) State-sponsored religious displays in the U.S. and Europe: introduction. In: Faculty publications. Paper 93. http://scholarship.law.stjohns.edu/faculty_publications/93, pp 1–6
Muselli L, Ceffa CB (2017) Libertà religiosa, obiezione di coscienza e giurisprudenza costituzionale. Giappichelli, Torino
Ninatti S (2008) Il rilievo dell'original intent nell'interpretazione dell'art. 7 della Costituzione italiana. In: Nicotra I, Giuffrè F (eds) L'original intent nella giurisprudenza della Corte costituzionale. Giappichelli, Turin
Noble TFX (1984) The Republic of St. Peter: the birth of the Papal State 680-825. University of Pennsylvania Press, Philadelphia
Nozick R (1974) Anarchy, state, and Utopia. Basic Books, New York
Partner P (1972) The lands of St. Peter: the Papal State in the middle ages and the early renaissance. University of California Press, Los Angeles
Pin A (2010) Laicità e Islam nell'ordinamento italiano. Una questione di metodo. Cedam, Padua
Pin A (2011) Public schools, the Italian crucifix, and the European Court of human rights: the Italian separation of church and state. Emory Int Law Rev 25(1):97–149
Pin A (2014a) Does Europe need neutrality? the old continent in search of identity. BYU Law Rev 605–634
Pin A (2014b) Religions, national identities, and the Universality of Human Rights. Oxford J Law Relig 3(3):419–439
Ravitch FS (2007) Master of illusion. The Supreme Court and the religious clauses. New York University Press, New York
Rawls J (1971) A theory of justice. Harvard University Press, Cambridge, MA
Rawls J (1985) Justice and fairness: political not metaphysical. Philos Public Aff 1985:225–291
Scharffs B (2017) Why religious freedom? Why the religiously committed, the religiously indifferent and those hostile to religion should care. BYU law research paper no. 17-01, 3 Feb 2017, p 5
Smith S (1995) Foreordained failure: the quest for a constitutional principle of religious freedom. Oxford University Press, Oxford
Smith SD (2014) The rise and decline of American religious freedom. Harvard University Press, Cambridge, MA
Taylor C (2009) The polysemy of the secular. Soc Res 76(4), 1143–1166
Taylor C (2010) The meaning of secularism. Hedgehog Rev 12(3):23–34
Tega D (2008) Imperfect symmetry. The Court of Strasbourg and the US Supreme Court on religious symbols in public spaces. EUI working paper RSCAS 2016/08

Temperman J (ed) (2012) The Lautsi papers: multidisciplinary reflections on religious symbols in the public school classroom. Nijhoff, Brill

Vanoni LP (2013) Laicità e libertà di educazione. Il crocifisso nelle aule scolastiche in Italia e in Europa. Giuffrè, Milan

Vanoni LP (2016) Pluralismo religioso e stato (post) secolare. Una sfida per la modernità. Giappichelli, Turin

Vanoni LP (2017) Argomentazione e principi giuridici: il caso della laicità. In: Nanni P, Rigotti E, Wolfsgruber C (eds) Argomentare per un rapporto ragionevole con la realtà. Itacalibri, Milan, pp 257–284

Venter F (2015) Constitutionalism and religion. Edwar Elgar Publishing, Chelternham, UK, Northampton, MA

Weiler JHH (2007) A Christian Europe? Europe and Christianity: rules of commitment. Eur View 6(1):143–150

Weiler JHH (2010) Lautsi: Crucifix in the classroom Redux. EJIL. https://www.ejiltalk.org/lautsi-crucifix-in-the-classroom-redux/

Whaley JD, Dreisbach DL (1999) What the wall separates: a debate on Thomas Jefferson's "Wall of Separation" metaphor. University of Minnesota Law School. Retrieved from the University of Minnesota Digital Conservancy. http://hdl.handle.net/11299/167975

Witte J, Nichols JA (2011) Religion and the American constitutional experiment. Westview Press, Boulder

Zagrebelsky G (2011) Scambiarsi la veste. LaTerza, Rome

The Blasphemy Laws of Pakistan: Experimenting with History and Tradition

Muhammad Ahsan Qureshi

Abstract The Blasphemy Laws of Pakistan are arguably the most controversial piece of legislation in the country's constitution. Rooted in its colonial past, the Laws have evolved with Pakistan and continue to hold tremendous importance in its identity formation. The Laws have been used by both religious and liberal agents to shape the meta-narrative and are often used by politicians to gain votes. An in-depth analysis of their formation and evolution can best explain how the Laws gained such prominence in the national discourse of Pakistan. The chapter starts with such an attempt. In order to provide a more contemporary understanding of how Pakistani society sees the Laws, discourse from leading newspapers is also captured and analyzed via the lens of Epistemic governance. The resulting analysis reveals religious traditions, religious historical and the nationalist historical roots of the Laws, explaining why they continue to dominate the national narrative in Pakistan.

1 Introduction

April 13, 2017, a charged mob walked towards the boys' hostel building in Abdul Wali Khan University in Mardan, Pakistan, looking for Mashal Khan. They found him hidden in his room. Dragging him out, they beat him, shot him and eventually let him bleed to death. The mob, amounting to hundreds, not satisfied with just killing the boy, decided to further insult him. Denuding his carcass, the mob continued to pelt his body with stones and to hit it with belts and ceramic pots. Had the police not intervened then, they would have burnt the body as well. Such was the anger and disgust against Mashal, an alleged blasphemer.

This chapter is a modified and amended version of the Masters Thesis of Mohammad Ahsan Qureshi submitted for the Master's Programme in Global and Transnational Studies at the University of Tampere, School of Social Sciences and Humanities, May 2017.

M. Ahsan Qureshi (✉)
Faculty of Social Sciences, University of Tampere, Tampere, Finland
e-mail: ahsan.qureshi@uta.fi

J. Giles et al. (eds.), *Law, Religion and Tradition*, Law and Religion in a Global Context 1, https://doi.org/10.1007/978-3-319-96749-3_2

The anger of those in the crowd had been building up for several months. Mashal was an intellectual, one who could not help but debate with people. Some of his debates were with religious people during which he would reveal contradictions within Islam. One such debate took place a day before his death and acted as the trigger point to his mob-lynching. In this conversation, he had offered his doubt on whether Adam and Eve were, in fact, the originators of humanity. On one retort, Mashal had inquired if humanity was a result of incestuous relationships between Adam and Eves' offspring. This claim irked the people with whom he was debating.

Previously, Mashal had addressed another sensitive issue by pointing towards corruption within his University. This took place in an interview with a private TV channel. The administration of the institution, angry at his criticism, sought to punish him. They collected a group of boys who were already annoyed about his religious debates and offered their assistance in intimidating him into silence. However, the group, which eventually swelled into an angry mob, got out of control. Fuming with anger against the alleged blasphemer, the mob charged towards the boys' hostel, shouting religious chants and pulling in more religiously charged university students. Mashal had no way to escape what came his way. The details of his horrific murder were caught on several mobile cameras and uploaded on social media sites. Leading newspapers also decided to publish the videos after heavily censoring them.

There were two peculiarities in the tragic saga of Mashal that caught the country off-guard. One was the location and the environment where the murder had taken place. While mob-lynching on blasphemy-related killings are not a rarity in Pakistan, they usually happen in social settings where a lack of education can be blamed. However, Mashal was killed within the premises of an educational institution. Hence, the murderers were, in a sense, educated individuals who had rationally decided that the repercussions of their actions did not outweigh taking revenge against an alleged blasphemer. In other words, the incident proves that the lack of education alone could not be blamed for such actions. Another peculiarity was how the media handled its reporting on the issue. While such incidents are usually reported in newspapers, with washed-out, stale details, this time, the media houses chose to show videos of the lynching after censoring them. The videos hence gave a more realistic and relatable presentation of what happened, explicitly revealing the full brutality with which Mashal was murdered.

While there was widespread condemnation on the ruthlessness with which he was killed, not many were sympathetic towards Mashal in the immediate aftermath of the killing. It was only after the authorities confirmed that he had not blasphemed that people, including the Prime Minister of the country, started offering support and compassion to his family. Others continued to blame him for debating controversial and sensitive topics. Local religious leaders, however, were not convinced and continued to call him a blasphemer, urging people not to offer or take part in his funeral prayers. Later, many took out rallies in support of his murder. Fearing its desecration, Mashal was not buried in a graveyard but on a piece of land owned by his father and his grave is under the constant surveillance by police. The investigation agencies have since indicted 58 people for the murder while three accused remain at large.

The incident of Mashal's lynching, although widely reported and discussed, was not entirely unique. Pakistan's history is filled with incidents where its Blasphemy Laws have been exploited for personal reasons. Draconian and vague in form and spirit, the laws have been criticized by human rights groups, and civil society members for going against numerous human rights conventions signed by the country (Julius 2016). Given the volatility of those who support the Laws, suggestions to amend them are very rare.

More recently, they have been further institutionalized by the State to censor opinions against either the government or the army. Five bloggers behind anti-army Facebook pages and blogs were abducted by the intelligence agencies at the start of 2017 and released after a few weeks. During their detention, media channels that are famous for their pro-army stance led a campaign against the abducted bloggers accusing them of running blasphemous pages and blogs. Since their release, the bloggers have moved abroad and stayed mostly underground, fearing for their lives due to the blasphemy charges. In December 2017, Pakistan's Islamabad High Court formally absolved them from the charges due to lack of evidence.

Any understanding of the usage of the Blasphemy Laws would prompt an in-depth recognition of their formation and evolution. Contrary to popular belief, the Laws are not derived from religious scriptures. Similarly, while the religious lobby did play an important part in their evolution, they were formalized by relatively liberal political leaders and used as tools to control narratives. This chapter will deal with the history of the Laws, connecting them to various traditions and dogmas. The first part will root the Laws in Pakistan's colonial past, recording their evolution until the present day. The second part will present an updated outline of the Laws, detailing their misuses and attempts at amendments. The third part will highlight the perceived historical and religious origins of the Laws, as found in columns of the leading newspapers of the country. In all these parts, an attempt will be made to highlight how religious and historical traditions have been used to impose particular definitions of the Laws. This will be especially obvious in the last part where verbatim script from newspapers will be highlighted to see this imposition as a form of epistemic governance.

2 History of the Laws

The Blasphemy Laws of Pakistan are rooted in its colonial past. Upon independence, the country inherited constitutional instruments from British ruled India. One such instrument was the Indian Penal code which already included a watered-down version of the Laws in it. This version was originally included in the Penal Code to mitigate tensions between the British colonists and the Indian Army subjects who had mutinied against them in 1857. The mutiny, allegedly, occurred due to the production of new bullet cartridges which had to be chewed before they could be used. To ensure that they did not dry up, they were laced with grease. A rumor spread that the grease used in the cartridges included animal fat, especially fat from cows and pigs (Dalrymple 2006). Cows hold religious significance in Hinduism and pigs are *Haram* (forbidden) in Islam. As the British were already seen as conquerors who, with their missionary projects, were trying to Christianize India, the army reacted sharply. Some soldiers refused to use the guns and mutinied against the officers. The mutiny eventually escalated into the "Indian rebellion" of 1857. After the dust settled and the rebellion was quashed, the British introduced religion-sensitive reforms in the constitution to avoid similar clashes in the future. A "Blasphemy Law", derived from the English Common Law, was part of these reforms. The Law maintained that everyone had a right to practice the religion of their choice. Moreover, it barred all insults to religions regardless of creed or religious affiliations. Put into place to ensure stability in the multi-religious society of India, the Law did not change until some 70 years later when it was revised and more articles were added to it.

In 1929 Mahashay Rajpal used his publishing company to print a book that ridiculed Muhammad, the Prophet of Islam. The publication angered Muslims who used the aforementioned Blasphemy Law in the Indian Penal Code to take him to court. While the court found him guilty of inciting religious hatred, the penal code did not detail any punishments. When Rajpal appealed against the judgement, the court acquitted him citing lack of legal tools to prosecute him further. The Muslim population felt cheated and their frustration grew. One of them, a young man named Ilm-u-din, decided to take matters into his own hands. He killed Rajpal, terming it as revenge for the Prophet. He was caught by the police, found guilty and hanged in 1929. As a result of the incident, the British amended the penal code adding article 295-A. The additional article stated:

> Whoever with deliberate or malicious intentions of outraging the religious feelings of any class of His Majesty's subjects, by words either spoken or written, by visible representations insults or attempts to insult religion or religious beliefs of that class shall be punished with imprisonment of either description for 2 years or fine or both.

This amended version of the Law was inherited by Pakistan when it claimed independence from the British on August 14, 1947. When the adopted Indian Penal Code was converted to the Pakistan Penal Code, the sentence for a blasphemer was increased from 2 to 10 years.

Since its adoption, the religious political parties have tried to use the Law against the Ahmadi sect of Islam. Founded in the 19th century in British Indian Punjab by Mirza Ghulam Ahmad, the sect claims to be devout Muslims. However, they differ from other Muslim sects with one of the core beliefs of Islam: the finality of Muhammad's prophethood. The sect claims that while Muhammad was the seal of prophets, he was not the last one and was followed by the founder of the sect. This puts them in direct opposition to the general narrative in Islam, making their association with the religion controversial.

Religious parties in British India had tried to put an end to the Ahmadi movement since its inception, but could not as they lacked influence in secular India. Also, given their lack of involvement in the independence movement for Pakistan, they failed to keep a check on the influence of Ahmadis in the lead up to independence. All their efforts were mostly ignored by Muhammad Ali Jinnah, the founder of Pakistan, who firmly believed in a pluralist society and insisted that one's religious beliefs had "nothing to do with the business of the state."[1]

Jinnah passed away only a year after Pakistan gained its independence, leaving a vacuum of leadership in the newly formed state. As distinct religious identity was the major driver of the independence movement and the most efficient tool to unify and motivate the country, religion was officially imbedded in the national narrative by the new leaders (Waterman 2014). On March 7, 1949, Liaquat Ali Khan, the first Prime Minister of the country, introduced the "Objectives Resolution" to the newly formed constituent assembly. The document, which was basically a preamble to the planned constitution, strongly supported the formation of a political framework based on Islamic principles (Bindra 1990). The religious parties, encouraged at this, started mainstreaming themselves into politics to be more influential in formulating the national identity. They also established themselves as the moral conscience of the government, checking it when it fell short of ensuring social ethics within society (Jalal 2014). The moral policing eventually led to the issue of the Ahmadis' claims on being muslims.

In 1949, *Ahrar*, a Deobandi Sunni organization, demanded that the Ahmadis should be officially declared heretics in the new Muslim State (Qadir 2015). When the demand was not accommodated, the general resentment against the sect grew even further. Another cause for distress was the presence and influence of Ahmadis in the State's infrastructure. Besides allowing them to hold important positions in the bureaucracy and army, the State also appointed Muhammad Zafar Ullah, an Ahmadi, to the post of foreign minister. The religious right felt that an Ahmadi could not represent a Muslim state in the international stage. In order to force the government to seek the resignation of Zafar Ullah, several religious parties gathered under Tahaffuz-e-Khatme-Nabbuwat (Movement for the Protection of the Finality of the Prophet) and started a national street movement (Haider 2011). The movement eventually demanded a complete, official ostracizing of the Ahmadis. The protests soon became violent leading to an organized pogrom of an estimated 2000 Ahmadis in Lahore (Ispahani 2017). The protests were quelled when the army took control of the city, marking the first of many martial laws in Pakistan's history. These protests interlaced the inherited blasphemy law with the Ahmadi issue, laying foundations for eventual additions to it.

When, in 1973, a new constitution was being drafted, the Ahmadi debate reignited. Interestingly this happened during the tenure of Pakistan's first democratically elected leader, Zulifqar Ali Bhutto. An Oxford graduate, Bhutto was the founder of the People's Party of Pakistan, a socialist party that is generally believed to be liberal. He formed his government in the aftermath of the 1971 civil war which led to the independence of Bangladesh. Given these were times of great identity crisis for the

[1] Muhammad Ali Jinnah's first Presidential Address to the Constituent Assembly of Pakistan (August 11, 1947) http://www.columbia.edu/itc/mealac/pritchett/00islamlinks/txt_jinnah_assembly_1947.html.

nation, Bhutto took upon himself to refound the nation's philosophy. Much like the leaders before him, he too decided to use religion as a unifying factor, and introduced measures to emphasize Pakistan's Islamic credentials. One of these constitutional measures was to put belief in the finality of Prophethood as a precondition to holding the office of President and Prime Minister.

Effectively barred from the top offices already, the religious parties now demanded a complete ostracizing of the Ahmadi sect. However, the pressure to dictate the definition of "being Muslim" was not purely local. The 1970s saw a tug of war between Iran and Saudi Arabia to dominate the global Islamic narrative. King Faisal, to counter the influence of the Shah of Iran, sought Pakistan's allegiance to Saudi's *Wahabbist* interpretation. In April 1974, the Rabita al-Alam-al-Islami (Islamic World Congress) held a meeting in Mecca where the attributes of being Muslim were discussed. The congress members also discussed the Ahmadi issues and, as a result, demanded that Muslim governments declare Ahmadi's to be non-Muslims (Jalal 2014).

Back in Pakistan, an eight-party religious alliance launched a 100-day campaign, leading to social unrest. Maulana Abul Ala Maududi, head of Jamaat-e-Islami, who had close connections with Saudi Arabia, played a crucial part in these protests. Yet again, the riots turned violent leading to 42 deaths, 27 of whom were Ahmadis (Kennedy 1989). As Bhutto wanted support for his newly formulated constitution, he gave in to the political demands and convened a special session of the National Assembly to discuss the Ahmadi issue (Shaikh 2009). In-camera proceedings held from August 5 to September 7 resulted in a unanimous recommendation to declare Ahmadi's as non-Muslims. As a result, the second amendment to the Pakistani constitution was passed and Ahmadis were officially declared as non-Muslims. Articles specific to their baring were added to the Blasphemy Law, acting as a stepping stone for further amendments in the future.

General Zia-ul-Haq, a military dictator who overthrew the government of Bhutto, sought the support of religious parties to justify his takeover. To appease them, he introduced several parallel religious laws and systems in the State's legal infrastructure which continue to exist today. This groundwork allowed further amendments to the Blasphemy Laws making it stricter and even more far reaching. In 1982, Zia's government decided to include the desecration of the Quran within the legal definition of blasphemy. This came in the form of the addition of article 295-B in the Blasphemy Law. Eventually, in 1986, article 295-C was added, bringing insult to the Prophet Muhammad within the legal definition of blasphemy as well. At the same time, the maximum sentence for blasphemy was increased from 10-years imprisonment to "life imprisonment or death". The option of life imprisonment was later challenged in a Federal Shariat court, a parallel religious court set up by Zia. That court ruled in favor of death as the only punishment for blasphemers.[2] As a result, the option of life imprisonment was removed, leaving death as the only punishment for a blasphemer. This was the last addition and produced what are now collectively termed as the "Blasphemy Laws of Pakistan". The amendments made during Zia's

[2]The Court order found in Sr. No 336 in: http://federalshariatcourt.gov.pk/Leading%20Judgements/decided%20shariat.%20cases.doc.

time included language which was vague and open to interpretations. In time, some politicians have suggested amending them to make them clearer but these suggestions have been violently rejected by the religious right who continue to hold great power amongst the people.

3 The Laws Today

Pakistan's Blasphemy Laws are generally seen by both local and international human rights activists as being in contravention of numerous human rights conventions signed by the country, and also as impeding the rights guaranteed by the State's own constitution (Julius 2016). Amendments made to the original Law, which was adapted from the Indian Penal Code, reflect today's society as increasingly intolerant. During British rule, prior to the independence of Pakistan in 1947, a total of seven cases were filed on blasphemy charges based on the original version of the Law (Shakir 2015). Post-partition until the amendments in 1980, eight cases were filed under the revised version Since the 1986 amendments during Zia-ul-Haq's tenure in 1980, the Laws have attracted a total of 1335 cases (Amnesty International 2016). Besides these cases, up to 51 of those accused have been killed extra-judicially, some dying moments after being acquitted by the courts (Supreme Court of Pakistan 2015). The mob justice related to the Laws is not limited to the accused alone, in fact, there have been several cases where neighborhoods have been burnt down as a response to a single person's action. The accusations of blasphemy are not limited to non-Muslims alone. Based on the same principle as the one that resulted in Ahmadi-specific amendments in the Laws, any one deviating from the dominant narrative of Islam is in danger of committing blasphemy. Moreover, the Laws are often used against business associates and to bully and intimidate people. As most claims have no tangible proof to support the accusations, the trials are usually based on hearsay and word of mouth. Those accused, are permanently tainted with the charge, leading to social exclusion. Many have to move to a different location and change their names, in fear of their lives and the lives of their loved ones. As the Judges are exposed to the same pressure from the religious lobby, trials are usually not very transparent. Similarly, lawyers who defend the accused are treated with hostility and are harassed within and outside the court. Due to these reasons, those accused and arrested, sometimes have to wait in jail cells for many years as they can neither find a defense lawyer nor a judge to take the case.

Given their ability to facilitate intimidation and the power and scope they provide to prosecutors, the Laws have found support in power hungry politicians, manipulative opinion makers and even local and international terrorist organizations. As stated above, the Laws were chiseled in their current form during the governments of liberal politicians who used them to gain support or increase their vote bank. Religious political parties often use these Laws to increase their popularity and to bully politicians. Moreover, the Laws have recently been cited in terrorist threats by organizations linked to Taliban and Al-Qaeeda, leading some scholars to include them as tools for militant ideology (Abbas 2013).

4 Attempts at Amendments

Discussions about the Laws have been mostly discouraged due to their sensitive nature. Their supporters have increasingly become more inflexible on discussing the Laws and are prone to become violent over any suggestion of amendments. While some local and international NGOs have been involved in movements for modifications, they have failed to convince politicians, media personalities and other opinion makers to debate them. As most of these cases happen either in rural areas or amongst poor families, they are not brought to the public's attention and so do not enter into the social discourse. However, this changed in 2010, when Salman Taseer, Governor of the biggest province of Pakistan, Punjab, visited Aasia Bibi, a woman accused of blasphemy, in her jail cell. She had been accused of saying derogatory words against Muhammad and the death sentence was subsequently pronounced by a local magistrate's court. After meeting her, Taseer held a press conference, insisting that her sentence was unfair and that he would seek a presidential pardon for her. He also insisted that the Laws, in their current form, were vague and were prone to exploitation and misuse. He insisted that they were man-made and hence could be modified. He pledged to lobby for their modification and refinement in the Parliament. His call was supported by Shahbaz Bhatti, the Federal Minister for minorities, who had earlier failed to get any support from the government.

There was widespread reaction to Taseer's statements. Religious parties took to the streets to protest against him, insisting that by calling the Laws "man-made", he too had blasphemed. They demanded of the country's Chief Justice, Iftikhar Muhammad Chaudhry, to take a *suo moto* (self-initiated) action against Taseer for abusing his powers as a Governor. They warned the President against intervening in the case and pardoning Aasia. The negative reaction to Taseer was not limited to the religious lobby alone. People from within the government refused to be associated with Taseer. Babar Awan, the Minister for Law and Justice, convened a press conference on the issue, stating that "in [his] presence as the Minister, no one should think of abolishing this law."[3]

On January 4, 2011, within weeks of the press conference, Taseer was assassinated by his own body guard as he came out of a restaurant in Islamabad. None of the other guards stopped Mumtaz Qadri, the assailant, who shot an estimated 36 bullets into Taseer. Qadri confessed to the murder, claiming he had killed for the sake of Muhammad. Two months later, Shahbaz Bhatti was assassinated by the Taliban for agreeing with Taseer and seeking amendments to the Laws.

---

[3]Interview: https://www.thenews.com.pk/archive/print/610178-babar-awan-says-no-one-can-change-blasphemy-law.

During his trial, Qadri was defended by the former Chief Justice of the High Court, who took his case voluntarily. Qadri had enormous support within the legal community. They came out in crowds to shower rose petals on him, and to garland him, whenever he was presented in the courts. The defense team challenged the death sentence at all levels of the court proceedings, insisting that Qadri could not be prosecuted for being a good Muslim. Their appeals were rejected by the courts. After the Supreme Court upheld the judgement, some media channels reported that Qadri made an appeal for a presidential pardon. The pardon was rejected as well. On February 29, 2016, more than five years after he killed Taseer, the death sentence was passed on Qadri. Although the government banned all coverage of his funeral, it still managed to attract thousands of people including representatives from the leading religious parties. His grave has since been converted into a mausoleum visited by many admirers every day.

5 Perceived Roots of the Blasphemy Laws Within the Media

Media, besides influencing society at large, also reflects how people think (Nawaz 1983). In that sense, the discourse reproduced in the media imitates the concerns and opinions of readers (Shoeb 2008). This is especially true for opinion pieces and columns in newspapers. The writings published in these sections voice the views of leading opinion makers and intellectuals. As they are not dependent on day-to-day reporting, the writers have the opportunity to critique subjects at length and in much more depth than conventional forms of reporting. Besides acting as "advocacy tools" to direct narratives (Sommer and Maycroft 2008), columns also represent the issues which the common man of the country is concerned about (Golan 2013).

Print media holds an exceedingly significant position in energy deprived nations such as Pakistan. Given the widespread lack of access to internet and the inability to use electronic hardware effectively, the less dependent, cheaper print media is the natural alternative source of information for most of the population (Fair et al. 2015). Moreover the Pakistani broadcast media tends to emotionalize and exaggerate reporting, in attempts to increase their ratings. Hence, in that sense, print media in Pakistan remains a preferred source of information and opinions and is seen as "credible and reliable" (Iqbal et al. 2013).

As discussion of the Blasphemy Laws are rare in Pakistan, not many history books deal with their roots and evolution. Similarly, afraid of volatile reactions, media houses generally avoid covering debates on the Laws from any angle deemed controversial. However, with the involvement of Salman Taseer and subsequent events that took place, the media finally began to shed some light on the discourse about the Laws. In the columns published in Pakistan's leading newspapers, analysts initiated discussions on the applicability and roots of the Laws, blending them in the context of national and international dynamics. Such columns in the leading newspapers of

Pakistan were captured and analyzed for this study. The English newspaper "*Dawn*" and the Urdu newspaper "*Daily Jang*" were used for the study. The rationale on choosing them lies in them being the most widely read newspapers in Pakistan in their respective languages. Also, each newspaper caters to a unique type of audience and hence could shed light on how opinions differed across society. *Dawn*, for example, pursues a left of center stance (Fair and Hamza 2016) and has an elitist readership (Akhtar 2009) whereas, the *Daily Jang* has a moderate conservative leaning (IMS 2009) with a more generic readership. Columns were collected from the day Taseer visited Aasia Bibi and held his press conference to a few weeks after Qadri's hanging. Overall, the data covered over 5 years of discourse on the Laws.

The columns were analyzed using the *Epistemic Governance* approach. Foucault (1991) defined governance as the ability to influence the "hopes, desires, or milieu" of the governed (Inda 2005). This understanding requires that the governed—the actors—are not passive. Hence policies can only be fully implemented if the affected themselves believe in them. This influencing can only take place when both sides seem to accept a common reality. In this way, both the columnists and the audience, engage in reciprocal convincing, till their perceived realities are similar. Alasuutari and Qadir (2014) see such engagements as "epistemic governance." According to this approach, actors believe in a set of imageries that direct how they respond to situations. The response can be influenced by engaging in epistemic work on these imageries. Such work must include shaping another's ontology of the environment, identifications and perceived norms. Hence, a compromise only makes sense when everyone in the discourse shares (accepts, if not embraces) a unique understanding of the reality.

With this framework in mind, data was broken down into imageries and units of epistemic work. Besides providing deep insight into how discourse on the Laws developed and contributed to the general narrative, the broken-down data also revealed different perceived roots of the Laws. These roots are briefly presented in the following pages, linking them to various assumed traditions.

5.1 Religion/Religious Laws

There was an obvious disparity in rooting the Laws in religion amongst the columnists. While a large majority of the columnists in *Daily Jang* implied that they were rooted in religion, the columnists in *Dawn* did not agree to the claim. While not many called them "man-made" explicitly, the *Dawn* columnists did write narratives that implied this. For example, writers called the Laws "poorly drafted", "astonishing", "ambiguous", "controversial", "piece of legislature", "a wrong inflicted on Pakistan's minorities", "draconian" and called their existence "sordid" and a "monstrosity". All these columnists were of the view that there was a need for amendments to the Laws to make them more accurate. However, none sought their abolition. In fact, the blame was always put on the religious leaders for pushing interpretations which were inhumane and contradicted the "peaceful" face of Islam. Recognizing how their word carried weight, the columnist urged the religious leaders to refrain from resorting to emotionalism or violence on any discussion about amendments to the Laws. Some of the columnists even blamed the religious leaders for not playing their part when the Laws were formed and included in the constitution, allowing certain extremist mindsets to dominate the narrative on blasphemy. Such writers were of the view that there should have been an elaborate public discussion on the subject and religious leaders from different sects should have been included in the conversation to reach a more well-rounded form of the Laws. However, these opinions were not unanimous. A small portion of columnists in *Dawn* did insist that the Laws were rooted in scripture and Salman Taseer had been "careless" to imply that they were man-made, however, yet again, the blame was put on religious personalities for inciting Qadri and pushing him to be anarchic.

Columnists in *Daily Jang*, with an exception of one columnist, were unanimous in insisting that the Laws were rooted in religion. Most of the writeups proved this connection by citing the Quran and *Hadith* (actions and sayings of Muhammad). Writing about the severity of the Laws, the columnists insisted that they, in their current form, were accurate and there was no room for leniency for a blasphemer. Quoting the Quran, one columnist insisted that "God himself was angry at those who insulted Prophet Muhammad" so there was no space to be merciful towards them. Others insisted that only Muhammad himself could forgive a blasphemer and no state authority had the right to pardon one. While some columnists insisted that reaction to blasphemy was due to an "unconventional" degree of devotion towards the Prophet, something that every Muslim possesses, others found the Laws and their severity very rational and a result of "1400 years long research, thought." Some columnists ridiculed the liberal elements within Pakistani society for criticizing the Laws, urging them that only Islamic Laws made sense in an Islamic state like Pakistan. Others, insisted that the attacks on or criticisms of the Laws were an international conspiracy against the Islamic identity of Pakistan.

5.2 Religious History

There was an obvious overlap between narratives which relied on religion and history to support their arguments. Such columnists quoted incidents during Muhammad's life to either support or criticize the Laws. Those who insisted that the Laws made no sense in Islam, quoted several examples of Muhammad's leniency and peace-loving nature. For example, an often-quoted incident was one where he went to nurse a Jewish woman who would usually throw trash on him but had been absent on that particular day. Other examples included his selfless forgiveness for the people of *Taif* who had pelted him with stones. As the legend goes, when Angel Gabriel was sent by God to suggest a punishment for the community, Muhammad refused, forgiving all of them. Others argued that Islam had historically "preached tolerance and diversity of faith in the most unequivocal terms." This was undertaken by citing several examples of Muhammad creating a society in *Madina* where people from different faiths managed to live peacefully. These examples were then compared with Pakistan where the Muslim readers were advised to protect the rights of the minorities living in the country just as the Muslims in *Madina* had protected the Jews from "prosecution at the hands of the medieval Christians in Europe and Byzantium."

On the other hand, those who supported the death penalty for blasphemy used the example of Muhammad forgiving everyone on his conquest of Makkah except those who had "mocked" or "jeered" at him. This particular incident was the most cited in several columns in *Daily Jang* and used to snub the claims of people who sought an *ijtihad*[4] on the issue. Others used names and experiences of renowned Muslim leaders to convince their readers to act in accordance with their creed. Interestingly, there was a degree of ambiguity in the references. For example, an incident of a certain Caliph during the *Usmania* Caliphate was used in one column. The Caliph had promised to wage war on France if they did not stop the production of a blasphemous theatrical play. The columnist insisted that France had ceased the production and praised the Caliph for his devotion and love for the Prophet. However, the name of the Caliph was not mentioned in the column. Similarly, another columnist urged the readers to stay true to the lineage of *Salaudin Ayubi*, not explaining what he meant by it.

5.3 Nationalist History

Both Muhammad Ali Jinnah and Muhammad Iqbal were often quoted by many columnists both in support and condemnation of the Blasphemy Laws. Jinnah, the founder of Pakistan was a great proponent for pluralism in society and was strictly against infusion of religion in politics. Iqbal, on the other hand, is widely considered the "spiritual founder" of Pakistan as he was the first person to envision a separate country for the Muslims of India (Khan 2012, 58). Both continue to hold a special place within national discourse and influence the meta-narrative on Pakistan's philosophical roots.

Columnists who insisted that the Blasphemy Laws were inconsistent with Jinnah's vision of the country quoted the speech he made on August 11, 1947 where he insisted that the state had nothing to do with religion. Basing their arguments on this speech, some columnists insisted that Jinnah wanted a secular country and "did not want to mix state matters and religion." By including laws such as the Blasphemy Laws, the columnist berated legislators and the governed on the grounds that "we failed the nation, and most of all we failed the creed of the man who made this nation."[5]

On the other hand, columnists who found the basis of the Laws in Jinnah's life presented a completely different picture of the founder. For example, they insisted that he was a "very religious person" who would have wholly agreed with the Laws. Moreover, most of this narrative cited Iqbal, especially detailing his reaction to

[4]Issues that cannot be solved using the Quran and Sunnah are allowed to be discussed by ulemas who can debate and reach a solution on them. This process is called as Ijtehad.

[5]Dawn 22/01/2011: Blind and stupid and savage by Ardeshir Cowasjee.

the Ilm-u-din case. As mentioned above, Ilm-u-din had killed the publisher of a defamatory book and was later hanged for it. According to the columnists, both Muhammad Iqbal and Jinnah had praised Ilm-u-din's actions. Iqbal, according to these columnists, convinced Jinnah to defend Ilm-u-din during his trial. Later, Iqbal led his funeral prayers and envied him for killing Rajpal.

Ilm-u-din was not the only murderer mentioned by the columnists who supported the Blasphemy Laws. Another case mentioned by the columnists was that of Amir Cheema who was a student in Germany who attempted to kill the editor of a newspaper which had reprinted the cartoons of Muhammad. Cheema was arrested and committed suicide while awaiting trial. The columnist who dedicated his column to him, repeated verbatim interviews and conversations with Cheema's father, calling his action "incomparably noble". All these accounts were designed to convince the reader that the Blasphemy Laws were derived from natural Islamic thoughts and actions and would have been supported by the founders of the country.

6 Conclusion

The Blasphemy Laws of Pakistan continue to be a controversial topic in the country and discourse on them remains limited. As is evident in this chapter, there are different narratives that are superimposed on each other to blur out their true history. These narratives are based in deeply rooted religious and historical traditions and are used by people in power to epistemically govern people into certain realities. This is most obvious with the insistence that the Laws are based on religious traditions when, as the write-up portrays, they are a remnant of Pakistan's colonial past. Similarly, by using them to incite and reiterate national and religious insecurities, politicians have been able to epistemically steer the population. By emphasizing one tradition over another, Pakistan has managed to change the core motivation and form of the original Law derived from English Common Law. This emphasizes the impact and influence of tradition as a form of epistemic governance and the method's ability to manufacture targeted realities.

References

Abbas SB (2013) Pakistan's Blasphemy laws: from Islamic empires to the Taliban. University of Texas Press, Texas

Akhtar RS (2009) Media, religion and politics in Pakistan. OUP, Karachi

Alasuutari P, Qadir A (2014) Epistemic governance: an approach to the politics of policymaking. Eur J Cult Polit Sociol 1(1):67–84

Amnesty International (2016) As good as dead. p 14. Retrieved from: http://www.refworld.org/pdfid/585a41704.pdf

Bindra SS (1990) Politics of islamization: with special reference to Pakistan. Deep & Deep Publications, New Delhi

Dalrymple W (2006) The last Mughal. Bloomsbury, London
Fair C, Hamza A (2016) From elite consumption to popular opinion: framing of the US drone program in Pakistani newspapers. Small Wars Insurgencies 27(4):578–607
Fair CC, Kaltenthaler K, Miller W (2015) Pakistani political communication and public opinion on US drone attacks. J Strateg Stud 38:6
Foucault M (1991) Governmentality. In: Burchell G, Gordon C, Miller P (eds) The Foucault effect: studies in governmentality. University of Chicago Press, Chicago, pp 87–104
Golan G (2013) The gates of column diplomacy: newspaper framing the 2011 Egyptian revolution. Int Commun Gazette 75(4):359–373
Haider Z (2011) Ideologically adrift. In: Lodhi M (ed) Pakistan: beyond the crisis state. Oxford University Press, Karachi, pp 113–130
IMS (2009) Between radicalization and democratization in an unfolding conflict: media in Pakistan. Published online July 2009
Inda JX (2005) Analytics of the modern: an introduction. In: Inda JX (ed) Anthropologies of modernity: Foucault, governmentality, and life politics. Blackwell, Oxford, pp 1–20
Iqbal A, Ali Z, Fatima S, Naseem S (2013) Comparative analysis of editorial treatment by Urdu press of Pakistan regarding elections 2008. Int Asian Res J 01(01):46–58
Ispahani F (2017) Purifying the land of the pure: a history of Pakistan's religious minorities. Oxford University Press, New York
Jalal A (2014) The struggle for Pakistan: a Muslim homeland and global politics. The Belknap Press of Harvard University Press, London
Julius Q (2016) The experience of minorities under Pakistan's Blasphemy laws. Islam Christ Muslim Relat 27(1):95–115. https://doi.org/10.1080/09596410.2015.1108639
Kennedy CH (1989) Towards the definition of a Muslim in a Islamic state: the case of the Ahmadiyya in Pakistan. In: Vajpey D (ed) Religious and ethnic minority politics in South Asia. Manohar 90, New Delhi, pp 71–108
Khan N (2012) Muslim becoming: aspiration and skepticism in Pakistan. Duke University Press, London
Nawaz S (1983) The mass media and development in Pakistan. Asian Surv 23(8):934–957
Qadir A (2015) When heterodoxy becomes heresy: using Bourdieu's concept of Doxa to describe state-sanctioned exclusion in Pakistan. Sociol Relig 76(2):155–176
Shaikh F (2009) Making sense of Pakistan. Columbia University Press, New York
Shakir N (2015) 'Islamic Shariah and Blasphemy Laws in Pakistan' the round table. Commonwealth J Int Aff. https://doi.org/10.1080/00358533.2015.1053235
Shoeb NF (2008) An analysis of Urdu and English editorial coverage of the 2007 emergency from Pakistani newspapers. Master's thesis, Georgetown University. Retrieved from: https://repository.library.georgetown.edu/bitstream/handle/10822/552894/shoebNadia.pdf;sequence=1
Sommer B, Maycroft JR (2008) Influencing public policy: an analysis of published column by academics. Politics Policy 36(4):586–613
Supreme court of Pakistan (2015) The state vs Malik Mumtaz Qadri. p 26. Retrieved from http://www.supremecourt.gov.pk/web/user_files/File/Crl.A._210_2015.pdf
Waterman D (2014) Saudi wahhabi imperialism in Pakistan: history, legacy, contemporary representations and debate. Socialinių Mokslų Studijos Societal Stud 6(2):242–258

An Analysis of Possibility of Fulfilling Gender Equality Within the Legal System of the Islamic Republic of Iran (IRI)

Marziyeh Bakhshizadeh

Abstract Iran, under the government of president Rouhani, adopted the 2030 Agenda for Sustainable Development, expressing its commitment towards its holistic and comprehensive implementation, albeit with some reservations expected from an Islamic country. The signing of the document was strongly criticized by the Supreme Leader, Ayatollah Ali Khamenei, who said this was not proper for an Islamic country, where Quran and Islamic rules are the benchmark for public and private living together. On June 23, 2017, the Supreme Council of the Cultural Revolution voted in favor of the non-implementation of the document of Agenda 2030 in Iran. Similarly, *the Convention on the Elimination of All Forms of Discrimination against Women* (CEDAW) was ratified by the reformist government of Mohamad Khatami, and was approved by the sixth parliament (2000–2004). However, the Guardian Council ultimately rejected it, arguing that it was incompatible with Islam. This chapter considers the traditional role accorded to women in the law of Iran in the light of the development of equality rights in international law. The two cases presented here are illustrations of two different interpretations of Islam and how these impact on equality rights and the traditional role accorded to women under law in Iranian society. What we see on the one hand is adoption by Khatami's or Rouhani's governments of important international agreements—the CEDAW and the 2030 Agenda—while on the other hand, both documents being rejected by the Supreme leader and fundamentalists in Iran because they are incompatible with Islamic values or teachings. This chapter will compare CEDAW as a set of criteria for gender equality with the current laws of the Islamic Republic of Iran. This comparison is necessary to recognize how CEDAW allegedly is in conflict with Iranian laws that are claimed to be based on Islamic laws. The aim is to illustrate the capacities, strengths and limitations of Islamic Laws for gender equality. Accordingly, this chapter aims to investigate the

This chapter is a modified version of ideas first expounded in a book by Marziyeh Bakhshizadeh entitled "Changing Gender Norms in Islam between Reason and Revelation", Barbara Budrich Publishers, June 2018.

M. Bakhshizadeh (✉)
Ruhr-University Bochum, Bochum, Germany
e-mail: Marziyeh.Bakhshizadeh@rub.de

J. Giles et al. (eds.), *Law, Religion and Tradition*, Law and Religion in a Global Context 1, https://doi.org/10.1007/978-3-319-96749-3_3

different interpretations of Islam to find out which interpretations are compatible with the global norms of justice and hence in accordance with gender equality.

1 Introduction

Today, incorporating gender equality into law is regarded as a requirement for fulfilling social justice and is encompassed within international rights frameworks and international development. Fulfillment of gender equality requires *inter alia* that nation states adopt legislation and programmes to provide women and men with equal opportunities, rights, and access to resources in all spheres of life, including economic, political and cultural dimensions. International development funders in Europe and the United States of America require that projects include proposals to track how women are treated, how projects might affect them, whether projects might have a negative impact on their well-being and treatment and how projects might improve their situation. The 2030 agenda for Sustainable Development Goals (SDGs) is a set of 17 "Global Goals" with 169 targets. This was adopted by 194 countries of the UN General Assembly on 25 September 2015. Among the SDGs, goals 4 and 5 focus on equal opportunities of education for girls and boys as well as gender equality and empowerment of all women and girls through providing equal access to resources in different dimensions of society. Promoting gender equality and empowering women is necessary to the success of all the other development goals (OECD).[1]

Iran, under the government of president Rouhani, adopted the 2030 Agenda for Sustainable Development, expressing its commitment towards its holistic and comprehensive implementation. Some reservations were to be expected given that Iran is an Islamic country. Signing the document was strongly criticized by the Supreme Leader, Ayatollah Ali Khamenei, who said this was not proper for an Islamic country, where the Quran and Islamic rules are the benchmark for public and private living together. On June 23, 2017, the Supreme Council of the Cultural Revolution voted in favor of the non-implementation of the document of Agenda 2030 in Iran.

Similarly, *the Convention on the Elimination of All Forms of Discrimination against Women* (CEDAW) was ratified by the reformist government of Mohamad Khatami, and was approved by the sixth parliament (2000–2004). However, the Guardian Council[2] ultimately rejected it, arguing that it was incompatible with Islam.

[1] OECD and Post-2015 Reflections (Gender Equality and Women's Rights in The Post-2015 Agenda: A Foundation for Sustainable Development) Element 3, Paper 1.

[2] Article 91 of the Constitution introduces the Guardian Council with the following terms: "With a view to safeguarding Islamic commands and the Constitution, so that the legislation of the Islamic Assembly are not in contravention with them, a council named the Guardian Council shall be established composed of the following: (1) Six clerics, just and acquainted with the needs of the time and problems of the day. These individuals will be appointed by the Leader or the Council of Leadership; (2) Six jurists who are qualified in various branches of law, from among Muslim jurists, introduced to the Islamic Assembly by the Head of the Judiciary and appointed with the approval of

This chapter considers the traditional role accorded to women in the law of Iran in the light of the development of equality rights in international law. The two cases presented here are illustrations of two different interpretations of Islamic tradition and how this impacts on equality rights and the traditional role accorded to women under law in Iranian society. What we see on the one hand is adoption by Khatami's or Rouhani's governments of important international agreements—the CEDAW and the 2030 Agenda—while on the other hand, both documents being rejected by the Supreme leader and fundamentalists in Iran because they are incompatible with Islamic values or teachings.

In this chapter, I will compare CEDAW as a set of criteria for gender equality with the discriminatory statutes in the current laws of the Islamic Republic of Iran (IRI). This comparison is necessary to recognize how CEDAW allegedly is in conflict with Iranian laws that are claimed to be based on Islamic laws. The aim is to illustrate the capacities, strengths and limitations of Islamic Laws for gender equality. Accordingly, this chapter aims to investigate the different interpretations of Islam to find out which interpretations are compatible with the global norms of justice and hence in accordance with gender equality.

In this regard, this chapter starts with an overview of the history of CEDAW, and then proceeds with a brief history of the IRI laws related to women. This section will be followed by an analytical comparison of CEDAW with the laws in the legal system of IRI regarding the main interpretations of Islam in Iran since the 1976 revolution. It then concludes with an explanation of the influence of social change on different interpretations of Islam and women's rights.

2 An Overview on the History of CEDAW

Since the 1940s, international law has seen the development of a new tradition, namely that of equality rights within the overarching framework of fundamental rights protection. While fundamental rights developed overtime, equality rights are a 20th century phenomena which have, in particular, challenged religious and cultural norms, requiring that faith traditions both seek to retain their integrity and also seek to adapt to contextualize themselves within this new rights framework.

---

the Assembly." Also according to article 96, the majority of the clerics of the Guardian Council will decide whether the legislation passed by the Islamic Assembly is in conformity with the precepts of Islam, while the decision with regard to the conformity of the acts with the Constitution comes from the majority of all members. A bill is passed into law after it is passed by to the Islamic Assembly, approved by the Guardian Council, and signed by the president (Kar 2010: 44).

2.1 The UN Convention

The first direct mention of elimination of discrimination based on sex, specifying 'the equal rights of men and women' and 'the fundamental rights of individuals, the dignity and value of human beings' is in the preamble of the Charter of the United Nations, established on October 24, 1945. Article 1(3) explains that one of the purposes of the UN is to promote and encourage "respect for human rights and for fundamental freedoms for all without the distinction of gender, race, language or religion" (Zwingel 2005, 77).

In order to advance "women's rights in the fields of politics, business, social life and education, and to treat problems in the sphere of women's rights urgently" (Gaudart 2007, 13), the Commission on the Status of Women (CSW) was established in 1947. CSW played an essential role in ensuring that the phrase 'equal rights of men and women' from the preamble of the UN Charter was retained in the Universal Declaration of Human Rights (UDHR) (Zwingel 2005, 86).

2.2 Declaration on the Elimination of Discrimination Against Women (DEDAW)

Despite the fact that the UN Charter and the UDHR recognized the status of women and promoted the rights of women and non-discrimination based on sex, the CSW was convinced that a universal document was required to fully protect and promote women's rights, since "the existing international human rights laws were not effectively addressing the specific disadvantages and injustices faced by women" (Hoq 2001, 680). Most of the specific disadvantages faced by women were not yet recognized as violations of human rights, but they were regarded as "cultural and traditional patterns" (Zwingel 2005, 90). In fact, general human concerns were restricted to men's concerns, neglecting those of women; "because men are generally not the victims of gender discrimination, domestic violence, or sexual degradation and violence, for example; these matters can be consigned to a separate sphere and tend to be ignored" (Charlesworth et al. 1991, cited in Edwards 2011, 45). Hence, it became necessary to ensure that the "experiences of women contribute directly to the mainstream international legal order; otherwise, international human rights law loses its claim to universal applicability" (Charlesworth 1995, cited in Zwingel 2005, 92). Human Rights Law was not able to address all violations of women's rights as it was confined to the public sphere and many violations occur in private and in family life, where "the perpetrator and the victim interact in the intimate sphere of a family" (Schöpp-Schilling 2007, 7). Therefore, issues such as 'honor killing' and the various forms of physical and mental violence committed against women in the family were outside the scope of the human rights law. Therefore, a gender-specific instrument was required that would provide the greatest potential to ensure substantive gender equality for women, in both the private and public domains (Hellum and Aasen 2013, 2).

The first step in creating a convention of this type was the adoption of the non-binding Declaration on the Elimination of Discrimination Against Women (DEDAW) in 1967. The Convention on the Elimination of Discrimination Against Women (CEDAW) was adopted on December 18, 1979. It was enforced on September 3, 1981, after being ratified by twenty member states (Zwingel 2005).

Currently, 189 states are parties to the convention and only six UN member states have not yet ratified or acceded to the Convention. These states include Iran, Somalia, Sudan, Tonga, Palau (signed on September 20, 2011) and the United States of America (signed on 17 July 1980). Ratification or accession by many states does not mean the "ban of discrimination against women on the grounds of gender and marital status or with the demand for equality, equal treatment and equal status of women and men." Some states have made reservations [Article 28(1) and (2)][3] and have not accepted all articles of CEDAW, justified by the incompatibility of these articles with their political, legal and religious arrangements. However, in practice, 'many reservations run counter to the objective and purpose of the relevant articles' (Schöpp-Schilling 2007, 8).

3 A Brief History of Changing the IRI Laws Related to Women

Attempts were made in Iran during the presidency of Seyyed Mohammad Khatami (August 2, 1997–August 3, 2005) to make amendments to laws relating to women. These were made in an attempt to enable Iran to join CEDAW.

At the beginning of Khatami's presidency, a reformist agenda was promoted 'from the Islamic Ideology to the Reform of Islam' (Amir Arjomand 2009). Despite Khatami's reformist actions, he encountered opposition from the fundamentalists that dominated the fifth Parliament. Under this context, many efforts were made to promote women's rights and while some were successful, the opposition blocked many reformist actions.

Khatami won the 1997 election with seventy percent of the vote, which demonstrates the hope and optimism of people for political reform and social change in Iran. Throughout both of his terms, Khatami advocated for freedom of expression, political tolerance, civil society, equal opportunities, rule of law, women's rights, and constructive diplomatic relations with other states. The United Nations endorsed Khatami's 'Dialogue of Civilizations and Cultures' and declared 2001 as the 'United

[3]**Article 28**: 1. The Secretary-General of the United Nations shall receive and circulate to all States the text of reservations made by States at the time of ratification or accession. 2. A reservation incompatible with the object and purpose of the present Convention shall not be permitted (CEDAW).

Nations' Year of Dialogue Among Civilizations.[4] Civil society prospered in this era with more press freedom, the closer coordination of all women activists, and the opening of the Center for Women's Participation. The center had the task of empowering women to run non-governmental organizations to reinforce women's participation in the sociopolitical, economic, and cultural processes of civil society and to provide women with more freedom in the public sphere (Sadeghi 2010). Many women's groups took advantage of Khatami's 'Dialogue of Civilizations' and sought to participate in various international meetings and conferences, particularly in Asia. These opportunities allowed Iranian women to share their experiences with other women activists, to gain new insights about women's issues in other regions, and to enter the global women's movement (Tohidi 2002). Khatami also promoted women's rights by appointing women to significant political positions. Masoumeh Ebtakar, the first female Vice President of Iran, was appointed as head of the Department of Environment and Zahra Shojaee was appointed as the director of the Center for Women's Participation. These appointments led to a change in public attitudes and behavior to take women's work more seriously (Tohidi 2002).

However, only a small number of legal reforms were passed during Khatami's presidency. The minimum age of marriage and the age of penal responsibility for girls increased from nine to thirteen, although girls as young as nine could be married with the permission of the court. Another reform lifted the ban on unaccompanied single women studying abroad on government scholarships. Women were also granted custody of boys and girls up to seven years of age (the previous law entitled mothers after divorce to have custody of boys up to two years and girls up to seven). Decisions about custody of children after the age of seven were given to the court. However, other reforms that promoted women's rights provided by the sixth Parliament were rejected by the Council of Guardians (Koolaee 2012). One such reform included the 'law on insurance for women' which was passed by the sixth parliament and ratified by the seventh. The law aimed to entitle women to family property at the time of divorce and it was particularly important for many women who did not undertake paid work. The seventh parliament also passed the 'equality in blood money insurance law' which stipulated that insurance companies are obligated to pay equal blood money to men and women, in the event that paying blood money was required (Koolaee 2012). Iran's abortion law was also amended in 2005, which stipulated that

> performing abortion by physicians is permitted with definite diagnosis of retardation or malformation of the fetus that is unbearable for the mother or life-threatening disease of mother by three specialist medical doctors and verification of Legal Medicine Organization (LMO). This act allows therapeutic abortion (TA) with [the] mother's consent, only before ensoulment that is considered [to take place] 4 months after conception. In addition, the list of maternal and fetal problems that legally justify TA is open and the LMO holds the authority to verify such diseases (Shamsi Gooshki et al. 2014, 77).

An important thing to note here is that according to this law, if a woman is pregnant as a result of rape, she still does not have the right to an abortion.

---

[4] United Nations Educational, Scientific and Cultural Organization (UNESCO). 2001. Dialog among Civilization.

Many of Khatami's reformist efforts were often blocked by the fundamentalists, so that he 'declared publicly that he lacks sufficient powers to implement the constitution and the rule of law' (quoted in Moghissi and Rahnema 2001). For instance, both the Guardian Council and the judiciary[5] (which have always been under conservative control)[6] limited policies by refuting legislation and pursuing legal action against anyone who challenged the system. These circumstances restricted the scope of freedom for the press and actions from civil society. The conservatives and fundamentalists remained rooted in the ideology that women must stay at home and perform household duties and raise children while men work to earn money and manage the family (Koolaee 2012).

One notable unsuccessful effort in this era was the attempt to engage with the Convention on the Elimination of All Forms of Discrimination against Women (CEDAW). CEDAW was ratified by the reformist government and approved by parliament. However, the Guardian Council ultimately rejected it, arguing that it was incompatible with Islam. The Guardian Council then disqualified most reformist candidates from participating in the seventh and eighth parliament elections, which enabled the fundamentalists to regain control of the parliament. However, the reformists in the seventh parliament (2004–2008) proposed two conditions on CEDAW, that "international institutions should not have the right to violate Islamic laws and that international courts should not intervene in the internal affairs of Iran." The proposal was rejected by the parliament, including the female representatives, even after identification of seventy clauses in CEDAW that violated Islamic laws. The conservative female representatives argued that CEDAW was based on the Western definition of women's rights, which was not acceptable in Iranian society. Some even claimed CEDAW created a more difficult economic situation for women since it would have banned polygamy (Koolaee 2012). The following section compares CEDAW with discriminatory provisions in the current laws of the Islamic Republic of Iran in order to recognize where CEDAW conflicts with Iranian laws.

Laws in the legal system of the Islamic Republic of Iran (IRI) incorporate several types of provisions. The most important provision is in the Constitution, which determines the general framework of the political and social systems of the country. The Civil Code is another main provision of the legal system, which consists of statutes and laws that deal with civic and social relations between individuals and various circumstances of their lives.[7] Another important provision of the legal system is the penal code, which covers all punishments and offences defined in the laws. This

[5]According to the Article 156 of the Constitution of the Islamic Republic, the judiciary is 'an independent power'. And according to article 157, the head of the judiciary is to be a just *Mujtahid* appointed by the Supreme Leader and serve for a period of five years.

[6]Since the head of judiciary and also six clerics of the Guardian Council according to the Constitution are appointed by the supreme leader, in fact, through these arrangements, there is a guarantee that if the elected president or the majority of the elected body of the parliament are not under the control of the conservatives, they would not be able to divert its policies from the policies of the supreme leader (See: Moghissi and Rahnema 2001).

[7]Encyclopedia Iranica. Civil Code (qānūn-e madanī) of Persia.

section provides a review of women's rights in the Iranian legal system in comparison with CEDAW.

4 Women in the Constitution

Women and their position in society are of the utmost importance for the Islamic government in Iran, as much as that their position is addressed in the preamble of the Constitution: "*because of great oppression women suffered under the old regime (Pahlavi's regime), they should benefit great restoration of their rights*." The Constitution states that the duty of the Islamic government to provide the necessary facilities to strengthen the basis of the family as the fundamental unit of society and the primary basis for development of society. Accordingly, it emphasizes that women are meant to take on the valuable and momentous task of motherhood and are released from being regarded as an object or instrument in the service of promoting consumerism and exploitation.[8]

While the preamble and Article 1 of CEDAW draws attention to the definition of discrimination and the point that 'the role of women in procreation should not be a basis for discrimination', the preamble of the Constitution of Iran aims to recognize the motherhood and rearing children as the main task for women, which affects other roles of women in the society.

Article 4 of the Constitution states,

> all civil, penal financial, economic, administrative, cultural, military, political, and other laws and regulations must be based on Islamic criteria.

Islam is the resource of legislation, which has serious implications on women's rights. Article 20 of the Constitution states that both men and women equally enjoy the protection of the law, as well as all human, political, economic, social, and cultural rights. However, this article does not recognize unconditional equal protection, but rather it conditions this protection of equal rights to be in conformity with Islamic criteria.

Article 21 of the constitution explains the government's obligations concerning women's rights in all respects, which are conditioned to be in conformity with Islamic criteria and implies unequal rights for men and women in policies, programs, and legislation undertaken by the government. This article lists specific goals that government must implement related to women's rights:

1. create a favorable environment for the growth of woman's personality and the restoration of her rights, both the material and intellectual;

[8]Preamble of the Constitution of the Islamic Republic of Iran. University of Nevada, Las Vegas.

2. the protection of mothers, particularly during pregnancy and childbearing, and the protection of children without guardians;
3. establishing competent courts to protect and preserve the family;
4. the provision of special insurance for widows, and aged women and women without support;
5. the awarding of guardianship of children to worthy mothers, in order to protect the interests of the children, in the absence of a legal guardian.

It is obvious that all of these objectives, considered by the Constitution for improvement of women's rights, are restricted to family and do not include any improvement for women's political, social, economic, or cultural rights. This depicts the priority of the role of women in the family rather than in the public sphere in the Constitution; in contrast Article 3 of CEDAW obliges states to take appropriate measures in all fields, particularly in terms of political, social, economic and cultural rights to ensure the full development of women in order to provide women's enjoyment of human rights and fundamental freedoms.

Accordingly, the Constitution of IRI as the main legal structure setting out the political and social system of the country does not recognize the full spectrum of equal rights for all citizens including men and women envisaged in international law, but rather has a more limited focus on women's issues relating to the primary role accorded to women as mothers.

5 Women's Rights in the Family Law

5.1 Minimum Age for Marriage

Though in 2002 the law was amended to increase the minimum age of marriage from 9 to 13 years for girls and from 15 to 18 years for boys, children can be married off by their father or paternal grandfather before legal age of marriage (Kar 2008). According to Article 1041 of the civil code,

> Marriage of girls before reaching the age of 13 full solar years and boys before reaching the age of 15 full solar years is subject to the permission of the Guardian and on condition of taking the child's best interest into consideration and approval of the relevant court.

This article is in contrast to the article 16 of CEDAW which prohibits child marriage.

5.2 *Choice of Spouse and Permission of Father*

According to Article 1070 of the civil code, the consent of both marrying parties to the marriage is the fundamental condition for the legality of the marriage. However, there are several limitations on the rights of a woman in this regard. To choose a spouse and enter into marriage, a woman who has not been married previously requires the permission of her father or her paternal grandfather, even if she has reached the full age of maturity. According to Article 1043 of the civil code,

> If, however, the father or the paternal grandfather withhold the permission without justifiable reason, the girl can refer [the matter] to the Special Civil Court giving full particulars of the man whom she wants to marry and also the terms of the marriage and the dowry money agreed upon and notify her father or her paternal grandfather through that Court of the foregoing particulars. The Court can issue a permission for marriage fifteen days after the date of notification to the guardian if no response has been received from the guardian to satisfy refusal.

Women are also not allowed to marry non-Muslims or foreign nationals without special permission of the government, according to Articles 1059 and 1061 of the civil code, respectively (Nayyeri 2013). As a result, the freedom of choice of spouse and entering into marriage stipulated in the Article 16(a, b) of CEDAW are not recognized in the Civil Code of Iran.

5.3 *Mahr (Dowry)*

Dowries are "*anything which can be called property and which can be owned and possessed as a marriage portion*" (Article 1078 of civil code), which is fixed "*upon the mutual consent of the marrying parties*" (Article 1080) entering into the marriage. Article 1082 of the Civil Code recognizes the wife as the "*owner of the marriage portion*" immediately after the performance of the marriage ceremony and gives her the authority to "*dispose of it in any way and manner that she may like*". The wife has the right to refuse starting sexual relations with her husband until he pays the entirety of the *Mahr*, stipulated by article 1085 of Civil Code.[9] Regardless of this provision, in actual societal practice, a woman only receives the marriage portion if the husband divorces her, rather than at the time of marriage.[10] After an amended act in 1997 due to hyper-inflation in Iran, women's *Mahr*, if agreed in cash, should be recalculated to take account of inflation and "it shall be paid in accordance with

[9]"As long as the mahr is not paid to her, the wife can refuse to fulfill her duties toward her husband, provided that the mahr is prompt. This refusal does not debar her from the right to nafaqa (maintenance)" (Nayyeri 2013).

[10]According to article 1092, "if the husband divorces his wife before the consummation of marriage, the wife be entitled to half of the marriage portion" (Nayyeri 2013).

the change of the annual price index at the time of payment in comparison with the time of the contract, which shall be calculated by the Central Bank of Iran, unless otherwise agreed by the spouses at the time of contract" (Kar 2008; Nayyeri 2013). *Mahr* is considered as an economic right, legally provided for women.

5.4 The Relation Between Husband and Wife

Entering into the marriage establishes certain rights and reciprocal duties between husband and wife (Article 1102 of civil code). They are "*bound to establish friendly relations*" and "*must cooperate with each other for the welfare of their family and the education of children*", as Articles 1103 and 1104 stipulates. Nonetheless, Article 1105 of the civil code recognizes "*the position of the head of the family*" as "*the exclusive right of the husband*". The cost of *nafaqah* (maintenance) of the wife, according to Article 1106, is at the responsibility of the husband in permanent marriages. Maintenance, according to Article 1107 of the Civil Code, includes "*all reasonable and appropriate needs of the wife such as dwelling, clothing, food, furniture, the cost of health and remedy, and a servant if the wife is accustomed to have servants or if she needs one because of illness or defects of limbs.*"[11] Though, as Article 1108 clarifies "*if the wife refuses to fulfill duties of a wife without legitimate excuse, she will not be entitled to the cost of maintenance.*" Duties of the wife include *tamkin* (sexual submission and obedience), meaning that a woman is obliged to meet her husband's sexual desires at all times. A woman's refusal to fulfill her husband's sexual needs is known as *nushuz* (disobedience), which leads to suspension of her right of maintenance. Therefore, there is no space for 'women's psychological needs and readiness' in sexual relations between wife and husband which may result in marital rape (Kar 2008).

Article 5 of CEDAW calls for the modification of the social and cultural patterns of the conduct of men and women based on inferiority or superiority of either sex or on stereotyped roles for men and women. However, the Civil Code of IRI, legally determines the head of family, defines the roles of bread-winner of the family and the duties of wives to their husbands, follows and strengthens the stereotypical roles for men and women.

Fundamentalists within the Islamic tradition argue that the Quran accords guardianship over women to men (4:34) as the head of the family. It regards men as the partner capable of providing financially for the family and having the decision making capacity. Javadi Amoli (2010) emphasizes first, that this superiority exists only in terms of the relationship between wife and her husband. Secondly, that this superiority does not indicate perfection and being closer to God, rather it is a form of responsibility and labor division. This does not mean that men are more virtuous. The essence of this superiority is one's duty towards others. In this sense, men are responsible for their wives and families (Javadi Amoli 2010, 325–326). Similarly,

[11]The cost of health and remedy is added to the article in 2002 (Nayyeri 2013).

Mesbah Yazdi argues that because men have more intelligence, they are responsible for the expenses of family and consequently they are more meritorious and befitting for managing the family (Mesbah Yazdi 2009, 241).

5.5 *Right to Work*

The right to work is considered an economic right, although as it is restricted for married women. The right to work for married women depends on husband's decision. The husband can, according to Article 1117, "*prevent his wife from [an] occupation or technical work which is incompatible with the family interest or the dignity of himself or his wife.*" However, the article does not offer any definition of 'family interest.' This ambiguity causes personal interpretations of 'family interest' to restrict a women's potential for a career. However, article 18 of the Family Protection Law gives the same right to the wife, though: "*the wife can also request a similar matter from the court. If doing so does not cause interruptions in the livelihood of the family, the court will prevent the husband from continuing at the job.*"[12] The husband's interpretation of 'family interest' or incompatibility does not need to be approved by a court in contrast to the women's request. Accordingly, women's right to work is not considered 'as [an] inalienable right of all human beings' as conferred in the Article 11 of CEDAW.

5.6 *Right to Movement and Freedom to Choose Residence*

A married woman cannot leave the country without her husband's approval. Article 18 of the Passport Law stipulates that she needs her husband's consent to obtain a passport to travel outside the country. Furthermore, according to Article 19 of the same law, a man has the right to impose a travel ban on his wife and request that her passport be seized.[13]

Articles 1005 and 1114 of the Civil Code provide men with the exclusive right to determine the place of their wife's residence: "*the wife must stay in the dwelling that the husband allots for her unless such a right is reserved to the wife.*" A wife, who leaves her husband's home against his will, is considered as *nashezeh* (disobedient), hence, disqualified from maintenance rights. According to Article 1115, "*If the existence of the wife and husband in the same house involves the risk of bodily or financial injury or that to the dignity of the wife, she can choose a separate dwelling*" (Nayyeri 2013); though, in these cases, the wife is required to prove to the court that she 'faces a significant risk of bodily harm, threatening her life and

[12] *Qanun-e Hemayat az Khanevadeh* (The family protection law of Islamic republic of Iran). Islamic Parliament Research Center.

[13] *Qanun-e Gozarnameh* (The Passport Law), available at: http://rc.majlis.ir/fa/law/show/96904.

personal safety.' Therefore, the same right for men and women to free movement and also to choose their residence and domicile, as mentioned in the Article 15(4) of CEDAW, are denied in the Civil Code of IRI.

5.7 *Polygamy*

Men have the religious and legal rights to have up to four permanent marriages at one point in time. Although this right is not explicitly stipulated in Civil Code, it is referred to in other articles such as the article on the law of inheritance. Also, Articles 1075–1076 of civil code recognize temporary marriage.[14]

In the Family Protection Act of 1968 and 1975, polygamy was restricted through the need to obtain permission of a court of law. According to Article 16 of the Family Protection Act, a man was allowed to marry a second wife only under specific circumstances as following: consent of first wife; inability of first wife to perform marital duties, failure of the first wife to be obedient to the husband; affliction of the wife, such as insanity or other difficult to cure diseases; conviction of the wife of a criminal offence; addiction of the wife to harmful substances; wife's abandonment of family life; wife's infertility; and disappearance of the wife.

Article 17 explains the procedure of second marriage, that "*The applicant must present two copies of the application to the court and explain his reasons. A copy of the application shall be sent to his wife. The court shall give the permission only when it has taken the necessary steps, and, if possible, has made an inquiry of the present wife of the man, in order to assure the financial ability of the man and of doing justice in the case of article 16(1). It is however the first wife's right in all cases to apply for divorce if she wishes*" (Nayyeri 2013). This article also defines a punishment term of six months to one year of imprisonment for a man who violates this rule, as well as for the Registry Officer and the new wife if she is aware of the former marriage of the man.

Though the Family Protection Law after the 1979 revolution was repealed, this article is still valid with a small change concerning the punishment of parties to the further marriage and the Registry Officer mentioned in the Article 17. In such manner, that there is not any punishment of parties, since the punishment is recognized as being against *shari'a*. Nonetheless, legally sanctioned polygamy is in direct contrast to the stipulation set out in article 16 of CEDAW which calls for equality in marriage and family relations such as the same rights and responsibilities during marriage and at its dissolution (Chinkin and Freeman 2012).

The reason for polygamy offered by fundamentalists within the Islamic tradition is based on the difference between men and women according to their physical and spiritual aspects. In terms of the physical, Mesbah Yazdi (2009) talks about women's menstrual cycle which makes them weak and frail. Within this cycle, it is necessary

[14]Article 1075: Marriage is called temporary when it is for a limited period of time. Article 1076: The duration of the temporary marriage must be definitely determined (Nayyeri 2013).

for them to have more rest. This condition results in particular distinctions in the social roles and expectations of men and women, and in turn becomes the basis for their rights in family life. Mesbah Yazdi also points out differences in terms of their sex organs. He explains that when women are pregnant or lactating, their sex organs are inactive while a man's sex organ is active all the time. This makes the function of each sex organ very different. As such, bio-psychological aspects should be considered when making laws. For instance, such aspects justify men's right to polygamy and temporary marriage during the time that the wife is not able to meet his sexual needs (Mesbah Yazdi 2009, 215–216).

5.8 *Punishment for Adultery*

Sexual intercourse outside of marriage is defined as a crime of *zina*. The punishment for *zina* committed by an unmarried person (*zena-ye-qeyre-mohsaneh*) is one hundred lashes; and for a married person (*zena-ye-mohsaneh*), is stoning to death (Article 225 of the new Islamic penal code). The punishment of stoning is defined for men and women; however, it is applied in greater proportion to women. Men can evade the conviction of adultery by claiming that they engaged in the relation through a temporary marriage which permits sexual intercourse with multiple wives at the same time outside of a formal marriage; while women are not afforded this option under the Iranian Civil Code (Nayyeri 2013).

5.9 *Inheritance*

Article 907 of the Civil Code determines the inheritance for daughters and sons from their parent:

> If the deceased leaves no parents, but has one or more children, [...] If there are several children, some being boy(s) and some girl(s), each son takes twice as much as each daughter.

According to Article 913,[15] the wife will only receive a quarter of the assets of the deceased spouse, if there are no children; and if there are children, her portion is reduced to one-eighth. According to Article 946 of the civil code,

[15] Article 913—"In all the cases mentioned in this subsection, whichever of the spouses that survives takes his or her share which shall be half of the assets for the surviving husband and one-quarter for the surviving wife, provided that the deceased left no children or grandchildren; and it shall be one-quarter of the estate for the husband and one-eighth for the wife if the deceased left children or grandchildren. And the remainder of the estate is to be divided among the other inheritors in accordance with the preceding articles" (Nayyeri 2013).

The husband takes inheritance from the whole of the effects of the wife.

The wife takes inheritance only from the 'moveable property' and 'buildings and trees'. It does not include land or farms, which are known as immovable property. Articles 946–948 explained this rule, though these were amended on January 25, 2009. According to the amended articles, "*the wife may inherit from 'the value' of her share from the land. In such cases the current value of the land shall be assessed and paid to the wife. But the main rule remained unchanged and women still may not inherit a share from a land, but from its value*" (Nayyeri 2013).

According to Article 942 of civil code:

> If there is more than one wife, one-fourth or one-eighth part of the assets, which belongs to the wife, will be divided equally among them.

Also, according to Article 949, if there is no other inheritor, the man inherits all the assets of his deceased wife, while the wife may only inherit a quarter of the assets and the rest belongs to the State. Therefore, women and men do not have the same rights to family benefits. This contrasts to the rights set out in Article 13 of CEDAW which articulates the equal right to access to financial benefits in family and all forms of financial credit.

The argument for women's inheritance is to be found in the Quran, which states that men's share is twofold of women's. Since men have the responsibility of providing for the family and for women's life expenses; and also having to pay *Mahr*, their greater inheritance should be considered as compensation for this inequality (Javadi Amoli 2010, 343; Mesbah Yazdi 2009, 240). Furthermore, Mesbah explains, if the share of man and women is equal, half of the society's economic and financial capital will remain useless and stagnant, because as Mesbah Yazdi argues, women can never be as economically active as men, though they can enjoy the benefits derived from the capital inherited by men. In other words according to fundamentalist Islamic tradition, men are producers and women are consumers (Mesbah Yazdi 2009: 268).

5.10 Transfer of Nationality

Article 976 of civil code deprives women of the right to pass on their nationality to their husbands and children. An amendment to this law in 2006 allows children of Iranian mothers, born in Iran after reaching the full age of 18, to apply for Iranian citizenship but only if their parents' marriage is officially approved.[16] Accordingly, women do not have equal rights with men concerning the transfer of nationality to

[16] *Qanun-e Taien-e Taklif-e Tabeieat-e Farzandan-e Hasel az Ezdevaj-e Zanan-e Irani ba Mardan-e Khareji* (The Law on Nationality of Children of Fathers of Foreign Nationality). Islamic Parliament Research Center.

their children, while the Article 9 of CEDAW emphasizes the right of "acquisition and retention of nationality and the transmission of nationality to children."

5.11 Guardianship Over Children

According to Article 1168 of the Civil Code, maintenance of children is both the right and duty of the parents, the right of guardianship over children and supervision of the affairs of children, according to Article 1181, is given to the father or paternal grandfather. For example, deciding on departure from the country for children below the age of 18 is possible only with the approval of the father or the paternal grandfather—the mother has no legal say in such matters (Kar 2008). Therefore, women do not have the same rights and responsibilities as parents in matters relating to their children, as demanded in Article 16 of CEDAW (part d and e).

5.12 Honor Killing

If a man discovers his wife with another man, he is legally allowed to kill his wife and her lover, according to Article 630 of the old Penal Code. This article, which remains unchanged in the new penal code, reads: "*When a man sees his wife committing zina (adultery) with another man, provided that he is certain that his wife is willing [to have sex], he can kill both of them in the same position; however if he knows that his wife acts under coercion, he may only kill the man [i.e. her rapist]. The same rule applies to assault and battery*" (Nayyeri 2013).

5.13 Right to Divorce

Women do not have the same right to the dissolution of marriage, as Article 16(c) of CEDAW mentions. Article 1133 provides the man with the right of divorce his wife whenever he wishes to do so; the woman is not entitled to the same right to divorce. According to Article 1130, women in certain circumstances "*can refer to the Islamic judge and request a divorce. When it is proved to the Court that the continuation of the marriage causes osr-va-haraj (intolerable difficulty and hardship), the judge can for the sake of avoiding harm and difficulty compel the husband to divorce his wife. If this cannot be done, then the divorce will be made on the permission of the Islamic judge.*"[17]

[17]Note added to Article 1130 in 2002: "the following circumstances, if proved in the relevant court, shall be considered as a case of *osr-va-haraj* (intolerable difficulty and hardship):

Nonetheless, women can benefit from a few measures to improve their domestic rights, such as 'marriage conditions' which must be published in marriage certificates.[18] These conditions have been in place since the beginning of Islam, according to Kar (2008) and "allow women to request certain rights, such as right to divorce, before the marriage takes place. If the man agrees to them, then the woman is entitled to request a divorce from a court whenever she chooses". Therefore, such conditions can replace the law, though they will never be a permanent status since many men will not agree to all the conditions.

An amendment to the law to improve the financial situation of a woman divorced by her husband is the right to receive *ujrat al-mithl* (wages for housework) from her husband for the whole time of their marriage. This is a monetary value on women's housework determined by the court as compensation for household services rendered to the husband. Despite all amended acts, a man still has unlimited power to divorce, and a woman has a conditional right to divorce that has to be proven in court. This unequal right requires woman, in most cases, to abandon all of her financial benefits, including her dowry, to obtain the man's acceptance to get divorce. Therefore men and women do not have the same right at marriage dissolution as mentioned in Article 16(c) of CEDAW.

5.14 Custody of Children

According to the Article 1169—amended in 2002— "*For the custody of children, whose parents are separated, the mother has priority until the age of seven; and then, custody will devolve upon the father*." This continues in a Note: "*After reaching seven years of age, in the case of dispute, considering the best interest of the child, the court*

1. The husband's leaving of marital life for, at least, six consecutive months, or, nine alternative months in a one year period, without any acceptable reason.

2. The husband's addiction to any kind of drugs or alcohol that, damages the marital life, and his refusal, or impossibility of compelling him, to quit the addiction in a period prescribed by the doctor. If the husband does not fulfill his promise [to quit], or, again begins his abuse, the divorce shall be granted by the request of the wife.

3. Final conviction of the husband to five years, or more, imprisonment.

4. Betray or any kind of mistreatment of the wife that is intolerable in the wife's condition.

5. Husband's affliction to incurable mental illnesses or contagious disease or any kind of incurable diseases that disrupts the marital life.

The circumstances mentioned in this article are not exhaustive and the court may grant the divorce in other cases that *osr-va-haraj* is proved in the court" (Nayyeri 2013).

[18] Article 1119: "The parties to the marriage can stipulate any condition to the marriage which is not incompatible with the nature of the contract of marriage, either as part of the marriage contract or in another binding contract: for example, it can be stipulated that if the husband marries another wife or absents himself during a certain period, or discontinues the payment of cost of maintenance, or attempts the life of his wife or treats her so harshly that their life together becomes unbearable, the wife has the power, which she can also transfer to a third party by power of attorney to obtain a divorce herself after establishing in the court the fact that one of the foregoing alternatives has occurred and after the issue of a final judgment to that effect" (Nayyeri 2013).

will decide who receives custody of the child" (Nayyeri 2013). However, this article is conditional. If a mother remarries, custody will devolve upon the father, even during the priority age (before the child reaches seven years of age), which is mentioned in Article 1170 of Civil Code. Such restriction is not valid for the father.

6 Women's Social, Economic, and Cultural Rights

Some articles on women's cultural, economic and social rights were mentioned in the family law, such as the right to work, dowry, maintenance, inheritance, stereotyped roles of men and women, right to transfer the nationality. Other women's issues in these areas are as follows.

6.1 Choice of Clothing

Women, both Muslim and non-Muslim, are required to wear clothing in accordance with the Islamic dress code. According to the Article 638 of Islamic penal code, "Women, who appear in public places and roads without wearing an Islamic *hijab*, shall be sentenced to between ten days to two months' imprisonment or a fine of fifty thousand to five hundred thousand Rials."[19]

The veil, according to fundamentalists, is necessary to temper sexual desire of men towards women (Mesbah Yazdi 2009). This allows men to maintain their loyalty to their wives and avoid betrayal of their family (Javadi Amoli 2010, 310–11). Refusal to wear the veil is a violation of God's right. Amoli argues: "Woman should completely understand that her veil is not only for herself so that she can say: I want to give up my right. Woman's veil is not related with husband so that he can say: I agree or not. The Veil is not a personal right of woman, it is rather a God's right that should be respected by woman" (Javadi Amoli 2010, 351). Amoli explains that when the Quran's speaks of the veil, it means that the veil is to respect and revere women, meaning that men should not look at them maliciously. This does not apply to non-Muslim women because non-Muslim women are deprived of this reverence. Amoli argues that the veil should not be regarded as a limitation since the Quran propounds that veiled women are an embodiment of reverence and grace of society and therefore, they are honorable (Javadi Amoli 2010, 350–352).

[19]Islamic Penal Code of the Islamic Republic of Iran—Book Five. 2013. The Iran Human Rights Documentation Center (IHRDC).

6.2 Age of Criminal Responsibility

According to Article 147 of the new Penal Code—approved in January 2012, states that "*The age of maturity for girls and boys are, respectively, a full nine (8 years and 9 months) and fifteen (14 years and 7 months) lunar years*." Therefore, if a girl aged 9 and a boy aged 15 commit crimes, they will be treated as adults.

6.3 Diya (Blood Money)

According to Article 544 of the new Penal Code (similar to Article 300 of the old Code), "*The diya (blood money) for murdering a woman is half that of a man*." Accordingly, if a woman is killed by a man, the murderer will be sentenced to death, only if the family of the murdered woman pays the murderer half of the blood money, as stipulated by Article 379; since the value of the blood money of the murderer is higher than that of the victim. A new solution for this unequal treatment is noted in Article 545, which provides:

> In all cases of homicide where the victim is not a man, the difference between the diya and the diya of a man shall be paid from the Fund for Compensation of Bodily Harms.

Also Article 554 explains

> The diya of [harm to] limbs and bodily abilities, up to one third of the full diya, is the same for man and woman; however if it reaches, or exceeds, one third of the full diya, the diya of woman shall be decreased to half.

In such cases, the difference is not payable from the Fund for Compensation of Bodily Harms (Nayyeri 2013).

Article 299 of the new Penal Code stipulates that if father or paternal grandfather murders his child or grandchild, the perpetrator does not face the death penalty; while, if a mother kills her children, and is proven guilty, then she will get the death penalty (Kar 2008).

The reason for blood money in the fundamentalist Islamic tradition refers to the importance of men's economic contribution. Amoli believes that in Islam, blood money is not based on human's spiritual value; rather it is based on a human being's economic contribution. Therefore, because man is the bread-earner of the household, his blood money will be of greater value than that of a woman. The difference between blood money of men and women does not add anything to men's status and does not lessen the value of women because some material and financial differences have no relation to spiritual status. There is no rational or traditional correlation between blood money and spiritual perfection so we cannot say the greater the sum of blood money, the more sacred is the soul of the person who has been killed or the closer he is to God (Javadi Amoli 2010, 345–348).

6.4 Testimony of Women

In many type of crimes, the testimony of women is not accepted in a court of law. For instance Article 119 states that

> Testimony of women, whether alone or together with men, may not prove livat (a homosexual act between men).

Article 199 of the new Penal Code explains the standard of testimony:

> The standard of testimony in all crimes is the testimony of two men, except in zina (illicit sexual intercourse), livat (homosexual act between men), tafkhiz (homosexual act between men without penetration), and mosaheqeh (homosexual act between women) which shall be proven by the testimony of four men. Zina may [also] be proven by the testimony of two men and four women, except in cases where zina is punishable by execution or stoning in which case then the testimony of at least three men and two women is required. In such cases, if two men and four women give testimony, it is only punishable by flogging. Bodily injuries, which require diya (blood money), may also be proven by the testimony of one man and two women.

Therefore, the testimony of two women is the same as that of one man (Nayyeri 2013).

The argument for the testimony of women offered by fundamentalists says that there are two requirements for witnessing: Firstly, the witness should be alert and clever in the instance of observing an event and he or she should be able to record the event exactly and with accuracy. Secondly, the witness should not be affected by emotions and passions at the time of testifying and must be able to explain what has been witnessed correctly and completely (Mesbah Yazdi 2009). Comparing traits of men and women, Mesbah Yazdi (2009) comes to the conclusion that men are more capable and meritorious with regard to both of the aforementioned aspects. Where there is no possibility to men's attestation, women's witness should be credited. In this case, because of the possibility of forgetting the event or being under effect of emotions and passions, a woman should be accompanied by another woman in order to minimise the inaccuracy of her attestation (Mesbah Yazdi 2009, 253–254). In this regard, Javadi Amoli (2010) believes that the Quran (2:282) also makes a comment about the credibility of women when it says that the testimony of two women is equal to one man's. This is not because of a deficiency in women's wisdom or a possibility of flaw and fault in recognition, but due to the fact that if one of them made a mistake, the other one will correct her. According to Amoli, women's domestic and child care responsibilities restrict their ability to observe and remember what they have witnessed. As such it is necessary to have two women so that if one forgets the other will remember (Javadi Amoli 2010, 344–345).

6.5 Homosexuality

Homosexuality is considered a crime, and those who commit homosexual acts will be severely punished.[20] Articles 127–134 deal with homosexual act between women, which will be punished by one hundred lashes. If the act is repeated up to four times, the accused shall be condemned to death (Kar 2008).

7 Women's Political Rights

There is no legal obstacle for women to work as a Member of Parliament or as a Minister in the government, although it does not seem women are allowed to perform all positions at all levels of government as stipulated in the Article 7 of CEDAW which includes the right to vote, the right to be elected to government positions, the right to participate in the government's decision making.

7.1 Women as Judges

After the 1979 revolution, women were removed from judicial bodies as officers of the court. Later, they were granted judicial standing and the right to serve as counselors, but women are still not allowed to issue and sign final verdicts (Kar 2008).

As Javadi Amoli (2010) and Mesbah Yazdi (2009) explain, some Islamic jurists believe that being male is not a requirement for being appointed as a judge in Islamic courts. However, in Shiite tradition, being male is a necessary condition. Having scrutinized various traditions in this regard, Amoli explains that certain responsibilities are for men, but women do not have to take them. Furthermore, being a judge in an Islamic court entails a responsibility to execute legislative punishments. Thus,

[20]"Article 234 of the new Islamic Penal Code states that for male same-sex conduct, the sodomizer, if found guilty of being involved in consensual same-sex relations, will receive 100 lashes, as opposed to the death penalty, which was required in the old Islamic Penal Code. The sodomizer will only be sentenced to death if he is involved in a permanent [heterosexual] marriage (*muhsan*) and he was involved in non-consensual sex (rape). Under Article 109 of the old Islamic Penal Code, punishment by death awaited both parties engaged in same-sex relations" (Jafari 2015: 24).

women can train students, hear trials and conduct consultation among other judges about cases but have no right to decide on the final sentence (Javadi Amoli 2010: 299–304; Mesbah Yazdi 2009, 229).

7.2 Women as President

Article 115 of the Constitution sets out the criteria for the presidential candidates applying an Arabic phrase '*rejal*' which means 'men'. The article states "*The President must be elected from among religious and political men*"; though it can be interpreted as 'personalities'. The task of interpretation of this Arabic phrase is given to the Guardian Council. The Council has never pronounced that being man is a precondition for the presidential candidate. Nevertheless the ambiguity within this article denies women the right to be president. This contrasts with the right to be elected to government positions and the right to participate in the government's decision making conferred in the Article 7 of CEDAW.

8 Islamic Law in Fundamentalist View

The *Shi'a* fundamentalist Islamic view of religion is that since religion is aimed at managing human society, and educating humankind, it is necessary to have rules and regulations in accordance with the requirements of society as well as human nature. According to fundamentalists, these regulations and laws have inevitably remained the same throughout human history. They argue this is because of the unchangeability of human nature (Javadi Amoli 2010). What does changes, are the manners and habits of human beings in the material world. Hence, in this view, only God has the right to legislate for human beings since only He knows human characteristics and the essence of human existence. As a result, humankind requires religion and revelation to manage their individual as well as social affairs to reach salvation and felicity in social and individual life (Javadi Amoli 2010). Accordingly, fundamentalists also reject the idea of the flexibility of laws according to time and circumstances. They argue "if the laws obey the times, then who should the times obey? That would imply that laws should follow the wishes of the people," (Omid 1994, 57) who are fallible and make mistakes because of their free will. From the fundamentalists' point of view, the law is responsible for controlling and conducting society. For this reason, human beings need to rely on eternal and absolute values, as well as on a set of laws and practices that are beyond time and the wishes of fallible people. Such eternal law, according to fundamentalists, can be found in Islamic law aimed at the salvation of human beings in this world and in the afterlife (Mesbah Yazdi 1999).

9 Women's Rights in Fundamentalist View

Women's rights from the fundamentalist perspective have been defined based on the notion of 'desert-based' justice (Kadivar 2013) originating from Aristotle's idea of distributive justice, which essentially means that individuals receive rewards based on their merits. Such an idea of justice understands inequality among persons as a natural order and people are accorded with unequal share of rights, depending on their merits. Justice in this sense means receiving rewards that are proportionate to one's merit and injustice is receiving more or less than which one actually deserves (Aristotle 2004, 118–120).

This concept of distributive justice is an idea that has been approved and used by Muslims in defining what justice means in Islam. Justice as 'putting everything in its place and giving everyone their proper rights' reflects Muslim philosophers' understanding of the Aristotelian notion, which justifies slavery and gender inequality. According to Tabataba'i, equality resulting from social justice does not mean that all social ranks are distributed equally among all members of society (Kadivar 2013, 219–222). This notion of justice is the basis for the fundamentalists' perspective on women's rights in Islam. They believe that some verses in the Quran talk of innate characteristics that are present in both, men and women. However, they also argue that men and women are by nature biologically different and thus any action taken against the intention of nature would result in a disaster. As Tabataba'i reasons,

> biologically, the average woman is inferior to the average man in brainpower, heart, veins and nerves, let alone height and weight. For this reason, women's bodies are softer and weaker and men's rougher and physically stronger; and women have gentler feelings such as love and tenderness and a greater interest in beauty and self-adornment, while men are more rational than women. Thus, women's life is emotional and men's life is rational. In Islam, the difference in social duties and obligations (of men and women) is due to their different emotional and rational faculties. For example, men are specialists in politics, law and warfare, where rationality plays a greater role, while women specialize in raising children and managing the household… Consequently, men have overall control because of their rationality, while women get more assistance because of their emotional advantages (cited in Kadivar 2013, 219–220).

As Motahhari argues, this disparity between men and women demands different rights, obligations, duties, and retributions. Only when rights are defined according to this natural order, can natural justice, domestic happiness, and social progress be achieved (Motahhari, cited in Kadivar 2013, 221).

Such views on gender differences are not mentioned in the Quran and of course are not restricted to the Islamic fundamentalist perspective; rather, it is a general debate with a long history that did not originate from a specific religion. Several productions of pop psychology mention that women and men are naturally opposed to each other in thinking, emotions and communication. For example the book 'Men Are from Mars, Women Are from Venus' which has sold more than 30 million copies and translated in forty languages, or an endless stream of articles on this subject in popular magazines all over the world, though most of their claims have been refuted by large amounts of research (Connell and Pearse 2015, 33). Fundamentalists are required to pay attention to the current debates on sex differences and gender studies as well as contribute to such discussions from a religious viewpoint. It would help them to protect their religious arguments from pop psychological views.

10 Egalitarian Justice and Women's Rights in Reformist View

Reformists, like other streams of Islamic thought, regard justice as the main objective of religion, thus every *shari'a* commandment should be 'an interpretation of what justice entails'. Therefore all precepts in the realm of human interaction have to be based on the principle of justice. Arguably there is no one eternal and fixed definition of the outworking of justice even if the basic concept itself may be eternal. The outworking of the concept of justice accords to conventions and practices over time and societies develop and advance. As a result, all *shari'a* non- worship commandments on women's rights which are related to social interactions cannot be eternal and immutable, but rather should be redefined based on the criteria of justice and collective human reasoning within current historical and social contexts.

Reformists believe in a rationalist perspective in Islam, "certain acts are either good or evil inherently, that is to say, without a ruling from [a] lawgiver" (Kadivar 2013, 217). They also recognize the capacity for reason, independent of revelation, to decide whether such acts are good or evil. Reformists consider rulings related to women's rights to be part of the realm of reason. This means that "when we are absolutely sure that the Lawgiver has not forbidden it, our rational ruling can be counted as a *shari'a* ruling" (Kadivar 2013, 217). Legal justice concerning men and women is a good thing according to reasonable people and practical reason. Since in their minds, legal justice as an outcome of rational faculty benefits the public, which is of interest to the whole human species and is necessary for the maintenance of order in human society. Similarly, legal discrimination and injustice causes harm and corruption for humanity, therefore, it is condemned by reasonable people as unwholesome and evil. Consequently, legal justice is sought by reasonable people in order to gain beneficial influence and to reject harmful consequences in human society. This is correlated with the *shari'a* rulings and the Lawgiver, "because it is a basic principle of the 'People of justice' that the Lawgiver is reasonable and in fact, is the head of all reasonable people" (Kadivar 2013, 217).

Accordingly, desert-based justice, once legitimate and acceptable, can no longer be of interest to human society, rather it is egalitarian justice which is more compliant with the spirit of the Quran and the essential message of Islam. What is important in defining rights is humanity in human spirit and nature, which is the basis for dignity and respect for all human beings regardless of gender, race, color, religion, political ideology, social status or any other attributes. Therefore, "humans have equal rights because they share this divine essence. Human dignity derives from this shared essence which is also the cause of equal rights. Human beings deserve the same rights because they share the same essence" (Kadivar 2013, 224). As a result, legal discrimination is in contradiction with human dignity. Furthermore, Kadivar points to the relationship between justice, dignity and the necessity of legal equality or, in other words, the correlation between dignity and egalitarian justice. In this way, dignity cannot be respected without justice in the form of legal equality for all human beings (Kadivar 2013, 225). In this regard, international law is acknowledged by reformists as an international legal criterion to protect the human dignity.

11 Conclusion

An overview on the laws of IRI concerning women's rights illustrates that men and women are not equal before the law, in contrast to the requirements of Article 15 of CEDAW. Women are not provided with equal rights in various aspects of cultural, social, economic, and political rights as well as on the matters of marriage and family relations. Although the preamble of the Constitution considers the duty of the Islamic government in strengthening the basis of family, and seeks to release women from being an object or instrument in the service of promoting consumerism and exploitation; the laws do not seem to be successfully releasing women from being an object or instrument in other respects. Regarding family laws, marriage is understood as an economic contract between a man and woman, so that the man gains household services and sexual ownership over his wife through the exchange of a dowry and maintenance as a sales price. In this perspective, a cooperative social relationship based on love, equality and partnership between parties of the family has no place, but rather it is based on the norms of authority and patriarchy. Therefore, women are still regarded as an object and instrument, though in the frame of family and in the service of husbands. Such a perspective that legitimizes a family based on relation between a head and subordinate with the obedience of wife to husband is unable to comply with women's rights, human rights, and fundamental freedoms. Consequently, this perspective is unable to provide women with life circumstances to facilitate individual self-realization and flourishing of human life appropriate to human dignity.

Among the various schools of Islamic thought, the fundamentalist view aims to impose norms, values and authority on all subsystems through the fulfillment of Islamic law without any alteration over time, which can lead to unacceptable discriminatory laws.

Reformists aim to present an interpretation of Islam in which Islamic laws are compatible with modern concepts, such as human and women rights. They apply different inner religious methods to address such modern concepts in the *sunna* and Quran. In this way, they offer an interpretation of Islam based on an egalitarian notion of justice, which is not only compatible with human rights and gender equality in general, but also acknowledge such concepts essential for Muslim society. Reformists have been successful in opening space for debate and accepting human and womens rights in society through their efforts to offer an interpretation of Islam based on an egalitarian view of human rights. Therefore, this view has changed some discriminatory Islamic laws in favor of women rights; though it has not been completely successful in changing patronizing perspectives on women. It seems such perspectives need further debate in order to attain a better understanding of human rights, justice, and gender equality.

This chapter concluded by considering a new form of reasoning which has emerged from the reformists. Reformists are gradually leaning towards increasing recognition of human reason and individual agency. According to this view, people living in the modern era have different ideas and worldviews from people who lived in traditional Islamic societies (Malekian 1381/2002). They are not aimed at finding modern concepts in *sunna* and Islamic law, but rather they believe that modern life needs modern means which do not necessarily originate from the *sunna* or Quran. Such concepts are outcomes of human reason and are required to achieve justice in the modern era. They reject the text-based definition of being Muslim and emphasize the role of faith, spirituality and religious experience (Mojtahed Shabestari 1389/2010); therefore, I would call this school of thought secular Muslim. On this matter, human beings are regarded as subjective agents who recognize and affirm their identities as Muslims, while also consciously choosing important aspects of religion that they think will enhance their spiritual experience. Secular Islamists challenge the notion of religion as closed, defined solely by text-based interpretation. In this way, the Muslim is not a passive believer that simply accepts a historical definition of being Muslim. This means that everything in history that has been understood as Islam and all historical events which have occurred in the name of Islam provide and determine a definition of being Muslim in the way that being Muslim means a commitment to following the definite set of rituals and precepts provided in the course of history (Mojtahed Shabestari 1389/2010). This perspective regards human reason as independent from revelation and acknowledges the autonomy and authority of human reason as a criterion for distinguishing good from evil. Hence, human reason is the foundation for defining and determining the rights and laws in modern society rather than the revelation as manifested in the Quran and *sunna* and Islamic laws. This view does not mean to reduce the impact of religion and faith on human life, but rather it leads to conscious religiosity and being Muslim in accordance with the human needs of modern time. In attaining religious and unitary experience a healthy society is required where social and political arrangements provide human beings with individual freedom and self-determination. Regarding this, various conventions on human and women's rights and gender equality have become more important, for they respect and protect individual rights in the society and promote the self-determination and freedom for every person in society. Therefore, such conventions are required for an Islamic society.

The issue of women's rights and gender equality receive more attention in the secular view; so that debates on women's rights have changed from mere reform of some Islamic laws on women's rights to a new view on individual agency and individual rights. It seems necessary that this interpretation of Islam should be discussed more in the public sphere; thereby enabling it to gradually find its place among various interpretations of Islam.

References

Amir Arjomand S (2009) After Khomeini: Iran under his successors, Oxford University Press
Aristotle (2004) The Nicomachean ethics. Penguin Classics, New Ed edition, London
Chinkin C, Freeman M (2012) Introduction. In: Chinkin C, Freeman M, Rudolf B (eds) The UN convention on the elimination of all forms of discrimination against women, a commentary. Oxford University Press, Oxford
Civil Code of the Islamic Republic of Iran. Iran Human Rights Documentation Center
Connell R, Pearse R (2015) Gender: in world perspective. Polity Press, UK and USA
Edwards A (2011) Violence against women under international human rights law. Cambridge University Press, New York
Gaudart D (2007) What are the origins of CEDAW? The history of the UN convention on the elimination of all forms of discrimination against women. In: Kölbl S (ed) What is CEDAW? The UN convention on the elimination of all forms of discrimination against women. The human rights of women and what they mean. Federal Chancellery-Federal Minister for Women, Media and Civil Service, Vienna, pp 12–16
Hellum A, Aasen HS (eds) (2013) Women's human rights: CEDAW in international, regional and national law. Cambridge University Press, Cambridge
Hoq LA (2001) The women's convention and its optional protocol: empowering women to claim their internationally protected rights. Colomb Human Rights Law Rev 32(1):677–726
Jafari M (2015) Islamic jurisprudence-inspired legal approaches towards male homosexuals in Iran. In: Lesbian, gay, bisexual and transgender rights in Iran. Analysis from religious, social, legal and cultural perspectives. International Gay and Lesbian Human Rights Commission
Javadi Amoli A (1389/2010) Zan dar Ayene-ye Jalal va Jamal (Woman in mirror the glory and beauty). Esra, Qom
Kadivar M (2013) Revisiting women's rights in Islam: 'Egalitarian Justice' in Lieu of 'Deserts-based Justice'. In: Mir-Hosseini Z, Vogt K, Larson L, Moe C (eds) Gender equality in muslim family law: justice and ethics in Islamic legal tradition. I.B. Tauris, New York and London, pp 213–234
Kar M (2008) Discrimination against women under Iranian law. Official homepage of Mehrangiz Kar
Kar M (2010) Constitutional obstacles: human rights and democracy in Iran, IHRDC
Koolaee E (2012) Women in the parliament. In: Povey T, Rostami-Povey E (eds) Women, power and politics in 21st century Iran. Ashgate, England and USA, pp 137–151
Malekian M (1381/2002) Ma'naviyat: Gohar-e Adiyan (1). In: Soroush A, Shabestari MM, Kadivar M (eds) Sonnat va Sekoularism (Tradition and secularism). Serat, Tehran, pp 267–306
Mesbahh Yazdi MT (1388/2009) Negahi Gozara be Hoquq-e Bashar az Didgah-e Eslam (A brief look on human rights in Islamic perspective). Moasese-ye Pazhouheshi-ye Emam Khomeini, Qom
Moghissi H, Rahnema S (2001) Clerical oligarchy and the question of 'democracy' in Iran. Iran Chamber Society
Mojtahed Shabestari M (18 Aban 1389/09 November 2010) Masael-e Asasi-ye Noandishi-ye Dini dar Iran-e Moaser (The main issues of religious intellectualism in contemporary Iran). An speech at the Knowledge and Research Institution
Nayyeri MH (2013) Gender inequality and discrimination: the case of Iranian women. Iran Human Rights Documentation Center, New Haven
OECD and Post-2015 Reflections (Gender equality and women's rights in the post-2015 agenda: a foundation for sustainable development) Element 3, Paper 1
Omid H (1994) Islam and the post-revolutionary state in Iran. St. Martin's Press, New York
Preamble of the Constitution of the Islamic Republic of Iran. University of Nevada, Las Vegas
Sadeghi F (2010) Bypassing Islamism and feminism: women's resistance and rebellion in post-revolutionary Iran. Revue des mondes musulmans et de la Méditerranée (Remmm) 128:209–228

Schöpp-Schilling HB (2007) What is CEDAW? Introduction to the UN convention on the elimination of all forms of discrimination against women. In: Kölbl S (ed) What is CEDAW? The UN convention on the elimination of all forms of discrimination against women. The human rights of women and what they mean. Federal Chancellery-Federal Minister for Women, Media and Civil Service, Vienna, pp 7–11

Shamsi Gooshki E, Mahmoud A, Neda A (2014) Abortion in Iranian legal system. Perspect Iran J Allergy Asthma Immunol 13(1):71–84

Tohidi N (2002) International connection of the Iranian Women's movement. In: Keddie NR, Matthee RP (eds) Iran and the surrounding world: interactions in culture and cultural politics. University of Washington Press, USA, pp 205–231

Zwingel S (2005) How do international women's rights norms become effective in domestic contexts? An analysis of the Convention on the Elimination of all forms of Discrimination Against Women (CEDAW). Doktor der Sozialwissenschaft. Fakultät für Sozialwissenschaft, Ruhr-Universität Bochum, Bochum

Tradition's Edge: Interactions Between Religious Tradition and Sexual Freedom

Frank S. Ravitch

Abstract This chapter considers the topic of same-sex marriage and the ordination of gay and lesbian clergy from the perspective of several religious traditions. The chapter focuses on the internal legal and theological struggles faced as these religions considered doctrinal and spiritual change to longstanding practices. Four religious traditions are explored: United Synagogue of Conservative Judaism; The Episcopalian Church; Japanese Zen Buddhism; and the Roman Catholic Church. Three of these four traditions have recognized and accepted same-sex marriage and ordination of gay clergy, but the processes through which they developed those responses, and their theological approaches, have been quite different. The fourth tradition, the Roman Catholic Church, had a different response than the other three traditions and this will be explored as well.

1 Introduction

In my recent book *Freedom's Edge: Religious Freedom, Sexual Freedom, and the Future of America*,[1] I addressed the ways in which religious freedom and sexual freedom can legally and socially coexist by seeking common ground even as people on both sides argue coexistence is unlikely. This chapter considers the topic of same-sex marriage and the ordination of gay and lesbian clergy from the perspective of several religious traditions. The chapter focuses on the internal legal and theological struggles faced as these religious traditions considered doctrinal and spiritual coexistence.

The chapter looks specifically at four religious traditions that have used different processes in addressing same-sex marriage and ordination questions. These traditions are: United Synagogue of Conservative Judaism; The Episcopalian Church; Japanese Zen Buddhism; and the Roman Catholic Church. Interestingly, three of these four

[1] Ravitch (2016).

F. S. Ravitch (✉)
Michigan State University College of Law, East Lansing, USA
e-mail: fravitch@law.msu.edu

J. Giles et al. (eds.), *Law, Religion and Tradition*, Law and Religion in a Global Context 1, https://doi.org/10.1007/978-3-319-96749-3_4

traditions have had similar responses to same-sex marriage, but the processes through which they developed those responses, and their theological approaches, have been quite different. The fourth tradition, the Roman Catholic Church, had a different response than the other three traditions and this will be explored as well.

Ordination of openly LGBT clergy members has long been an important question for some religious traditions. More recently, performing same-sex marriages or recognizing same-sex marriages has come to the fore as an important issue. For some religions there is no conflict between their traditions and theology and the ordination of LGBT clergy or the performance and/or recognition of same-sex marriages. For other religions these issues raise complex and important theological questions. And for some religions ordination of LGBT clergy and even recognition of same-sex marriage pose insurmountable theological and/or traditional hurdles.

As we will see, the processes involved in resolving questions about change can have an impact on the ways in which various religious traditions adapt to these questions. Moreover, the nature of the religion can make a significant difference in both the processes used to answer these questions and the specific answers on each issue. For example, there are significant differences between the processes used by religions with established hierarchies, such as the Episcopalian Church and the Roman Catholic Church and religions with a mixture of congregational and hierarchical elements such as synagogues that are part of United Synagogue for Conservative Judaism and Japanese Zen Buddhist temples. Neither of the latter two are purely congregational, but neither have a traditional hierarchy that can mandate what Congregations do on unsettled theological issues.[2]

Significantly, however, the process does not dictate a specific outcome. As we will see the Episcopalian Church has embraced ordination of LGBT clergy members and same-sex marriage, but the Roman Catholic Church has not. Both United Synagogue for Conservative Judaism and Japanese Zen Buddhism have allowed, to differing degrees, ordination of LGBT clergy and have embraced, again to differing degrees, same-sex marriage. In both of these traditions individual synagogues or temples have latitude to decide for themselves what to do about these questions depending on the circumstances.

The reason I selected these four traditions for discussion is the very different processes they used to come to what are sometimes similar answers, and more importantly, the fact that all four had to grapple with significant theological and traditional questions that required interpretation, and they confronted these questions in a rather open and public manner (in the case of the Roman Catholic Church the processes were less public, but the debates within the Church became highly publicized). Therefore, as we explore these four religions it is important to consider both the process and the result. Since many readers of this chapter may be less familiar with United

[2]For example, United Synagogue of Conservative Judaism requires member synagogues to follow a number of requirements, including being strictly Kosher, but individual synagogues and their rabbis maintain quite a bit of freedom regarding other religious and governance issues. The United Synagogue of Conservative Judaism, Standards for Congregational Practice (1959, last amended in 2017), http://www.uscj.org/LeadingKehilla/Leadership/StandardsforCongregationalPractice.aspx (visited Sept. 3, 2017).

Synagogue of Conservative Judaism and Japanese Zen Buddhism than they are with the two Christian traditions, I will provide some background information on United Synagogue and Japanese Zen at the beginning of the sections addressing each.

2 United Synagogue of Conservative Judaism

The United Synagogue of Conservative Judaism (USCJ) is an important movement in the Jewish tradition that seeks to uphold Jewish law (Halacha) and traditions in the modern world. The term "conservative" in this context has nothing to do with politics and everything to do with conserving Jewish tradition in a changing world. For lack of a better reference point, readers might most easily view this movement as promoting adherence to Halacha and tradition, while adapting that law and tradition—where it is possible to do so without violating Halacha and its interpretive methodologies—to changing circumstances.

The Committee on Jewish Law and Standards is perhaps the most important venue for addressing the interpretation and application of Halacha to a variety of situations. It was this committee that addressed the issue of LGBT rights for USCJ. It did so through a Responsum, which is a written reply by a rabbi or rabbis to questions raised about the meaning or application of Jewish Law. The members of the Committee on Jewish Law and Standards are rabbis generally considered to be leading scholars of Halacha.

The process was thorough and detailed, and there were dissenting and concurring opinions to the Responsum. The Responsum focused on in this chapter was issued in 2006 to address questions of LGBT rights including ordination of openly gay clergy and same-sex unions, along with an important follow up in 2012 addressing same-sex marriage ceremonies.[3]

The 2006 Responsum was the result of a four-year process of study and discussion addressing the halachic questions surrounding LGBT rights.[4] The 2012 paper was issued, in part, to respond to a number of questions about same-sex marriage ceremonies that arose after the 2006 Responsum was issued.[5] The Responsum focused on the meaning of the biblical text relating to sexual relations between men and men and women and women, as well as Talmudic and post Talmudic rabbinical interpretations.[6] It also focused on the scientific and social scientific data showing that sexual orientation is not a choice,[7] and the negative impact that social stigma and lack of recognition of sexual identity within a community can have on gays and

[3]Dorff et al. (2006, 2012).

[4]Nevins (2017).

[5]Dorff et al. (2012).

[6]Dorff et al. (2006).

[7]*Id* at 2–4.

lesbians.[8] This latter point became quite important when the Responsum turned to the discussion of *Kvod Habriot*, which can be translated as "human dignity."[9]

The result of the 2006 discussions was a split opinion allowing ordination of openly gay and lesbian rabbis as well as same-sex commitment ceremonies, and complete acceptance of openly gay members and their significant others on the same terms as heterosexual members.[10] The majority opinion, which favored inclusion, recognized that the biblical text is quite prohibitive of anal sex between men, but noted that this does not answer the question in light of the importance of human dignity in Halacha and Jewish tradition.[11] Moreover, all members of the Committee, including the rabbis who dissented, recognized that recent scientific and social scientific information makes it clear that people do not choose their sexual orientation.[12]

The debate centered more heavily on the meaning and scope of rabbinical prohibitions on same-sex relationships in light of Talmudic and post Talmudic rabbinical interpretations,[13] and on the relationship between these interpretations and the biblical, Talmudic, and post Talmudic discussions of the importance of *Kvod Habriot* (human dignity).[14] The debates also focused on the processes for changing prior understandings of Halacha, and whether such changes are acceptable and if so under what circumstances.[15]

The Responsum explains that the concept of human dignity–*Kvod Habriot*–and its legal implications require a fresh look at the strict rabbinical restrictions in light of modern understandings and science.[16] Human dignity under Halacha requires that people be treated with kindness and that people should not be humiliated.[17] By denying LGBT Jews rights and recognition within the community their sense of isolation and humiliation would be increased and that is not in keeping with human dignity.[18] The Responsum explains that the principal of "*gadol kvod habriot shedocheh lo ta'aseh shebaTorah*," which means that human dignity is so important that it can override negative commandments in the Torah. It thus can be applied to overcome earlier rabbinic interpretations that conflict with human dignity, especially in light of the recent scientific understandings of sexual orientation that earlier rabbis did not have.[19]

This is especially true when the biblical commandments do not specifically address a given situation. For example, the Responsum explains that the biblical

---

[8] *Id* at 2–4, 15–17, 19–20.

[9] *Id* at 9–20.

[10] Nevins (2017).

[11] *See generally*, Dorff et al. (2006).

[12] *Id* at 2–4; Nevins (2017).

[13] Dorff et al. (2006), at 4–8.

[14] *Id* at 9–17.

[15] *See generally*, *Id*.

[16] *Id* at 9–17.

[17] *Id*.

[18] *Id* at 2–4, 9–17.

[19] *Id* at 8; Nevins (2017).

text does not specifically address lesbian relations or gay relations other than anal sex.[20] The broader prohibitions on same-sex relations arose from rabbinical interpretations of the biblical text, and even here famous rabbis such as the Rambam (Maimonides) and the Ramban (Nachmanides) disagreed on the scope of sexual prohibitions.[21] Maimonides' more restrictive interpretation garnered majority support for hundreds of years as a fence around the biblical prohibition so that people would not be tempted to violate that prohibition, but Nachmanides' less restrictive interpretation fits better with much of what we know today about the nature of sexual orientation.[22]

In Halacha rabbinical interpretations are exceptionally important, but this does not mean they must override principles such as human dignity, especially when they are not based in a specific biblical prohibition, but rather serve as a fence around those prohibitions.[23] Nowhere in Halacha or Jewish tradition are people expected to remain celibate, and the earlier broad rabbinic prohibitions on same-sex relations came about at a time when it was believed that by avoiding same-sex relations people would settle back into a heterosexual lifestyle with traditional marriage, etc.[24] The Responsum clearly states that today we know this is an incorrect assumption.[25] It violates human dignity to expect people to remain celibate, especially when we now know that sexual orientation is not something that can be changed and that the specific biblical prohibition is only on anal sex between men and not on other forms of same-sex relations, sexual orientation generally, or same-sex relationships generally.[26]

In this regard the Responsum explains that Jewish gay men are expected to avoid anal sex because of the clear biblical prohibition, just as heterosexual men and women are to avoid certain sexual practices such as sex during a woman's period under Halacha,[27] but of course there is no way—at least not within Conservative Judaism—for the religion to monitor private sexual practices, so this is ultimately between each person and G-d, and between each person and his or her relationship with Halacha.[28] The Responsum is clear that all other forms of sexual intimacy between men and men and women and women do not violate Halacha.[29] Moreover, the 2006 Responsum was clear that Conservative synagogues can recognize same sex relationships, and the 2012 addition explains that this includes same-sex

---

[20]Dorff et al. (2006), at 4–8.

[21]*Id* at 4–8.

[22]*Id* at 5–8.

[23]Id at 8.

[24]*Id* at 8.

[25]*Id* at 2–4, 8.

[26]*See generally, Id.*

[27]*Id* at 4–5.

[28]*Id* at 8, 17.

[29]*Id* at 5, 7–8.

marriages.[30] Moreover, the 2012 addition sets forth model ceremonies that can be used for same-sex marriages.[31]

3 The Episcopalian Church

The processes used to make decisions on theological questions in the Episcopalian Church are quite different from those used by United Synagogue. The Episcopalian Church is generally considered a hierarchical church while as noted above United Synagogue has more of a congregational structure. Yet, the results of the decision-making processes, and even the timing of those results, are quite similar.

The Episcopalian Church consecrated its first openly gay bishop in 2003.[32] In 2009, the Church's General Convention passed a resolution explaining that anyone can be called by G-d regardless of sexual orientation.[33] Most recently, in 2015 the General Convention amended the church canons so that marriage rites are available to everyone regardless of sexual orientation.[34]

This progress has come at a cost for the Episcopalian Church, however, as some churches have attempted to leave the national church, and in other cases dissent has been strong.[35] Moreover, it has led to some friction with the broader Anglican community to which the Episcopalian Church is connected.[36] The Church has worked to avoid disunity by recognizing not only the rights of dissenting clergy not to perform same-sex marriages,[37] but also the direct recognition that Episcopalians and Episcopalian Clergy of good faith can disagree on issues such as ordination of openly gay clergy and same-sex marriage.[38] Still, there are a number of ongoing situations involving church schisms resulting from LGBT rights issues.[39]

The Episcopalian Church is governed by a structure through which local churches are located within a diocese.[40] At the top of the structure is a legislative body called the General Convention, which meets about every three years.[41] The General Convention

[30]Dorff et al. (2012).

[31]*Id.*

[32]Ogden (2017).

[33]The Acts of Convention, *Reaffirm Participation in the Anglican Communion While Acknowledging Differences*, Resolution Number 2009-D025 (2009).

[34]The Acts of Convention, *Amend Canon 1.18 (Of the Solemnization of Holy Matrimony)*, Resolution Number 2015-A036 (2015).

[35]Jones (2012); McBeth and Sykes (2011).

[36]O'Halloran (2014).

[37]The Acts of Convention, *Amend Canon 1.18 (Of the Solemnization of Holy Matrimony)*, at Sec. 7.

[38]The Acts of Convention, *Reaffirm Participation in the Anglican Communion While Acknowledging Differences*.

[39]Jones (2012); McBeth and Sykes (2011).

[40]*Church Governance*, http://archive.episcopalchurch.org/governance.htm.

[41]*Id.*

is bicameral. It is composed of the House of Bishops (which is composed of active and retired bishops) and the House of Deputies (which is composed of laypeople and clergy elected by each diocese).[42] For present purposes it is important that the relevant legislation affecting LGBT rights was passed by the General Convention so it is binding on the church as a whole. Still, the General Convention included language making clear that every clergy member and congregation has the right to make their own decisions about what is acceptable for a given local church.[43]

In 2003, the Episcopalian Church consecrated Gene Robinson as Bishop for the Diocese of New Hampshire. He was the first openly gay Bishop in the Episcopalian Church.[44] Some members of the church vocally protested against the consecration, and there were even some church schisms in response to the consecration.[45]

In a 2009 resolution titled, *Reaffirm Participation in the Anglican Communion While Acknowledging Differences*, the General Convention recognized that gays and lesbian members of the church are welcomed and can be called by G-d, and that this includes calls to the clergy.[46] The resolution stated clearly, however, that members were "not of one mind, and Christians of good conscience disagree about some of these matters."[47] This was followed in 2012 by passage of a provisional service for same-sex unions, and by an open prohibition against discrimination aimed at transgendered individuals.[48]

In 2015, the General Convention amended the church canons to recognize same-sex marriage and the church issued updated ceremonies for same-sex marriage and unions.[49] The General Convention again recognized that there may be disagreement on these issues and left discretion to individual clergy members and churches to decide whether to solemnize or bless a marriage.[50] Moreover, as with same-sex marriages within United Synagogue, the new Episcopalian canons make clear that same-sex spouses have the same rights and are bound by the same duties as heterosexual marriages.[51] The new canons have led to significant fallout and there are

---

[42] *Id.*

[43] See, The Acts of Convention, *Amend Canon 1.18 (Of the Solemnization of Holy Matrimony)*, at Sec. 7.; The Acts of Convention, *Reaffirm Participation in the Anglican Communion While Acknowledging Differences.*

[44] *See*, Ogden (2017).

[45] Jones (2012), McBeth and Sykes (2011).

[46] The Acts of Convention, *Reaffirm Participation in the Anglican Communion While Acknowledging Differences.*

[47] *Id.*

[48] The Acts of Convention, *Adopt Statements on Threats Against Sexual Minorities*, Resolution Number 2012-D061 (2012).

[49] The Acts of Convention, *Amend Canon 1.18 (Of the Solemnization of Holy Matrimony)*; *Supplemental Materials, Appendices of the Report of the Standing Commission on Liturgy and Music*, https://extranet.generalconvention.org/staff/files/download/13068.pdf (last visited 9/7/2017).

[50] The Acts of Convention, *Amend Canon 1.18 (Of the Solemnization of Holy Matrimony)*, at Sec. 7.

[51] The Acts of Convention, *Amend Canon 1.18 (Of the Solemnization of Holy Matrimony)*, at Sec. 4.

a number of churches experiencing schisms and/or seeking re-affiliation with other Anglican churches.

The Episcopalian Church has been quite progressive compared to some other large Protestant churches in the U.S. and around the world, much to the ire of some of its Anglican Church cousins.[52] So why has the Episcopalian Church been able to adapt its traditions to be more welcoming to LGBT members of its community? There seem to be a number of reasons for this, but the best resource for this is the document produced by the church's Task Force on the Study of Marriage, which was appointed by the General Convention to study and report on these issues.[53]

The task force explains that the Anglican tradition—of which the Episcopalian Church is part—explores scripture, tradition, and reason when addressing important theological questions.[54] The Task Force explains in its report that it approached marriage "not as a matter of dogma or core doctrine, but as a concern of pastoral and moral theology."[55] This explains why the Task Force evaluated not only the biblical text, but also understandings of that text over time, and the changes in circumstances and information that have come about over the years. Since moral values affect the understanding of doctrine on these issues, the changes in understandings of sexual orientation are relevant to how the church should view marriage.[56]

The Task Force viewed the institution of marriage—for those who are called to it—as a religious calling and important to G-d's purpose.[57] Moreover, the Task Force explains there is a transformational aspect to faith, and that marriage too is transformational. The Task Force found these themes to be reflected in the Gospels.[58]

A lot of attention was also paid to the ways in which the institution of marriage has itself changed in society over time, as well as how church doctrines have responded to that change. It also explores the evolution of the canon law in response to the changes in church practices.[59] The Task Force openly took a holistic look at scripture and evolving tradition, as well as at current understandings and context, as it reasoned through the complex questions raised by same-sex marriage.

In fact, one need look no further than an important subsection of the 2015 Resolution recognizing same-sex marriages to see that the openness on LGBT issues reflects the church's holistic view of scripture, tradition, and reason. That subsection includes a declaration that must be signed by both parties to a marriage, including same-sex marriages:

> We understand the teaching of the church that God's purpose for our marriage is for our mutual joy, for the help and comfort we will give to each other in prosperity and adversity,

---

[52] O'Halloran (2014).

[53] Task Force on the Study of Marriage, https://extranet.generalconvention.org/staff/files/download/12485.pdf (last visited on 9/7/2017).

[54] *Id* at 9.

[55] *Id* at 10.

[56] *See generally, Id.*

[57] *Id.*

[58] *Id.*

[59] *Id.*

> and, when it is God's will, for the gift and heritage of children and their nurture in the knowledge and love of God. We also understand that our marriage is to be unconditional, mutual, exclusive, faithful, and lifelong; and we engage to make the utmost effort to accept these gifts and fulfill these duties, with the help of God and the support of our community.[60]

The Church was firm that same sex marriage does not change the goals and structure of marriage, and found the basis for same sex marriage in its traditional sources.

4 Japanese Zen Buddhism

To understand Japanese Zen Buddhist structure it is important to know what we are talking about when using the term Japanese Zen Buddhism. There are multiple schools of Japanese Zen Buddhism. The focus in this chapter is on the Rinzai School, which is also connected to the Ōbaku school for some purposes.[61] There are several other Zen sects in Japan, including the Sōtō school, which is the largest.[62] Moreover, Zen has spread throughout the world and Zen sects can be found in the United States, Europe, Australia and elsewhere. Since our focus will be on the Rinzai school, what follows is limited to that school; although other schools have agreed with the ideas expressed.[63]

A Rinzai school Buddhist temple called Shunkoin has famously been performing same-sex wedding ceremonies since 2011.[64] This is noteworthy because Shunkoin is an ancient sub-temple within the Myōshinji Temple,[65] which is one of the most important Temples in the Rinzai School and houses the central offices for the Rinzai School of Buddhism.[66] Shunkoin itself was established in 1590 C.E.[67]

There is no inherent conflict between same-sex marriage and Zen practices.[68] As explained below there is, however, a relevant precept that has been interpreted differently by a few unrelated Buddhist schools. Of course, not just Shunkoin Temple as a member of Rinzai sect Zen Buddhism, but many other Zen Schools, including those outside of Japan, have come to recognize same-sex relationships as consistent

---

[60] The Acts of Convention, *Amend Canon 1.18 (Of the Solemnization of Holy Matrimony)*, at Sec. 7.

[61] Borup (2008).

[62] *Id.*

[63] *See, e.g. A Universal Statement of Marriage Equality from the Zen School of Buddhism in Australia* (Australian Zen Institute 2016) (statement supporting marriage equality bill signed by leaders of several Zen Buddhist schools in Australia and elsewhere).

[64] O'Donoghue (2016).

[65] *Id.*

[66] Borup (2008), at 12–20.

[67] Shunkoin Temple Website: History of Shunkoin Temple, http://www.shunkoin.com/direction.html (last visited on 9/19/17).

[68] *See* O'Donoghue (2016); *Universal Statement of Marriage Equality from the Zen School of Buddhism in Australia*; Dynes (1990); Aitken (1995).

with Zen teachings and practice.[69] Some have even published statements in English on the topic.[70]

The term Zen is a Japanese derivation of a Chinese term and it means "exacting meditation."[71] Of course, meditation is an important practice for Zen Buddhists.[72] Also important to Zen Buddhism is an ancient Buddhist teaching called the "Four Noble Abodes."[73] These abodes consist of: compassion, kindness, equanimity, and joy in the attainment of others.[74]

Traditional Buddhist teachings do not directly address questions about sexual orientation, but they do address questions about sex and human nature. In Zen Buddhism these issues are reflected within one of the precepts accepted by all Zen Buddhist clergy and followers. The precept addressing these issues can be translated as: "I take up the way of not misusing sex."[75] This has been interpreted by some Buddhist sects to oppose same-sex relations and marriages,[76] but among the Mahayana schools of Buddhism, to which Zen belongs, there has generally been more acceptances of homosexuality and LGBT rights.[77] Many Zen clergy view the prohibition on "misusing sex" as a rejection of abusive, non-consensual, or self-centered, exploitive sex.[78] Yet, the genders of the partners involved are not the focus.[79]

Unlike United Synagogue and the Episcopalian Church there has been no formal statement recognizing same-sex marriage issued by the Rinzai school. This may be a result of there being no inherent conflict between Zen and same-sex marriage and/or because of the fact, discussed below, that there is no nationally recognized right to legally sanctioned same-sex marriage in Japan. Of course, the fact that same-sex marriages have been performed at Shunkoin for years has not raised religious condemnation or prohibition on the practice from within the Rinzai school,[80] and other Zen leaders and sects have strongly supported same-sex marriage.[81]

In Japan, same-sex marriage is not yet legal at a national level so the ceremonies performed at Shunkoin do not create any sort of legal marriage rights, but they can be very meaningful for those involved. This is consistent with marriage in general

---

[69] *Id* (all sources).

[70] *Universal Statement of Marriage Equality from the Zen School of Buddhism in Australia.*

[71] Aitken (1995).

[72] Borup (2008); Aitken (1995).

[73] Aitken (1995).

[74] *Id.*

[75] *Id.*

[76] O'Donoghue (2016), at 171.

[77] *Id.* at 168–171; *Universal Statement of Marriage Equality from the Zen School of Buddhism in Australia*; Baroni (2002).

[78] Aitken (1995); *See, e.g. Universal Statement of Marriage Equality fromthe Zen School of Buddhism in Australia*(Australian Zen Institute 2016) (statement supporting marriage equality bill signed by leaders of several Zen Buddhist schools in Australia and elsewhere).

[79] *Id* (both sources).

[80] O'Donoghue (2016).

[81] *See* note 68 and accompanying text.

in Japan. Getting married simply requires the couple to go to the city offices and finalize the documents recognizing the marriage. This is separate from the Kekkon-shiki (marriage ceremony) that may be performed at a religious institution or secular marriage venue. In fact, there is no legal need for a Kekkon-shiki and people have such ceremonies mostly for themselves and their families, colleagues, and friends. Thus, if a local government decides to recognize same-sex marriage or same-sex unions it becomes a legal right regardless of whether there is a ceremony as long as the couple fills out, and the city approves, the relevant documents.[82]

5 The Roman Catholic Church

The Roman Catholic Church has explicitly rejected recognition of same-sex marriage and the ordination of gay clergy members.[83] The church has issued statements, however, making clear that its rejection of same-sex marriage and ordination of openly gay clergy is not based in animus toward members of the LGBT community as human beings, but rather is a reflection of Catholic teachings relating to sex, marriage and natural law.[84] The Church views LGBT issues as an internal struggle for those who identify as gay, lesbian, or transsexual,[85] and opposes some forms of discrimination against members of the LGBT community. There has been significant discussion, debate and reflection within the Church on these issues.

The Roman Catholic Church has addressed the questions of ordination of gay clergy and same-sex marriage in separate documents. As to ordination or entrance into seminary, the Church has stated:

---

[82]Takarazuka Becomes Fourth Municipality in Japan to Recognize Same-sex Unions, The Japan Times (May 31, 2016); *Sapporo to Join Other Cities in Recognizing Same-sex Partnerships as Marriages*, The Japan Times (Dec. 22, 2016).

[83]*Instruction Concerning the Criteria for the Discernment of Vocations with regard to Persons with Homosexual Tendencies in view of their Admission to the Seminary and to Holy Orders*, issued by the Congregation for Catholic Education, Rome, Memorial of St Charles Borromeo, Patron of Seminaries (approved and ordered published by Pope Benedict XVI, Aug. 31, 2005) (concerning ordination) (hereinafter "2005 Statement"); *Considerations Regarding Proposals to Give Legal Recognition to Unions Between Homosexual Persons*, Congregation for the Doctrine of the Faith (approved and ordered published by Pope John Paul II, March 28, 2003, publication by Congregation for the Doctrine of the Faith, June 3, 2003) (same-sex marriages and unions).

[84]*See, e.g. 2005 Statement*, at Sec. 2 ("Such persons must be accepted with respect and sensitivity. Every sign of unjust discrimination in their regard should be avoided. They are called to fulfil God's will in their lives and to unite to the sacrifice of the Lord's Cross the difficulties they may encounter").

[85]*Persona Humana: Declaration on Certain Questions Concerning Sexual Ethics, Sacred Congregation for the Doctrine of the Faith*, at Section VIII (approved and ordered published by Pope Paul VI on Nov. 7, 1975, published by the Sacred Congregation for the Doctrine of the Faith, Dec. 29, 1975).

> [...] The Church, while profoundly respecting the persons in question, cannot admit to the seminary or to holy orders those who practise [sic] homosexuality, present deep-seated homosexual tendencies or support the so-called "gay culture" (footnotes omitted).
>
> Such persons, in fact, find themselves in a situation that gravely hinders them from relating correctly to men and women. One must in no way overlook the negative consequences that can derive from the ordination of persons with deep-seated homosexual tendencies.
>
> Different, however, would be the case in which one were dealing with homosexual tendencies that were only the expression of a transitory problem - for example, that of an adolescence not yet superseded. Nevertheless, such tendencies must be clearly overcome at least three years before ordination to the diaconate.[86]

In the recent document, *The Gift of the Priestly Vocation*,[87] the above-mentioned view was quoted with approval.[88] Thus, contrary to what some news stories have suggested, the Church does not accept members of the LGBT community into the clergy even if they remain celibate. Being gay or lesbian is treated by the Church as a sort of disorder that should not deny gays and lesbians respect as human beings, but with which the Church expects them to have to struggle and repress.[89]

While some have argued that the term "homosexual tendencies" might refer to homosexual acts rather than orientation,[90] that interpretation seems in conflict with the more stringent language issued by the Church on this issue that refers both to "homosexual acts" and "homosexual tendencies."[91] In fact, the Church went beyond the above prohibition to make it clear that it does not accept the "don't ask, don't tell" approach:

> [...] The spiritual director has the obligation to evaluate all the qualities of the candidate's personality and to make sure that he does not present disturbances of a sexual nature, which are incompatible with the priesthood. If a candidate practises [sic] homosexuality or presents deep-seated homosexual tendencies, his spiritual director as well as his confessor have the duty to dissuade him in conscience from proceeding towards ordination.
>
> It goes without saying that the candidate himself has the primary responsibility for his own formation. He must offer himself trustingly to the discernment of the Church, of the Bishop who calls him to orders, of the rector of the seminary, of his spiritual director and of the other seminary educators to whom the Bishop or major superior has entrusted the task of forming future priests. It would be gravely dishonest for a candidate to hide his own homosexuality in order to proceed, despite everything, towards ordination. Such a deceitful attitude does not correspond to the spirit of truth, loyalty and openness that must characterize the personality of him who believes he is called to serve Christ and his Church in the ministerial priesthood (footnote omitted).[92]

---

[86] *2005 Statement*, at Sec. 2.

[87] *The Gift of the Priestly Vocation: Ratio Fundamentalis Institutionis Sacerdotalis* (issued and ordered published by Pope Francis, Vatican City, Dec. 8, 2016).

[88] *Id* at 81–82.

[89] *Persona Human: Declaration on Certain Questions*, at Sec. VIII.

[90] Cameli (2016).

[91] DeBarnardo (2016).

[92] *2005 Statement*.

As for same-sex relationships, Pope Francis has stated openly that he seeks to minimize discrimination against members of the LGBT community,[93] but this does not mean that the Vatican is currently ready to accept same-sex marriage.[94] The Church has addressed same-sex relationships, especially marriage. The official position of the Church is that same-sex marriage goes against the teachings of the Church. In coming to this conclusion, the Church considered scripture, natural law, and reason.[95]

The Church has stated that recognition of same-sex relationships conflicts with biblical prohibitions and with what the Church views as the nature of marriage as being between a man and woman with procreative possibilities.[96] The Church's view is that same-sex relationships go against natural law and therefore even without the scriptural concerns such relationships can not be sanctioned by the Church.[97] The Church position also argues that recognition of same-sex relationships violates the concept of "right reason,"[98] which is connected with natural law and may be most effectively defined in the *Catechism of the Catholic Church*[99]:

> The natural law, present in the heart of each man and established by reason, is universal in its precepts and its authority extends to all men. It expresses the dignity of the person and determines the basis for his fundamental rights and duties:
>
> For there is a true law: right reason. It is in conformity with nature, is diffused among all men, and is immutable and eternal; its orders summon to duty; its prohibitions turn away from offense [...]. To replace it with a contrary law is a sacrilege; failure to apply even one of its provisions is forbidden; no one can abrogate it entirely (footnote omitted).[100]

Given the Church's view that recognition of same-sex relationships violates scripture, natural law, and right reason, the Roman Catholic Church reaches a different conclusion from the religions discussed above.[101] It is interesting that some of the base texts are the same for United Synagogue, the Episcopal Church, and the Roman Catholic Church. It may be that the differences lie in the respective views of natural law and its relationship to the principle of human dignity. That is a question for another time as this chapter is limited in scope. Questions regarding different views

---

[93] *Post-Synodal Apostolic Exhortation Amoris Lætitia of the Holy Father Francis to Bishops, Priests and Deacons, Consecrated Persons, Christian Married Couples, and All the Lay Faithful on Love in the Family*, (Issued by Pope Francis on April 8, 2016) (hereinafter "*Amoris Laetitia*").

[94] *Considerations Regarding Proposals to Give Legal Recognition to Unions Between Homosexual Persons*, Congregation for the Doctrine of the Faith (approved and ordered published by Pope John Paul II, March 28, 2003, publication by Congregation for the Doctrine of the Faith, June 3, 2003) (applicable to same-sex marriages and unions).

[95] *Id.*

[96] *Id.*

[97] *Id.*

[98] *Id.*

[99] *The Catechism of the Catholic Church*, Article I, Section 1954, available at http://www.vatican.va/archive/ccc_css/archive/catechism/p3s1c3a1.htm (last viewed on 9/15/17).

[100] *Id.*

[101] *Considerations Regarding Proposals to Give Legal Recognition to Unions Between Homosexual Persons*, Congregation for the Doctrine of the Faith (approved and ordered published by Pope John Paul II, March 28, 2003, publication by Congregation for the Doctrine of the Faith, June 3, 2003).

of natural law, natural rights, and their relationship to human dignity in religious traditions is a topic that could fill libraries. This chapter simply seeks to inform you about the ways in which four religious traditions have addressed LGBT rights.

6 Conclusion

Three of the four traditions addressed in this chapter have historical and theological legacies that would seem to have made recognition of LGBT rights harder. Yet, two of these traditions, United Synagogue of Conservative Judaism and the Episcopalian Church, recognized other overarching values from within those traditions that allowed for the inclusion of same-sex marriage and ordination of openly gay clergy. The third tradition, the Roman Catholic Church, also engaged in a process to address these questions, but could not recognize these rights as consistent with its traditions.

All three of these are "Western" religious traditions. The chapter also looked at Zen Buddhism, which has also been welcoming to same-sex marriages and ordination of openly gay clergy. There is less of a doctrinal and historical rejection of LGBT rights in Zen Buddhist traditions, but there has been interesting engagement with these issues from within Zen Buddhism.

All of the traditions addressed in this chapter have consciously addressed the question of LGBT rights from within tradition. The processes were often different, but the study of the ways in which religions address LGBT rights from within their religious traditions is an important issue that is often overlooked in the broader debates about LGBT rights. This study can help enrich the broader discussion and is necessary to understand why there are so many different positions on LGBT issues from within different religious traditions. Hopefully, other scholars will explore these questions in the context of other religious traditions.

References

Aitken R (1995) Written testimony to the commission on sexual orientation and the law. Zen Buddhist perspective on same-gender marriage, 11 Oct 1995. http://www.qrd.org/qrd/religion/zen.buddhist.perspective.on.same.sex.marriage. Last visited on 19 Sept 2017

Baroni HJ (2002) The illustrated encyclopedia of Zen Buddhism. Rosen Publishing Group, New York, p 288

Borup J (2008) Japanese Rinzai Zen Buddhism: Myōshinji, a living religion. Brill, The Netherlands.

Cameli RLJ (2016) How to understand the gift of the priestly vocation (Ratio fundamentalis institutionis sacerdotalis, 2016) On the question of homosexuality. L'Osservatore Romano, 18 Dec 2016

DeBarnardo F (2016) Did the Vatican ban gay priests or not? National catholic reporter, 27 Dec 2016

Dorff R, Nevins D, Reisner A (2006) Homosexuality and human dignity & Halakhah: a combined responsum for the committee on jewish law and standards. 6 Dec 2006

Dorff R, Nevins D, Reisner A (2012) Rituals and documents of marriage and divorce for same-sex couples, 31 May 2012
Dynes WR (ed) (1990) Encyclopedia of homosexuality, vol I at 170. Routledge, UK
Jones BD (2012) Litigating the schism and reforming the canons: orthodoxy, property & the modern social gospel of the episcopal church. Golden Gate UL Rev 42:151
McBeth IA, Sykes JR (2011) Comment, The unavoidable ecclesiastical collision in Virginia. Richmond J Law Pub Interest 19:509
Nevins DS (2017) Conservative Halakhah and homosexuality: an insiders view of the 2006 CJLS gay vote. My Jewish Learning. http://www.myjewishlearning.com/article/conservative-halakhah-and-homosexuality. Last visited on 3 Sept 2017
O'Donoghue JJ (2016) Kyoto Monk on a mission opens his doors to diversity. The Japan Times, 16 Mar 2016. https://www.japantimes.co.jp/community/2016/03/16/our-lives/kyoto-monk-mission-opens-doors-diversity/. Last visited on 19 Sept 2017
Ogden J (2017) Communion in crisis: Gene Robinson, the Episcopal church, and the Anglican communion, case studies in ethics. https://kenan.ethics.duke.edu/wp-content/uploads/2012/08/AnglicanCommunionCase20151.pdf. Last visited on 2 Sept 2017
O'Halloran K (2014) The Church of England-Charity law and human rights at Chapter 5. Springer, Berlin
Ravitch FS (2016) Freedom's edge: religious freedom, sexual freedom, and the future of America. Cambridge, Cambridge University Press

The Inverted Relationship: Constitutive Theory of Law and the Enforcement of Orthodoxy in Book XVI of the Theodosian Code

Ryszard Bobrowicz

Abstract This paper focuses on the question if, and if so how, the Theodosian Code, the first legal codification of the Roman Empire and its book devoted to religion, Book XVI, facilitated the formation and enforcement of the concept of orthodoxy and its boundaries. It uses the propositions of the Cognitive Science of Religion to advance a new understanding of the shift towards orthodoxy, as the process in which legitimate representations were reified in formal processes, and it applies findings from cultural and social studies to establish two ways in which law could exercise constitutive influence and operate as one of such processes: by establishing categories based on socially salient marks, and by instilling specific narratives. The analysis of the Code's context gives affirmative answer to the question 'if'. Christianity emerged as a hybrid creation, and the orthodoxy was an effect of the process of discernment, which was furthered by the progressing Christianisation of the Roman Empire, developments in Roman Law, and the use of coercion, turning law and religion into a cooperative enterprise. This was advanced by the Code's insistence on two "orthodoxies", legal and religious, which was achieved through unification, universalisation and clarification of the existing laws, as well as categorisation and ordering of different social spheres. The close analysis of Book XVI showed continuation of these developments and aims. The Code enforced orthodoxy both directly, by being a formal reifying process itself, and indirectly, by facilitating other processes of that kind. The orthodoxy was construed through doctrine, extra-doctrinal pronouncements that enforced narratives such as the apostolic continuity, precedence of the right belief before heresy or Roman primacy, and introduction of a coherent, empire-wide religious policy that stratified society according to religious affiliation. Differentiation between Catholic Christians, heretics, pagans, Jews and apostates helped in the process of self-identification and discernment of orthodoxy, while the flattening of non-orthodox on subsequent levels provided means for their rhetorical and legal rejection. The paper ends by proposing further research directions, such as comparison with the Justinian Code, or application of the theory presented here to other historical and contemporary developments.

R. Bobrowicz (✉)
Faculty of Theology, University of Copenhagen, Copenhagen, Denmark
e-mail: ryszard.bobrowicz@gmail.com

J. Giles et al. (eds.), *Law, Religion and Tradition*, Law and Religion in a Global Context 1, https://doi.org/10.1007/978-3-319-96749-3_5

1 Introduction

That the spheres of law and religion are best kept apart seems to be a commonplace baseline, at least in the Western hemisphere. And yet, these two disciplines rarely stand afar. Quite the opposite, law and religion are deeply interrelated, influencing one another in a complex manner. And while in a secular fashion we tend to focus on the way religion influences law, the latter may equally affect the former. Moreover, this influence may touch upon religion's core principles, and matters of such importance as the question of what constitutes 'orthodoxy'. In this paper, I argue that law can be a powerful formatter of orthodoxy, both directly, by exercising what is called the 'constitutive effect', and indirectly, by enforcing other formational processes.

I want to exemplify this by focusing on the formation of Christian orthodoxy after its ascension to power in the late fourth and early fifth century. This subject gathered renewed attention when Walter Bauer published "Orthodoxy and Heresy in the Earliest Christianity." Bauer's main thesis contested the 'classical' theory of the development of orthodoxy, which was furthered by such writers as Eusebius and presented orthodoxy as the primary Christianity, with heresies as some secondary deformations of the original. The so called 'Bauer Thesis' stated that what was later rewritten as 'orthodoxy' was just one of the primary versions of Christianity, but the one that later succeeded through the enforcement of political power.[1] Translated into English in 1970, Bauer's ideas were subject to a wide range of discussions. And while many criticised him for stretching the evidence,[2] his input reoriented the narration of orthodoxy, advancing questions of why and how orthodoxy succeeded.[3]

Since Bauer's time, the methodological framework of history changed significantly. The development of the linguistic turn, as well as new research currents, such as cognitive studies, cultural analysis and the social sciences, introduced numerous new ideas which allowed for a better operationalisation and understanding of the matter in question. These developments were shared by jurisprudence, changing completely the way we approach law and religion, and highlighting their interconnected character. This allows the researchers to go beyond the traditional dichotomies. In this paper, I will tackle one of such dichotomies by answering the following questions: if, and if so, how, did the Theodosian Code, the first public codification of Roman Imperial Law, and its treatment of religion in Book XVI facilitate the process of reification and sanctification of orthodoxy and its boundaries? This will be done in four main sections. The first will present the theoretical framework of the paper. The second will present the most important background information. The third will analyse the Code, with a special focus on Book XVI. Finally, the fourth will draw conclusions and point to some possible further applications.

---

[1] Bauer (1971), p. 229.

[2] See Turner (1954), Roberts (1979), Robinson (1988), Pearson (1990).

[3] See Hartog (2015).

2 Theory

The notion of orthodoxy draws a strict line between 'ancient' and 'modern' religions, making it hard to work with Christianity in its early context. A good answer to that problem was proposed by a new field of research called the 'Cognitive Science of Religion' (CSR). Jesper Sørensen points out that most of the efforts to conceptualise religion focused for a long time around the struggle for a 'magic bullet', that is, a single theory that could explain all religious phenomena at once. However, none of the subsequent theories were able to satisfy this requirement. As Sørensen argues, this was due to the fact that the term 'religion' is of non-scientific origin and thus cannot be easily and sharply defined. For the purpose of scientific inquiry, it has to be 'refracted' into its constitutive parts, which can be studied on a more solid and tangible basis. This allows for an application of the methods developed for non-religious phenomena to study religious ones.[4]

Using this approach and applying methods of cognitive studies, Roger Beck was able to compare Christianity and Mithraism. To do so, he came up with a new definition of doctrine as "that which within the given religious group is negotiated (or negotiable) concerning legitimate representations."[5] Mithraism, which, simultaneously to Christianity, developed during the first three centuries, had what Beck calls a "fluid doctrine", that is, in which legitimate representations were constantly negotiated between the public and the private. Christianity, on the other hand, negotiated these legitimate representations in formal processes over time, and thereby reified and sanctified them.[6] This difference paves the way for a reformulation of Bauer's problem; instead of asking why an 'orthodox' version of Christianity could have prevailed over others, the following questions may be posed: why and how exactly these legitimate representations were reified and sanctified in the formal processes?

The 'why' question requires an extensive investigation of its own; one which cannot be fully satisfied in a work of this size. Following Bauer and his adherents, I will concur with the view that the tools that came with political power allowed for this petrification. Elaine Pagels argues that persecutions most likely constituted an important factor, which helped both orthodoxy and ecclesiastical structures to prevail, and opened the road to further development.[7] On the other hand, Karl Noethlichs states that it was the "revolution from the top" that created the necessary background for the formation of orthodoxy. As he notes, from the beginning of Rome's existence there were two basic modes in which the ruling interfered with religious practice: by correcting the practice and by managing foreign influences. It was therefore not a novel activity for the emperor to adjudicate over disputes, as Constantine did in the case of Donatist controversy to introduce a "united simplicity closer to the truth and better for religion".[8] In this, as Eusebius notes in the *Life of Constantine*, he positioned

[4]Sørensen (2005), pp. 467–468.

[5]Beck (2006), p. 94.

[6]Ibid., 95.

[7]Pagels (1979), p. 98.

[8]Ibid., 119.

himself as the "bishop appointed by God over those outside" the Church.[9] However, this was not the last of such interferences, and, starting with the Arian controversy, the emperor began to resolve questions of a theological nature. Through the adjudication in subsequent cases of a similar character, the stress began to be increasingly put on both internal belief and external form. This is how emperors became the enforcers of 'orthodoxy', understood not only in the narrow understanding of doctrine, but also extra-doctrinal marks.[10] As Noethlichs points out, "with the arrival of Christians at the centre of power, these debates took on a new urgency and a new form, the result of seeking an "absolute truth", the fruit of combining monotheism, Judaism and Hellenic philosophy."[11] The Theodosian Code formed an important milestone in this process of progressing Christianisation as the first attempt at empire-wide unification in the sphere of religion, that gathered and ordered all of the developments from the time of Constantine up until its publication.

On that account, the second part of the above-mentioned question, that deals with the ways of petrification, can be studied on a much more solid and narrow basis. While the creeds and canons may be the first that come to mind when thinking about the sources of petrification, legislation, although less obvious, may be an equally powerful formatter of orthodoxy. Two recent turns in legal research, cultural and cognitive, introduced what is termed by scholars the 'constitutive theory of law.' As Austin Sarat and Jonathan Simon put it, "[c]ultural analysis and cultural studies suggest that law operates largely by influencing modes of thought, rather than determining conduct in any specific case. It enters social practices, and is 'imbricated' in them, shaping consciousness and making asymmetries of power seem, if not invisible, then natural and benign. Law is, in this sense, constitutive of culture, a part of the cultural processes that actively contribute in the composition of social relations."[12] In a similar vein, Clifford Geertz argued that law is not only reflective, but also constitutive and constructive of social categories.[13] While we are used to treating the spheres of law and fact separately, the first as normative, and the second as descriptive, the difference is not that clear. In fact, Geertz continues, we should not see law as a precise tool for satisfying needs or even interests, but rather a meaning giving process, in which law becomes a part of 'local knowledge.'[14]

A more cognitively oriented explanation was proposed among others by Eric Mitnick, who argued that "legal institutions participate in the construction of social identity types through the processes of categorisation that are intrinsic to the operation of a legal system."[15] As he notes, ever since the famous study by Gordon W. Allport on the nature of prejudice,[16] a growing body of literature has been devoted to the

---

[9]Eusebius (1999), p. 161.

[10]Noethlichs (2006), pp. 116–118.

[11]Ibid., 119.

[12]Sarat and Simon (2001).

[13]Geertz (1983), p. 218.

[14]Ibid., 213.

[15]Mitnick (2007), p. 828.

[16]Allport (1979).

study of social cognition, based on the following assumption: the limited character of human cognition creates the need for cognitive efficiency, which is achieved through the process of categorisation.[17] Subsequent research showed that categories are built through socially salient essential marks, based on power relations. Simultaneously they remain "fuzzy", that is, not all essential marks have to be ascribed to the subject of categorisation in order for it to be put in a certain category.[18] Dealing with social, rather than personal identity, law is interested in the ascription of social memberships, rather than individual traits, and because of that, it is one of the category creating processes.[19] However, it differs by having a formalised system of categorisation, in which legal texts introduce categories that are later precisely applied by legal officials.[20]

This is why, in this paper, I aim to analyse the Theodosian Code and investigate if, and if so, how the orthodoxy was enforced, and its opponents legislated away. Apart from straightforward doctrinal formulation, I will, first and foremost, focus on finding the essential marks of categories created by this legislation to see which social identities, and which underlying power relations, were either introduced or created by that Code. Additionally, I will trace the narratives that were selected and a specific understanding of different social experiences that was promoted by the legislation. Both of these tasks will be the subject of the following part. However, before approaching the Theodosian Code itself, it is important to understand the earlier developments in Christianity and Roman Law that allowed for its constitutive influence, both widely discussed in the research literature.

3 Historical Background

3.1 Christianity and Hybridity

As pointed out in the introduction, the 'classical view' on the development of 'orthodoxy' assumes that it was handed down straight from Christ and the apostles, and was a primary Christianity from which the subsequent heresies deviated. This view has two presuppositions that some historians find problematic: the notion of apostolicity of orthodoxy, and, in turn, its primacy over "heresy." It must be noted, however, that this view does not imply that there was no diversity in the earliest Christianity; it only holds that since the beginning there were measures of assessing what is the "right", or in other words, "orthodox" Christianity.[21] These presumptions were contested, among others, by Walter Bauer, who argued that in many geographical locations the

[17] Mitnick (2007), pp. 832–833.

[18] Ibid., 840.

[19] Ibid., 846–47.

[20] Ibid., 843.

[21] Köstenberger and Kruger (2010), p. 99.

orthodoxy was preceded by some other version of Christianity, like Marcionism or Gnosticism, and Rome was the only majorly "orthodox" region. The developments in Christianity were therefore moving rather from "error" to the "truth", and the Roman option finally prevailed. As I have mentioned in the introduction, Bauer's view was criticised for stretching the evidence but proved to be immensely fruitful for further research. Contemporary authors, such as Einar Tomassen or Bart Ehrmann, argued that the diversity in the early Church was even more prominent than in Bauer's view, and that "until the middle of the second century no group had excluded others from the general definition of "Christian"."[22]

The most recent view escapes the dichotomy of early and late Christianity and argues for hybridity instead. One of its representatives, Rebecca Lyman, argues that it is incredibly hard, and probably counterproductive, to differentiate between orthodoxy, heresy, philosophy, Judaism or Hellenism, when talking about the earliest Christianity. All of these were an intermingled mixture that produced a diversity of outcomes, from which only certain ones prevailed. There was therefore no "primary Christianity" or even "Christianities" in the strict sense, but orthodoxy was something that emerged from that "boiling pot" over time as a cultural hybrid that consciously separated itself from its roots and claimed the role of "the definitive and universal truth."[23]

It is not to say that there were no commonalities between the early Christians. As Rowan Williams points out, even Gnostics shared the conviction that the relationship between a believer and God results from specific historical activities. But there was no universal agreement in the matter of continuation of these historical mediations, such as gospel, sacrament, succession etc.[24] Richard Lim puts it in the following words: "frequently sectarian in a sociological sense, early Christian communities endured institutional fragmentation, schisms, and mutual accusations of heresy. Recurring admonitions to beware the "false teachers" and their heterodidaskalia in early Christian texts bespeak a dynamic climate of claims and counterclaims. In this environment, the church universal and apostolic succession were ideals favoured and promoted by certain Christians in their struggle for advantage or survival."[25]

Moreover, Christianity did not differ as much from its Roman environment as is often assumed. Roman religion, it is argued, was alien to struggles over orthodoxy and heresy, and because of that engaged in polemical debates and allowed for competition between rivalling viewpoints and beliefs. However, this picture is too simplistic. Like Christianity, Roman Hellenism was not a static entity, and to a similar extent it had its own struggles for unity. The questions of exclusivity and syncretism were present in both. And although there was a difference of degree, in the second and third

[22]Jeffrey Bingham (2006), p. 60.
[23]Lyman (2003), p. 221.
[24]Williams (1989), p. 17.
[25]Lim (2001), pp. 199–200.

centuries it was not uncommon for groups to struggle over truth, as well as the shape and self-understanding of their communities.[26]

As Williams points out, the earliest debates in Christianity have not yet set the grounds for discussions, but only worked them out in practice, and through that established the conditions under which the future arguments were supposed to be conducted.[27] And these criteria were being formed through hybridity, that is the process of discernment based, and deeply anchored, in the contemporary culture. Because of that, it mirrored, and yet was subversive towards the existing state of fact. As Lyman writes: "In late antiquity, Christian "orthodoxy" as a rhetorical presentation of transcendent identity could become a dominant form of "Hellenism" as a universal system because it occupied many of the same cognitive and authoritative spaces (…) This is not a transformation of "Hellenism" by "Christianity" or a cultural takeover by an external "third race," but a reconfiguring within the religious culture itself as a means of understanding ontological universality and multiple cultural identities."[28]

Due to this hybrid character, Christian truth was supposed to be recovered, among others, by contrast with error, found in both external (Judaism, Hellenism) and internal (heresies) sources.[29] Christianity refused to associate itself with them, and by that it entered 'mimetic tension',[30] verging between continuity with its background and superseding it at the same time, and claiming to be the sole rule of truth. As Lyman writes:

> This claim to transcendence and cultural inclusivity was the source of its dynamism and of its need for innovation and conflict—a need that remained at odds with other equally strong claims for doctrinal stability and unity, and eventually, even, the preservation of imperial peace.[31]

Once Christianity came into power, what had started between intellectuals and operated inside and between local communities, converted into a dispute over dominance. The basic grounds for the argument were laid down, and the equality of disputing parties began to diminish. Fowden argues that the idea of a universal community of believers, which followed Christianity from the beginning, was adapted by Constantine and put into practice. In his pronouncements, preserved mostly in Eusebius writings, one may reconstruct an ideal image of a Christian Roman empire, that would become a single religious community. In this image Christendom would be ruled by the guidance of Holy Spirit under the scriptural and episcopal authority, with one Emperor ruling under one God and guarding the external affairs of the Church.[32]

And yet, as Richard Lim points out, the ideal of Constantine was confronted with a paradoxical reality. Despite political triumph, the disputes inside the Church did

---

[26]See Bingham (2006), p. 47.

[27]Williams (1989), pp. 8–9.

[28]Lyman (2003), p. 220.

[29]See Osborn (1989), pp. 40–57.

[30]See Stark and Bainbridge (1996).

[31]Lyman (2003), pp. 221–222.

[32]Fowden (2001), pp. 89–90.

not silence, but rather multiplied and deepened. The practice of those who were excluded to further their cause by founding new communities flourished. The rising inflammatory points rose around the Donatist and Arian controversies, as well as Melitian schism in Egypt. Even after the imperial imposition of orthodoxy under Theodosius I the religious landscape of the empire remained highly diverse. The establishment churches coexisted and competed with nonconforming communities. Moreover, heresies found suitable allies in the neighbouring states, such as the Sassanian Empire in the case of Nestorians and Monophysites, or Germanic kingdoms in the case of Arians.[33]

Instead of achieving a religiously united empire, Constantine struggled to obtain even basic Christian unity. The Council of Nicea in 325 was supposed to introduce harmony and prevent future ruptures. But by presiding over it the emperor rather unintentionally began to promote episcopal authority, as it was with the bishops whom he negotiated, as they were the leading men of Christianity. This had two main results: on one hand, it disturbed the previous balance of ascetics, confessors and aristocratic patronage; on the other, it caused the local bishops to aspire for more control.[34] The system of enforcing Church decisions changed as well, and the use of state coercion emerged. As Fowden writes: "Before Constantine, Christian congregations enforced their decisions by excluding those who did not comply. Under Constantine, the church succumbed to the temptation to repress its deviants, and with fatal logic made the emperor God's active representative on earth."[35] All this, instead of pacifying the quarrels, inflamed them by multiplying issues to fight over, and urging the dissident groups to develop their own internal authority structure.[36]

The intensification of the debates had one severe effect: it resulted in the petrification of arguments. As Lim writes, a "number of ad hoc textual weapons were sent into the fray, often for defence. Ready-made responses or retorts [...] were provided to arm common as well as elite Christians against anticipated questions [...] In short, no effort was spared to prevent Christians from engaging in frank and unmediated exchanges over particular theological issues."[37] Creeds were of limited help. Too short creedal declarations could not satisfactorily guarantee the enforcement of orthodoxy, and required further interpretation. Those that were to precise were subject to criticism and espoused controversy. This is why the solidification included the authority of the "Fathers of the Church", whose writings began to be used as the safe point of stability. "This combination of diachronic and synchronic consensus circumscribed the ability of individuals, even trained dialecticians, to pose fresh questions and arguments in council."[38] From now on, the ultimate criterion of orthodoxy began to be compliance with the established consensus, and the emphasis

[33]Lim (2001), ibid., 196–97.

[34]Ibid., 201.

[35]Fowden (2001), ibid., 90.

[36]Lim (2001), ibid., 208–09.

[37]Ibid., 203.

[38]Ibid., 204.

was put on the examination of written evidence, which mirrored the senatorial and legal methods.[39]

All of these developments laid the ground for law to become an important point of reference for established Christianity. Its hybrid character allowed for the general compatibility with social structures of the Roman Empire. The imperial cooperation with ecclesiastical hierarchy facilitated gradual inclusion of orthodoxy in the law and deepening segregation of different Christian groups. The petrification of argument, on the other hand, highlighted the importance of written sources and aligned the methods of jurisprudence with those of apologetics.

3.2 Roman Law—From Obedience to Mind-Shaping

The end of the third century observed the dying breath of the principate, which, as George Mousourakis notes, had two main problems: the emperor had rather weak authority and the administrative structure of the Empire did not fit its area and military reality. The solution to both came in the form of a new order introduced by Diocletian. This new order, *tetrarchy*, brought in three main changes: co-regency, absolutisation of imperial power and transformation of administration into a "rigid bureaucratic system."[40] While the classical era was ruled by jurists, presenting a great variety in legal thought, the late empire strove for the establishment of the rule of law and put much more emphasis on imperial constitutions, curtailing the possibility of its excessive modification.[41] As Padovani and Stein write, "The jurists, having established what was the civil law, wanted to preserve and re-state it rather than reform it. When the empire became Christian in the fourth century, very little change in the civil law was needed to accommodate the new orthodoxy."[42] Because of that legislative focus shifted towards public law. In this way, the Roman Empire entered its last phase known as the dominate.

The systemic changes were followed by the introduction of a completely new intellectual base for Roman Law. In the principate "the divine justice had little to do with human religious administration".[43] As Tacitus wrote, referring to the emperor Tiberius' maxim, "*deorum iniurias dis curae*".[44] This changed in the beginning of the fourth century. To justify the "Great Persecution" of Christians in the years 303-313 Diocletian had to introduce a new theoretical basis. As Elisabeth DePalma Digeser points out, apart from reifying the classical jurisprudence, tetrarchy reached for Neoplatonic thought. This reconfigured the direction of the relation between law and religion for the next centuries. The authority of Ulpian was applied to strengthen

[39]Ibid., 205.

[40]Mousourakis (2015), p. 23.

[41]Tuori (2004), p. 336.

[42]Padovani and Stein (2007), p. 30.

[43]Bingham (2006), p. 45.

[44]"Wrongs done to the gods were the concern of the gods." Tacitus, *Annals* 1.73.5.

the connection between religion and national identity. In that way, one's adherence to licit religion became equivocal with the question of state obedience. Neoplatonic thought was used to put forward the conception of law as the divinising agent within the polity. Writings such as Plato's *Laws* were used to justify the necessity of coercion in the area of religious conformity. These, once introduced into the "Roman system", remained in it through the time of Christianisation.[45]

And what about the law's applicability? For a long time, the dominant conception assumed that it was more or less uniformly applied in the whole empire. Authors such as Edward Gibbon in his famous "History of the Decline and Fall of the Roman Empire" argued that all conquered nations completely blended into one, resigning from struggles over any kind of independence and distinction.[46] However, as Tuori points out, the unitary conception of Roman Empire proved to be untenable and recent scholarship has corrected this view. The "quasi-modern state" theory was replaced with one much truer to the sources conception of a "heterogeneous empire, in which local rules and customs" were often more prominent than the imperial provisions.[47] The proclamation of Constitutio Antioniana, which granted citizen rights to all free men of the Empire, did not result in an instantaneous adoption of Roman civil law by *peregrini*, and some scholars argue that no such adoption ever occurred. However, a certain level of adoption had to happen. As Tuori argues, we can find the confirmation of this in the spread of law books and legal manuals such as the Syro-Roman Law book, or the existence of the barbarian codes. However, it was not a straightforward application, but rather a process of imitation based on coexistence with the local law. Roman Law, states Tuori, left a certain dose of discretion to the new provinces, and was never consciously installed at all levels.[48]

Clifford Ando presents a slightly different perspective and, drawing on Weber and Habermas, argues that the normative power of rules is always based both on the individual's recognition of them as binding and the knowledge that others think the same. The enormity of the Roman Empire ruled out the use of coercion as the only source of motivation for compliance with law. Law had to operate within the framework of rational explanation to influence the internal motivation of its subjects. To do that, a tool of imperial ideology was introduced to, above all, impose a specific rationality.[49] By referring to Pierre Bourdeu's concept of habitus, Ando continues that Roman imperial ideology was, as pointed out in the previous section, a constitutive process. As he writes, "a habitus, or an ideology, is a system of belief that channels rather than stifles creativity: habitus is generative. Roman imperial ideology need not, therefore, have been monolithic or even universal (…) The emperors and governing class in Rome did not have to provide their world with Scripture, but merely with a system of concepts that could shape, and in so doing slowly unite, the cultural scripts

[45] DePalma Digeser (2006), pp. 68–75.

[46] Gibbon (2013), p. 43.

[47] Tuori argues in fact that "in the Rome of scholarship it is sometimes difficult to discern the difference between ancient Romans and dead Germans." See Tuori (2007), p. 43.

[48] Ibid., 43–50.

[49] Ando (2000), pp. 77–78.

of their subjects."[50] Both pre- and post-Constantinian empire used ideology to shape the way of thinking of their subjects, enforcing a division between the thinkable and unthinkable. That is why, among others, the illusion of republic remained a constant throughout the existence of the empire, hiding the extra-constitutional nature and arbitrariness of imperial power.[51] However, with the transition to dominate the empire became much more involved in the spreading of imperial ideology. As Harries writes, "Probing further, it may be argued that Roman Law became the victim of a deep-seated conflict within Roman society between rules, which were universal, and power, which was arbitrary."[52]

To what extent then did legislation have an effect on an average citizen of the Roman Empire, especially in the far-away provinces? The central Roman government made sure that the cooperation with provincials was as seamless as possible. The ways of dissemination of new laws differed depending on the anticipated outcome. Laws were written on bronze and marble in those cases that were to arouse authority. Whitened boards and papyrus were more convenient for quickly spreading the laws. Another thing that had to be taken care of was the high rate of illiteracy. That is why the laws were not only published in a written form, but also recited on a few separate occasions. Imperial magistrates did not require the empire's population to be literate, but to have access to a literate person.[53] Moreover, legal texts, even if not used as laws, served a descriptive role. Most people could not rely on other sources of information, such as private correspondence, which is why official documents provided the main way of gathering knowledge about the world. That is also why administrative documentation and legal proceedings constituted an important reference for historians, with authors such as Polybius or Livy referring to them sparingly, and Eusebius using them to a greater extent.[54] In that way law not only informed the present, but the past as well.

The law was, therefore, not fully obeyed in the whole empire, and, quite frequently, it was not even meant to. As Harries notes, laws were often introduced to give a general direction rather than strict guidance.[55] This was especially true in the case of Codes. They were similar to modern constitutions in the sense that they provided basic principles of conduct and thinking.[56] Moreover, as Harries argues, treating Roman law in terms of "obedience" and "functionality" is essentially mistaken. On one hand, emperors were striving for clear-cut laws, on the other, they exercised a conscious policy of non-interference with local customs and habits.[57] As Boudewijn

[50] Ibid., 23.

[51] Ibid., 28–32.

[52] Harries (2004), p. 77.

[53] Ando (2000), pp. 96–104.

[54] Ibid., 120–29.

[55] Harries (2004), p. 96.

[56] Harries (2007), p. 94.

[57] *Law and Empire in Late Antiquity*, 5.

Sirks points out, rather than aiming at absolute conformity, laws were designed to effect in social change, a task they could, and did, satisfy.[58]

4 Analysis

The publication of the Theodosian Code was a quite extraordinary achievement that required a massive amount of effort. As Tony Honoré points out, for people to leave their everyday chores and pursue the project that would take a significant amount of their work and time, and the results of which would, most probably, not be seen by its creators, had to be an outcome of special circumstances. The most direct of those included a burning crisis in the form of the progressing conflict between the western and eastern parts of the empire that threatened to destroy its unity and prosperity, and necessitated immediate and profound action.[59] It could not be resolved as long as ignorance of the valid precepts prevented the proper enforcement of the emperor's will and encouraged abuse by different parties.[60] The aim was to eliminate the ambiguities in law and to curtail the endless jurisprudential debates, that, in the emperor's view, could have subverted its proper exercise.[61] The main goal focused on the introduction of unity in both legislation and jurisprudence, which, in turn, would function as a safeguard for the unity of the empire. Orthodoxy in law appeared as a survival tool.

The Theodosian Code strengthened the rule of law and changed a long-standing emphasis on private law, shifting it towards public law.[62] It also established a number of general rules as foundational for the legal system, including prohibition of legal ignorance,[63] or non-retroactiveness of law.[64] The most profound change in legal theory concerned the fact that the laws were taken out of their original context, and received universal and empire-wide validity instead. Before the proclamation of the *Codex Theodosianus*, constitutions were mostly published for a specially designated region or in special circumstances. From the time of the Code's proclamation forward, all general laws were enacted for the whole area of the empire and applied uniformly.[65] Simultaneously, specific interpretative rules aimed at the removal of contradictions from the law were introduced. From that point on, specific law was supposed to be favored over the general one[66] and the posterior law had priority

[58]Sirks (2013), p. 476.

[59]Honoré (1986), p. 176.

[60]Humfress (2006), p. 254.

[61]Harries, *Law and Empire in Late Antiquity*, 60.

[62]Honoré (1986), p. 169.

[63]CTh 1.1.2.

[64]CTh 1.1.3.

[65]Honoré (1986), p. 178.

[66]CTh 1.1.4.

over the prior.[67] The Code provided specific conditions under which the writings of jurists could be used.[68]

The Code did a lot to secure the primary place of Catholic Christianity in the general structure of the empire, including three main developments. First, it separated the subject of religion into an individual book, including criminal laws, that were otherwise collected in Book IX, a development which in itself signalled a change in thinking. Second, the naming of the books and titles had a clear aim to draw a sharp line between licit and illicit religiosity. Finally, all pre-Constantinian emperors were presented as lacking legislative capacities and their laws discarded, introducing an appearance of radical discontinuity. Simultaneously, however, by relying on *edictum perpetuum,* the Theodosian Code operated within a certain vision of civil society, instead of fully restructuring Rome's social order.[69] Instead of rebuilding it from scratch, the Code revised the rules of the game, transferring power to the new social class and making a change in the main sources of social prosperity.[70]

Thus, two orthodoxies, one legal and one religious, joined their efforts in the production of the Code's last book. Book XVI, devoted fully to religion-related matters, consisted of eleven thematic sections and the content of each is ordered chronologically. It opened with the section entitled "*De Fide Catholica*", signifying that the Catholic faith was meant to be the new religious fundament of the empire, and setting the tone for the whole book, sketching the boundaries of acceptable and introducing the narrative framework in which the book operated. It also introduced three main directions which constituted the orthodoxy's main considerations: definition, privileged character, and the limitations of both. Finally, it summed up the role that law was meant to play in the enforcement of the right belief. And the rest of the book remained true to these themes.

The introduction of orthodoxy's definition was gradual. CTh 16.1.1, the first constitution of Book XVI, introduced first *homines christianae religionis adposuerit*, the people of Christian Religion, as a distinct category. Following it CTh 16.1.2, contained the first positive formulation of the rules of the right belief in imperial constitution.[71] In this constitution the emperor expressed his will for people to adhere to a specific religious tradition. This was followed by its legal definition, based on doctrinal references, but also extra-doctrinal marks, such as ecclesiastical reference, apostolic discipline and evangelical doctrine and the introduction of the category of "Catholic Christians" (*christianorum catholicorum*). By that, however, the law entered into a dialogue with the contemporary debates, instituting certain debated principles, and posited itself as an important point of reference for establishing what should be included within the range of Catholic Christians.

Proper ancestry was established through two aspects. The right religion was that transmitted *from* Peter the Apostle *to* the Romans, both quite controversial. The

---

[67] CTh 1.1.5.

[68] CTh 1.4.1–1.4.3.

[69] See Ando (2006), pp. 126–133.

[70] Sirks (2013), p. 471.

[71] See Stachura (2006b), p. 325.

controversies around the apostolic succession were covered in the previous section. Here I would only like to add that the Eusebian narrative from "*Historia Ecclesiastica*", which firmly sided with the unified apostolic continuity, was still treated with a healthy dose of scepticism by the Theodosian Code's contemporaries, even by those who shared his viewpoint. One of Eusebius' successors, writing a century after Socrates Scholasticus, in a new version of "Church History" criticised him for "being more intent on the rhetorical finish of his composition and the praises of the emperor, than on an accurate statement of facts."[72]

The notion of Roman primacy and centrality with regards to orthodoxy also went against the grain of some pretending to the name of Christians at that time. Rowan Williams, drawing on Henry Chadwick, describes two different ways in which the Early Christians perceived themselves: "elliptical" and "circular." As he writes, the former described Christian congregations as "the network of communities linked by their common origins in Jerusalem and the events transacted there at the navel of the earth", while the latter as "the unified institution with a definable centre providing a norm or touchstone for right belief." At first compliant with each other due to the centrality of Jerusalem, these two self-perceptions started to conflict when Rome became a pretender to the central position, forming two rival conceptions of authority. And while Rome never fully ousted the elliptical concept, it aligned with the aims of the Empire, and received full legal support, of which, among others, CTh 16.1.2 is the evidence.[73]

Apart from ancestry, the ecclesiastical reference was provided to indicate who possessed authority in assessing the orthodoxy. The Bishop of Rome, Damasius, covers the first reference, and the Bishop of Alexandria the second. By pointing to the former, and by calling him *pontifex*, Jasper notes, the primacy of Rome in the West, and the role of the pope, was clearly established and strengthened.[74] The second reference had a similar effect, because, as Ożóg and Wójcik note, the Alexandrian church was the usual eastern "contact" of Rome.[75] It also strengthened the doctrinal proclamations because, as Sidney Z. Ehler and John B. Morrall point out, the Egyptian See was one of the strongest defenders of the Trinitarian position.[76]

The notion of apostolic discipline once again referred to the narrative of apostolic continuity, while the evangelical doctrine introduced scriptural authority in the matter of religious beliefs. All of this was finished with what may be described as the doctrinal, or dogmatic, articulation, that is the belief "in the single Deity of the Father, the Son, and the Holy spirit, under the concept of equal majesty and of the Holy Trinity."[77] But, as Ożóg and Wójcik point out, this theological formulation was quite vague, as it did not specify some important concepts like consubstantiality,

---

[72]Nicene and Post-Nicene Fathers, Second Series (1890), p. 1.

[73]Williams (1989), p. 1; Drawing on: Chadwick (1959).

[74]Jasper (2001), pp. 8–10.

[75]Ożóg and Wójcik (2014), 2*.

[76]Ehler and Morrall (1967), p. 7.

[77]Pharr (1969), p. 440. "... *Patris et Filii et Spiritus Sancti unam deitatem sub parili maiestate et sub pia Trinitate credamus.*"

and left a lot of room for either further refinement or change of thought.[78] In such a way this proclamation of orthodoxy remained doctrinally inclusive, giving more prominence to extra-doctrinal determinants.

A more in-depth picture was presented by the subsequent CTh 16.1.3, which ordered the transmission of all churches to the orthodox, once again defined through doctrine and episcopal authority. However, these two notions were much more detailed and extensive than in the previous definition. Doctrine was further specified as a belief in the Father, the Son, and the Holy Spirit of one majesty, virtue, glory and splendour without any dissonance, while the concept of Trinity as the assertion of three Persons and the unity of the Divinity. Here, as Christine Shepardson points out, further refinement of doctrinal formulation was an effect of the immediately preceding Council of Constantinople, which proclamations were enforced by this constitution.[79] And, as this council confirmed and expanded the Nicene Creed, CTh 16.1.3. the protected orthodoxy received the title of *Nicaenae fidei*.

Moreover, as Raymond Van Dam writes, this law explicitly "defined orthodoxy in terms of preferences of various prominent bishops."[80] The ecclesiastical reference was much more extensive, pointing out exactly who should serve as the example of faith. This constitution, unlike the former, did not only point to one example for Eastern and Western parts of the Empire, but indicated a whole number of priests, with special references for, among others, the Orient, Dioceses of Asia or Diocese of Pontus. As Errington notes, this practical test for orthodoxy was important for two reasons: on one hand, it helped to define heretics as those who opposed specific members of the clergy, and, more importantly, informed on who constituted a good fit for taking over the churches of the opposed.[81]

Further definitions found in other sections confirmed that orthodoxy was not only about doctrine. The most notable example may be found in CTh 16.4.6. In this constitution, published at the end of 404 and directed against John Chrysostom,[82] the emperors Arcadius, Honorius and Theodosius deemed illicit all of the assemblies that, although orthodox in doctrine, convened outside of the legitimate churches. Once again, the ecclesiastical reference was used as the means to show those, to whom adherence was necessary if one should remain within the frame of legality. Bishops Arsacius, Theophilus and Porphyrius were presented as *antistites sacrae legis*, or, in other words, representatives of the Christian faith.[83]

Other pieces of legislation substantiated the importance of traces presented in *Cunctos populos*. Doctrinal precepts were invoked in the CTh 16.5.38, while scriptural authority, apostolic origin and tradition can be found in CTh 16.6.2, chronologically the earliest definition of the right belief. The most in-depth doctrinal explication, however, was made in the CTh 16.5.6, which directly referred to the fragments of the

[78] Ożóg and Wójcik (2014), 2*.
[79] Shepardson (2014), p. 18.
[80] Van Dam (2002), p. 240.
[81] Errington (1997), p. 441.
[82] See Constas (2003), p. 27.
[83] See Pharr (1969), p. 450.

Nicene Creed and mentioned all of the terms subject to controversy. Yet, it was put much deeper into the book, in the section concerned with heretics. The reason for that might be quite simple—the first section aimed, first and foremost, at the introduction of Catholic Faith to the general public. Thus, it needed to provide easy categorisation tools for the assessment of who counted as orthodox. On the other hand, the main aim of the CTh 16.5.6 was, as María Victoria Escribano Paño points out, to outline "the intellectual, moral and religious profile of the heretic."[84] The definition of orthodoxy was here a ground for adjudication of what should be considered heresy, in addition to condemnation, and not as a standalone evocation.

It is interesting to note that the term "orthodoxy" itself, used in its adjectival form, appeared only in polemical surrounding. It was mentioned only in contrast with un-orthodox religious affiliation,[85] gatherings,[86] churches,[87] writings,[88] or rites and festivities,[89] This was due to the fact that, as will be argued below, the non-orthodox accounted for an important point of reference in self-identification of the orthodox, operating on increasingly important binary oppositions. The orthodoxy forged its boundaries in the fire of polemics.

But the definition of orthodoxy was not only necessary for assessing the boundaries of the licit. Being categorised as orthodox equipped the group with a whole range of advantages. In fact, the earliest legislation included in Book XVI, CTh 16.2.1, published on the October 31st, 313 or 319,[90] long before the introduction of any legal definition of Catholic Christianity, already divided between the faction of heretics (*haereticorum factione*) and the clerics of the Catholic Church (*ecclesiae catholicae clericos*), granting the latter certain privileges. Simultaneously, preventing or hindering these concessions in any way was positioned as contemptuous and established as a delict. The orthodox had also been under the protection of criminal law. The aforementioned CTh 16.2.1 secured all men of the Catholic Christian church from any harassment by other groups pretending to the name of Christian. And as the example of CTh 16.1.4 and CTh 16.4.1 shows, this included also the harassment from other orthodox representatives. The same applied to the harassment by pagans[91] or Jews[92] and secured both, places and people.[93] The orthodox belief itself was under similar protection, as CTh 16.4.2 introduced strict prohibition of any kind of public disputes around the religious matters or counsel giving. Even ignorance or negligence towards the *divinae legis* could have been punished as sacrilege.[94] This

[84]Paño (2010), p. 111.

[85]CTh 16.4.6.

[86]CTh 16.5.6.

[87]CTh 16.5.57; 16.5.65.

[88]CTh 16.5.66.

[89]CTh 16.6.6.

[90]See Pharr (1969), p. 441.; Ożóg and Wójcik (2014), 6*.

[91]See CTh 16.1.1; 16.2.5.

[92]See CTh 16.8.5; 16.8.18.

[93]See CTh 16.2.31.

[94]See CTh 16.2.25; See Robinson (2007), p. 133.

was followed by a number of privileges for clergy, including exemption from public service,[95] tax exemptions,[96] in later legislation widened to family and servants,[97] or even *privilegium fori*, a separate jurisdiction which entitled Christian clergy to be tried by "their own" in special ecclesiastical courts.[98]

But the full significance of the term 'orthodox' was coming to light only in contrast with the non-orthodox. Although wary at first, it did not take long before Constantine took first steps in the formation of the new religious system of the privileged and repressed. As Humfress writes, "[i]n his attempts to urge the formation of a 'Catholic' and universal body of belief for an imperial church, the Emperor Constantine resorted to the sanctions of law in an attempt to enforce the anathemas against Arius and those 'of his opinions', pronounced at the Council of Nicaea."[99] Thus, while orthodoxy constituted the cornerstone of all religious matters addressed in the Theodosian Code, the condemned were the ones who got most of the attention. The unwanted behaviour and adherence presented by those pretending to the name of Christians, and non-Christians alike, received a lion's share of space in Book XVI. And four main groups of those whose status quickly degraded may be recognised: heretics, having the most "prominent" place, pagans, Jews and apostates.

The legislation in the Code did not leave any doubts about the multiplicity pretending to the title of Christians. While CTh 16.1.1 introduced "men of Christian religion" (*homines christianae religionis*), CTh 16.1.2, pointed out that only some of them were supposed to be included in the narrower category of Catholic Christians (*christianus catholicus*). All others were charged with adherence to heretical dogmas (*haeretici dogmatis*). And yet, over the course of the fourth century, it often proved to be unclear what counted as heretical, and what was assessed as the right religiosity, the problem that, among others, posed a great risk for the interests of the emperors. As Malcolm Errington argues, there were two main reasons that made a clear separation and condemnation of heretics crucial for the rulers of the Roman Empire: "theologically-salvationist" and "administrative-financial".[100] The legislation included in Book XVI aimed at satisfying both of these. Thus, the former found a response in the way heresy was defined, while the latter in the way it was characterised.

The first of the above-mentioned reasons pointed to the change in the role of Christianity. On one hand, it was supposed to play the leading role in the protection of the Empire, and, on the other, in the enforcement of the position of the emperor, who was supposed to become "God's vice-gerent on earth."[101] Heresy, as a phenomenon, threatened both of these by being an *error*, persistence in which could have dramatic consequences. By being in the near proximity to orthodoxy, but straying from it at

[95]See CTh 16.2.1; 16.2.2; 16.2.8; 16.2.9; 16.2.11; 16.2.15; 16.2.19; 16.2.26.

[96]See CTh 16.2.1; 16.2.8; 16.2.36.

[97]See CTh 16.2.10; 16.2.14.

[98]See CTh 16.2.12; 16.2.41.

[99]Humfress (2007), p. 225.

[100]Errington (2006), p. 171.

[101]Ibid.

the same time, and by posing as "the rightful religion",[102] heresies constituted yet another point of mimetic tension for orthodoxy. This posed a number of threats, from political to spiritual, thereby making them the ultimate enemies of the state. As Roger Scruton writes, "[i]n religious belief and observance … it is not the large differences that count but the small ones. (…) For those in the vicinity of real religion, the world presents a stark and disturbing choice between the absolute safety of the orthodox creed, and the mortal danger of denying it from a position within its territory. Heresy and sacrilege are dangerous because they threaten the community; the meticulousness of the religious rite is a sign that religion is not merely a system of belief, but a criterion of membership."[103] To do away with error was therefore of vital importance, because it threatened the religious foundations of the whole empire. Through persistence and through the practice of false rites, the error was transformed into sacrilege (*sacrilegium*),[104] superstition (*superstitio*)[105] and profanity (*profanus*).[106]

Thus, heresy was defined in two stages. The most common way of delimitation was that of negation. As shown above, every definition of orthodoxy, *a contrario*, signified what should be labelled as heretical.[107] But while negation was a dominant way of defining heresy, it was not exclusive. Indirect definitions were followed by direct ones, with the first instance in CTh 16.5.28. While still negative and extremely inclusive, this constitution brought some 'positive' content to the label of heretics, presenting them as those who "deviate, even in a minor point of doctrine, from the tenets and the path of the Catholic religion."[108] As Ożóg and Wójcik note, this definition for the first time clearly pointed out that heresy was seen as one-directional movement, going from the right religion to deviation from it.[109] Thus, on one hand, it underlined the narrative of the primacy of orthodoxy. On the other, it tried to rhetorically perform *reductio ad absurdum*, by explicitly arguing that heresy negates right religion by straying from the tenets of Catholicism.[110]

The theologically-salvationist reasons constituted only a half of the picture. The other half concerned much more pragmatic administrative and financial spheres of the empire. Over the course of the fourth century local churches and their representatives amassed an enormous amount of capital, privileges and influence, in many places comparable to that of imperial administration.[111] The separation of those who strayed from orthodoxy was therefore a question of power relations and the burdens that

---

[102] CTh 16.5.56; 16.6.4.

[103] Scruton (2007), pp. 7–8.

[104] CTh 16.2.25; 16.5.8; 16.6.4.

[105] CTh 16.5.48.

[106] CTh 16.5.41; 16.6.2.

[107] See also CTh 16.4.6; 16.5.53.

[108] Pharr (1969), p. 455.

[109] Ożóg and Wójcik (2014), 57*.

[110] As Ożóg and Wójcik point out, such reasoning was explicitly performed in CTh 16.6.4, where the practice of baptism was presented as losing its point with repetitions. See ibid., 84*. Similar in CTh 16.5.5.

[111] Errington (2006), pp. 171–172.

government had to endure. Moreover, the law was not always easy to enforce which necessitated involvement of the local population to enforce its proper application. Thus, legal measures against heretics aimed not only at denying them privileges, but also at depriving them of any legal and social standing. The legislation was designed to prevent heretics from taking part in any sphere of social life and make them highly unattractive for all of the others. But to do that, a narrative providing justification for the above had to be built. And the main way of achieving this was through characterisation.

Thus, any mention of heresy was always followed by a series of invectives, the spectrum of which was quite wide. And while pejorative ascriptions differed between views regarded as heretical, the purposeful tactic of flattening differences, to which I will return, made such statements more or less equally applicable to all factions included under the label of "heretics". The main tropes, as exemplified in CTh 16.5.6, included accusations of criminal behaviour, such as obstinacy (*obstinantia*), fraud (*fraus*) and deceit (*dolus*), while implicating that heretics were mad (*vesanos*) and demented (*dementes*).

The accusations of *fraus* and *dolus* did not only imply malice and general untrustworthiness of heretics, but also provided an excuse for different treatment of heretical groups by different emperors, who could have based their decisions on fraudulent elicitation or deceit. Under Roman Law any legal relations or contracts founded on error resulted in their complete voidance. Because of such narrative, it seemed only natural that the constitutions and rescripts based on misinformation caused by heretics should have automatically lost their validity. Bad faith, persistence in error and inducing it in others justified further deprivation of their legal personality.[112]

The narrative of bad faith was also exhibited through the heretics' lack of willingness to improve, which is related to another accusation, that of *obstinantia*. As subsequent laws pointed out, although heretical beliefs were formerly condemned,[113] the heretics still 'held dearly to their errors'[114] and did not respond to any rational argumentation. Quite the opposite, the attitude of heretics was on numerous occasions referred to as boldly (*ausus*) acting against the law.[115] And, as the narrative went, the good will of the emperors and the concessions made by them did not have any positive response.[116]

While then heretical belief itself was equal to error, persistent obstinacy was equal to madness. Heretics and their beliefs were on multiple occasions referred to as mad (*vesanos*),[117] demented (*dementes*),[118] and their actions described as a frenzy (*furor*).[119] All of the above made heretical factions equal with radical criminal organ-

[112]See CTh 16.5.48; 16.5.49; 16.5.58.

[113]CTh 16.5.5; 16.5.7; 16.5.49; 16.5.52.

[114]CTh 16.6.2.

[115]CTh 16.5.5; 16.5.54; 16.5.57; 16.5.58.

[116]See Cth 16.5.23 and CTh 16.5.25.

[117]CTh 16.1.2; 16.5.25; 16.6.7.

[118]CTh 16.1.2; 16.5.6; 16.5.24; 16.5.32.

[119]CTh 16.5.6; 16.5.25; 16.5.31; 16.5.32; 16.5.60; 16.6.2; 16.6.7.

isations. Not only did they break the law by acting against and harassing orthodoxy, but they deliberately exercised their bad faith, thereby committing a number of criminal offences, harming not only themselves, but also the rest of the population and the empire as such, which made them condemnable by God, first, and the imperial law, second.[120] Hence, those who willingly adhered to such doctrines deserved damnation themselves, meriting punishment.[121] Thus, CTh 16.5.40 established heresy as a crime of public law and the urgency of persecution was underlined with the semantics of contamination,[122] contagion[123] and pollution.[124] It was the responsibility of every citizen of the Roman Empire to counteract, from average civilians, who were encouraged to denunciate,[125] to officials, who were punished for not ensuring that the law was enforced.[126]

Definitions and characterisation of heretics cannot be separated from the ways in which they were catalogued and categorized. There were major differences between factions and individuals within them, and the Code gave the evidence to that fact by explicitly recalling a number of heresies under multiple names.[127] Some constitutions were focused on an individual group, other included multiple heresies, while yet another focused on the phenomenon of heresy as such. The reasons for such variations in indication were the primary circumstances of these constitutions, as at first anti-heretical legislation was rather reactionary, aiming at specific movements in specific situation. As Noethlichs writes, "[t]he multitude of names for types of heretics shows how difficult it was for the state to repress them, and it was the heretics, assembling in groups in their places of worship, that tended to provoke the state into action."[128] A progressive change in the attitude towards heretics also included a gradation of heresies,[129] as some were seen to pose a bigger threat than the others.[130] To the multiple heresies the legislation added three more groups: schismatics (*schismaticos*), Manicheans, and astrologers (*mathematicos*).

At first, in individual constitutions, different heresies and categories were treated separately and often hierarchically. Some factions received complete condemnation, while others were only deprived of orthodox privileges. However, the compilation of the Theodosian Code began to change this, progressively levelling out the differences

---

[120] CTh 16.1.2; 16.5.5; 16.5.13; 16.5.34; 16.5.35; 16.5.61; 16.6.2.

[121] CTh 16.1.2; 16.5.5; 16.5.13; 16.5.15; 16.5.45; 16,5,56; 16.6.5.

[122] CTh 16.5.6; 16.5.26; 16.6.1.

[123] CTh 16.5.20; 16.5.44; 16.5.56; 16.5.62; 16.5.64; 16.6.4.

[124] CTh 16.5.20; 16.5.26; 16.5.40; 16.5.52; 16.6.2; 16.6.5; 16.6.6.

[125] CTh 16.5.9.

[126] CTh 16.5.40; 16.5.46; 16.6.4.

[127] These include: *apollinariani, arriani, caelicolae, donatistae, encratitas, apotactitas, hydroparastatas, saccoforos, eunomiani, fotiniani, fryges, montanistae* (also as *pepyzitas*), *iovinianae, nestoriani, novatiani, priscillianistas, protopaschitas, sabbatiani, tascodrogitae.*

[128] Noethlichs (2015), p. 26.

[129] Like Novatians, who, while having lower status than orthodoxy, were not as strictly treated as the other groups. See e.g. CTh 16.5.2.

[130] See CTh 16.5.65.

between them. While gradation still could find expression in one of the latest constitutions, 16.5.65, they only differed with regards to the measures that should be taken against them, and not as to what the codification presents as mischievousness. This is evidenced by CTh 16.5.60, which reads: "We execrate, namely, the Eunomians, the Arians, the Macedonians, and all the others whose sects it disgusts Us to insert in Our most pious sanction, all of whom have different names but same perfidy."[131]

As Paño argues, the main aim of the Code was to make a joint label of heresy the "epitome of moral evil".[132] The means used to achieve that consisted of multi-level rhetorical flattening. First, adherents of specific beliefs were simplified and generalised into one unified group under the name of their founder. Second, different heresies were flattened into one phenomenon, that of heresy, thereby making what was at first used against a specific group in specific circumstances label-wide applicable. Third, by flattening different groups, such as Manicheans, schismatics and astrologers into one group, the negative characterisation of each and every one of them was applied to all of the others. For example, as Paño points out, the inclusion of astrologers in the mix built a strong association between heresy and *malificum*,[133] a strategy beneficial for two reasons. On the one hand, it sat well with the general population, as both heretical and magical books shared the form of the *codex*, and thereby looked similar enough to be difficult to differentiate for an average citizen of the Roman Empire. On the other, the authentic fear of magic that was on the verge of panic at that time made it easier to convince people to cooperate and denunciate heretics,[134] thereby further marginalising them and depriving them of social standing. Moreover, it instilled fear of being labelled as heretic, due to disastrous consequences that could have come from it.[135] Such treatment was planned to sway people away from the theological debates, dividing society into the orthodox, and a whole multiplicity of what has been seen as essentially the same: a false belief.

And yet, there were still reasons to retain the individual naming of heresies in the legislation. Listings of heresies accounted for supplementary indicative definitions of heresy. Like the names of orthodox bishops were recalled to signify the right adherence, named heresies served the purpose of delimitating those who strayed.[136] It must be noted, however, that such listings were never enumerative, always leaving space to name new movements.[137] Moreover, named heresies were rarely further defined, leaving a considerable amount of discretion to those enforcing the law, the orthodox clergy, and the previously mentioned heresiography.

Simplification of groups, that were often incoherent and greatly varied internally, was also very potent rhetorically. The first level of flattening focused on labelling

[131] Pharr (1969), p. 462.

[132] Paño (2010), p. 110.

[133] Ibid., p. 108.

[134] Ibid. 105.

[135] Ibid., 111–12.

[136] Pharr (1969), p. 452. Similarly, CTh 16.5.5; 16.5.7; 16.5.9; 16.5.11; 16.5.13; 16.5.48; 16.5.59; 16.5.60; 16.5.65.

[137] See CTh 16.5.12; 16.5.43.

heretical factions with the names of their founders.[138] This created a much less nuanced and singular group opponent based on the views of one specific person, presented as the founder, and thereby the first to deviate from orthodoxy. Such association of heresy with a specific person diminished its authority, positing it as man-made invention, and once again confirmed the primacy of orthodoxy. All subsequent developments in the points of disagreement were not only disregarded, but also left unspoken and thereby non-existent in the mainstream consciousness. Establishing such "correct" naming was also a counter-measure against the self-identification of such groups. Any attempts to acquire a specific name was ruled out by the legislation as fraudulent. As CTh 16.5.7 reads, the heretics were prohibited from "defend[ing] themselves with dishonest fraud under the pretense of those deceptive names by which many … wish[ed] to be called and signified as of approved faith and chaste character."[139] Thus, constitutions like CTh 16.5.66 strived to once and for all establish specific names as licit, while legislating away all of the others.

By contrast, persistent non-naming of the opponent on one hand discredited specific movements as a group, but, on the other, left it a space for return. Such treatment was, among others, the fate of John Chrysostom's adherents in the CTh 16.4.6. To name the movement with the name of Chrysostom could raise his status in that group and further empower him, and, simultaneously, strengthen the group internally. Thus, leaving the new movement unnamed in the legislation had a pragmatic sense. Additionally, it left the space for Chrysostom's later rehabilitation. Furthermore, denying specific names was used more generally as the method of belittling in the Theodosian Code. Thus, heretics were denied the name of Christianity,[140] their clergy was denied the names of priests[141] and bishops, who in some way failed to heresy, were to be deprived of their ecclesiastical status.[142] Similarly, the name of the "church" was restricted only to orthodox buildings.[143]

Finally, as Flower points out, listings of heresies bore similarity to the previously-mentioned and popular at the time heresiologies, and by that, also to earlier encyclopaedic writings. Such constitutions like CTh 16.5.65, the most comprehensive listing of heresies up to 428, showed off the learning and skill of the legislator and established the authority of the Code in that matter. Systematization implied reliability, ensuring an in-depth knowledge of the described movements, and thereby sanctioning the categorisation established through such naming. Simultaneously, heresiological likeness allowed the legislation to become a heresiographical writing itself, thereby posing the law as a vital and significant point of theological reference. Therefore, it provided the Code with both descriptive and normative value.[144]

---

[138] See CTh 16.5.6.

[139] Pharr (1969), p. 452.

[140] CTh 16.5.5.

[141] CTh 16.5.5; 16.5.19; 16.5.24; 16.6.7.

[142] CTh 16.5.28.

[143] CTh 16.1.3.

[144] Flower (2013), pp. 173–196.

All of this was followed by a number of reprobative measures that aimed at undercutting social and legal standing of heretics. They were denied the right to any privileges and all rescripts issued for their benefit were annulled.[145] They were punished for manifestation of their belief, which included, among others, gatherings, practice of rites not in congruence with the Catholic faith or ordination of clergy, as well as mere adherence.[146] Those who were found guilty of such crimes were liable for punishment, with the most common sanctions encompassing infamy, proscription (*proscriptio*),[147] that is confiscation of all property, exile or deportation[148] and, less often, death.[149] Additionally, all of the means by which a person could function in the Roman society were taken away from them. They were denied the right to make a valid will, fideicommissum, donation and could not have been anyone's heir,[150] all of which were, according to Stachura, logical follow up to infamy.[151] They were deprived of the right to draw up a valid contract.[152] They were also unable to enter any provincial capital, and could not get closer to Rome than 100 miles,[153] which further hindered their ability to change their devotion, grow economically or climb the social ladder.[154] As Barnard writes, "[t]he effect of these punishments and disabilities was to marginalise sectarians legally, socially, economically and geographically."[155]

The above description shows a complex picture of legal and linguistic measures that were introduced to sort "right" and "wrong" Christians, denying the right to that name to the latter. But such treatment in Roman Law was not exclusive to Christianity, and did not begin with its domination. As Noethlichs argues, the processes of universalisation started with Decius, who, in his decree, was the first to introduce it in the form of sacrifices in honour of the emperor. Irrespective of one's precise beliefs, everyone in the empire became a part of such unified cult in which the emperor served "as guarantor of divine benevolence for all" that constituted "the first step toward an imperial religion that was no longer limited to a specific city".[156] And, even earlier, it was common to punish violations in the religious sphere with criminal measures, social ostracism and, finally, divine disfavour.[157] This was followed, as

---

[145] See CTh 16.5.1; 16.5.6; 16.5.16; 16.5.37; 16.5.51; 16.5.52.

[146] CTh 16.5.3; 16.5.4; 16.5.5; 16.5.6; 16.5.9; 16.5.10; 16.5.11; 16.5.12; 16.5.14; 16.5.15; 16.5.19; 16.5.20; 16.5.23; 16.5.26; 16.5.30; 16.5.33; 16.5.36; 16.5.43; 16.5.45; 16.5.51; 16.5.52; 16.5.53; 16.5.57; 16.5.58; 16.5.65.

[147] CTh 16.5.3; 16.5.4; 16.5.7; 16.5.8; 16.5.21; 16.5.33; 16.5.34; 16.5.40; 16.5.45; 16.5.46; 16.5.51; 16.5.56; 16.5.58; 16.5.63; 16.6.4; 16.6.5; 16.6.7.

[148] CTh 16.5.6; 16.5.11; 16.5.13; 16.5.14; 16.5.18; 16.5.19; 16.5.20; 16.5.29; 16.5.30; 16.5.31; 16.5.32; 16.5.34; 16.5.45; 16.5.46; 16.5.52; 16.5.53; 16.5.56; 16.5.58.

[149] CTh 16.5.34; 16.5.51; 16.5.56.

[150] CTh 16.5.7; 16.5.9; 16.5.17; 16.5.25; 16.5.49; 16.5.54; 16.5.55; 16.5.56; 16.5.57; 16.5.58.

[151] Stachura (2006a), p. 52.

[152] CTh 16.5.40; 16.5.46; 16.5.64.

[153] CTh 16.5.62; 16.5.64

[154] McMullen (1964), p. 50.

[155] Barnard (1995), p. 128.

[156] Noethlichs (2015), p. 17.

[157] Ibid., 16.

Stachura points out, by a new self-understanding of imperial power in dominate, with such pre-Constantinian emperors as Diocletian or Maximinus undertaking similar measures against the Manichaeism or Christianity.[158] It was the emperor's task to bridle the chaotic social reality of the empire, and order it in the manner that would get rid of anything that threatened its peace, well-being and stability.

Constantine's shift towards Christianity did not introduce a radical break from the earlier attitude of law towards religion, but rather changed its subject. Thus, the individual laws included in the Theodosian Code were not revolutionary in themselves, but rather an effect of a long process of changes and development. However, as Sirks argues, the substantial change introduced by the Code encompassed introduction of a coherent, empire-wide and full-scale religious policy, that categorised different religious options, something never done before.[159] The endgame of this policy was to create a "homogenous, orthodox, Catholic empire,"[160] and the division between orthodoxy and heresy constituted only a part of it. Thus, not only heretics had to endure repressive measures, but also everyone else who did not adhere to orthodoxy, divided in the Code into three remaining categories: Jews, pagans and the apostates.

Already the division itself deserves attention. First, it introduced another level of flattening, especially with regards to the terms *paganus* and *apostate*. Second, its separation of Jews and Pagans from heretics went contrary to the established tradition of heresiography. The aforementioned *Panarion* indicated both post-Christian and pre-Christian heresies, with Judaism and Hellenism[161] among the latter.[162] The Theodosian Code rejected this "wide" understanding of heresy and established its own narrower label. Thus, on one hand, the general aim of the emperor required that all of the non-orthodox should be equally rejected, to which the Code gave recurring evidence.[163] Simultaneously, however, the structure and content of Book XVI clearly distinguished between them, introducing hierarchy of treatment.

The reason for that seems quite straightforward. The enforcement of orthodoxy through ultimate flattening of the non-orthodox into one diverse, but equally rejected group was the end game of the governing, but reality of the early fifth century was far from achieving that state. While the co-existence of heresy alongside orthodoxy posed a threat of riots, the opposite was true for pagans or Jews. Even after a century of increasingly repressive legislation a simple ban could have resulted in radical shock and upheaval. The middle steps were needed, and the Theodosian Code had to balance between distanced tolerance and further repression. Its strategy included stratification of society on the basis of religious affiliation, closure and hierarchical treatment of the thus created categories. The new order aimed at bringing a considerable change in both individuals and society. It assumed that the orthodox were the only ones to enjoy the full spectrum of social possibilities, possess wealth and serve at prestigious

---

158 Ożóg and Wójcik (2014), XXXVI.

159 Sirks (2013), p. 475.

160 Noethlichs (2015), p. 25.

161 Synonymous to paganism. See Kahlos (2007), pp. 20–21.

162 Epiphanius of Salamis (2009), pp. 18–22.

163 See e.g. CTh 16.5.46; 16.8.19.

public posts.[164] Religious affiliation became the most important social marker, even more influential than previously dominant birth rank, influencing all major aspects of one's life, and the "true baptism" served as an equivalent of the entrance fee to the most prestigious social class.[165] Simultaneously, it introduced a specific wording, that used ambivalence and similarity as two means of gradually achieving a unified, non-orthodox category in the future.

Wilken points out, that although pagans and Jews were seen as a similar threat, the continuing powerful presence of Jewish communities required the maintenance of certain privileges for the latter.[166] These included, among others, exemptions from compulsory public service,[167] and protection against different kinds of maltreatment, such as violent attacks and humiliation.[168] Simultaneously, specific measures were established to prevent Judaism from developing or spreading in any way. Jews were put in a position inferior to Christians, with severe punishments reserved for those who disturbed the converts to Christianity,[169] married Christian women,[170] forced conversion to Judaism on their slaves or circumcised any Christian in general. [171] They were denied the right to serve in most of the public services,[172] they could not possess slaves from other religions,[173] and were prohibited from building new synagogues.[174]

Pagans were in an even worse situation, one that on many accounts resembled the status of heretics. They were prohibited from practicing their faith in any way, which especially applied to sacrifices, both daily and nocturnal,[175] in public or in secret.[176] The same applied to divination,[177] veneration of images,[178] banquets and celebrations,[179] all of which could have resulted in severe punishments, including high fines, confiscation of the property used for such activities, proscription, exile and even death. All of the previous privileges conferred to pagan priests, ministers, prefects and hierophants were rejected and serving on such posts condemned and punishable by law.[180] Pagans were also unable to join the imperial service or become

[164] Sirks (2013), pp. 471–474.

[165] Noethlichs (2015), pp. 19–20.

[166] Wilken (1980), pp. 466–470.

[167] CTh 16.8.2; 16.8.4; 16.8.13; restricted partially in CTh 16.8.3.

[168] CTh 16.8.1; 16.8.9; 16.8.10; 16.8.11; 16.8.12; 16.8.21; 16.8.26.

[169] CTh 16.8.5.

[170] CTh 16.8.6.

[171] CTh 16.8.26.

[172] CTh 16.8.16; 16.8.24.

[173] Most notably Christian slaves, to which the whole Title 9 of Book XVI is devoted.

[174] CTh 16.8.22; 16.8.25; 16.8.27.

[175] CTh 16.10.2; 16.10.5; 16.10.6; 16.10.8; 16.10.12.

[176] CTh 16.10.1.

[177] CTh 16.10.9.

[178] CTh 16.10.10.

[179] CTh 16.10.19.

[180] CTh 16.10.14; 16.10.20.

either administrator or judge.[181] Their temples were supposed to be closed, shrines not approached, altars destroyed and statues torn from foundations.[182]

These differences in rights and repressive measures were accompanied by a gradual change in language. Many laws, including those inclined towards a bigger dose of tolerance, contained linguistic hostility, which, on one hand, indicated the emperor's disapproval for all non-orthodox, and, on the other, served the purpose of equalising them in the matter of fact, while retaining difference in the matter of law. It should not come as a surprise then, that the characterisation of Jews and pagans followed the tropes known from legislation on heresy. All three were accused of following error, criminality, bad faith, and insanity,[183] which made them into condemned and, ultimately, equally repulsive beliefs. The language used in their description drew widely on the long-standing legislative tradition. As Paño writes, "[t]he illicit in the sphere of religion at Rome had traditionally been constituted by terms such as *nefas, scelus, pollutio, sacrilegium, superstitio, perfidia, furor*. As antonyms of the concept *pietas*, they had served to blacken those who acted against the claimed public good in a religious or moral context."[184] All of these terms in some version can be found in the characterisation of the non-orthodox.

The use of polemical and denigrating characterisation had an important reference. As Kahlos argues, both of these linguistic strategies were extensively employed by another Christian genre, namely, polemical writings. Such characterisation of the opponents had as its main aim creation of binary oppositions, which, however, were not aimed, first and foremost, at the non-orthodox, but rather Catholic Christians themselves. Clear division of the world into "us" and "them" provided an important aid in self-identification, setting the boundaries, and showing where "Catholic" or "Christian" ended, and "the other" began.[185] As the above analysis shows, the Theodosian Code mimicked these strategies, operating on such dichotomies as orthodox and non-orthodox, Christian and non-Christian, *religio* and *superstitio*, licit and illicit, truth and error, rationality and insanity, simplicity and perversion, and many others, thus further developing the traits known from polemical writings. Additionally, the fact that Jews, pagans and heretics were singled out built multi-dimensional oppositions, that, on a higher level, isolated the orthodox from the non-orthodox, but on a lower level, separately distinguished Catholic Christianity from its different sources of influence.

In this way, a clear hierarchy of mutually defining Catholic Christians as the only truly legitimate religious group, and equally condemned, but differently repressed non-orthodox, with Jews at the top, pagans and heretics respectively was created by the Theodosian Code, determining more or less clear boundaries of social strata. Noethlichs points out, that law did not leave much room for change in one's social status. Not only heretics, but all non-orthodox were left with only two options. Either

[181]CTh 16.10.21.

[182]CTh 16.10.4.

[183]CTh 16.8.7

[184]Paño (2010), p. 110.

[185]Kahlos (2007), pp. 1–9; 103–110.

they could have converted to Catholicism, or became invisible.[186] But, as Ramsay McMullen argues, such division and ordering of society was far from the actual situation. The fourth century observed an enormous rise in social mobility, with the examples of complete change in social status, vocation and religious affiliation becoming much more common than before. The laws included in the Theodosian Code and its construction "bespoke frustration" of the emperors, who were unable to order their empire and make sure that every branch of society functioned properly.[187] This frustration resulted in the most severe treatment of those who transgressed the established categories, as they threatened the rising role of Catholicism and its identity.

Thus, the last religious category, which received a separate title in Book XVI, was that of the apostates, that is those who "forfeited their baptism" and took a "step back" towards the erroneous beliefs. To renounce Catholicism by becoming a pagan, Jew or heretic constituted the gravest of possible sins, and endured the full power of imperial repression. The apostates were practically obliterated from public activity of any kind, and, as CTh 16.7.4 reads, completely excluded from society. They couldn't make valid wills,[188] acquire inheritance[189] or give donations.[190] They were supposed to be persecuted without limitation, and their apostasy could have been established even after their death, with full legal consequences. They were unable to give testimony, endured infamy and were supposed to be stripped off of any privileges that would be due to them according to their birth rank, situating them in an inferior position in social strata than the lowest class.[191] And, according to their new affiliation, they were supposed to be punished above the normal limit of the sentence.[192] But, most severely, they were denied the right to ever improve their situation, as penance did not bring any effects in this case, and repeated conversion was straightforwardly banned.[193] Devoid of any rights, they were supposed to remain among the others, enduring the full spectrum of humiliation.

5 Conclusion and Further Direction

The main research question posed by this paper is: if, and if so, how, did the Theodosian Code help in shaping the concepts of "orthodoxy" and "heresy"? The above analysis shows clearly that it had every opportunity to exercise an important, if not decisive influence on the formation of these notions. Until the publication of the

[186]See Footnote 160.

[187]McMullen (1964), pp. 49–50.

[188]CTh 16.7.1.

[189]CTh 16.7.2.

[190]CTh 16.7.7.

[191]CTh 16.7.5.

[192]CTh 16.7.3.

[193]CTh 16.7.4

Code, the Roman Empire perfected the ways in which law was published and disseminated, which allowed it to penetrate the whole Roman Society, despite the high levels of illiteracy. The main principles of the Theodosian Code and its structure further facilitated the understanding of the law, and separation of the book on religion especially pronounced its ordering of religious matters. This was supported by the fact that law served as the main source of information for a majority of the imperial population.

The use of middle steps, the general focus on "orthodoxy" in law and the grounding of new categories and concepts in well-established rhetoric and ideas, additionally eased up the possibility of social change, the task around which the *Codex Theodosianus* was consciously oriented. Introduced in the beginning of the fourth century a new intellectual base established the link between state obedience and religious adherence, and justified the use of coercion in religious matters. The changes in Christianity and its alignment with the imperial ideology also fostered cooperation with law on that matter, due to polarisation of disputes, petrification of arguments, and mirroring of senatorial and legal methods in their examination of written material, which resulted in reduction of the complexity of "the other". All of that resulted in law and religion becoming co-dependent enterprises, influencing each other to a great extent in the process.

Further operationalisation of the query showed that the shift towards orthodoxy included the reification of legitimate representations in the formal processes. As the close analysis of the Code's text showed, it aided this shift directly, by being a reificatory force itself, as well as indirectly, by facilitating other formal processes. The former operated especially through the enforcement of specific doctrinal pronouncements. The latter operated through extra-doctrinal marks, such as creedal, conciliar and ecclesiastical reference. Both of these were further strengthened through creation of specific categories based on socially salient marks and instalment of specific narratives as being the only valid ones. In this way, the Theodosian Code exercised what is called "the constitutive effect", creating patterns of thinking and functioning in Roman society, drawing boundaries between the thinkable and unthinkable.

The Code therefore clearly differentiated between licit and illicit religiosity. Catholic Christianity was separated from the "people of Christian religion" as the only valid religious affiliation. Its definition included doctrinal pronouncement, with direct borrowings from the formulations of the Nicean and Constantinopolitan councils. This was supported by extra-doctrinal marks, such as ecclesiastical reference, adherence to which was necessary in order to remain orthodox in the eyes of the law, apostolic discipline, evangelical doctrine, peaceful character or, quite notably, proper ancestry, which was followed by a narrative of two primacies: the primacy of orthodoxy before heresy, enforced further by the definitions of heresy, and the primacy of the Roman Church.

The term "orthodox" itself was used only in polemical context, which revealed an important tendency in the ordering of religiosity in the Code. The boundaries of the licit were built in juxtaposition to the illicit, and created in that way binary oppositions helped in further struggle for self-identification of the former. The orthodox and non-orthodox were therefore mutually defining, and the fact that the exact pronouncement of the right belief was still in formation moved the centre of gravity to those who in any way conflicted with it. Thus, an extensive part of Book XVI was devoted to those who, as the narrative went, deviated from orthodoxy, that is heretics, as well as those, who did not yet vanish or accept the new faith, that is Jews and pagans.

The mix of religious and political reasons led to strict conjunction of the religious affiliation and social position, thereby making the latter relational as well. The privileges for orthodox and the repressive and reprobative measures towards the non-orthodox further perpetrated the differences between the two, making them into a conceptual and real divide. The position and prosperity of the orthodox was meant to further convince about their righteousness, while the lack of social and legal standing of the non-orthodox evidenced the dual condemnation of them by God first, and the emperor, second. The use of coercion by law and the introduction of hierarchy required justification, which resulted in the specific ways of characterisation. Thus, the combination of traditional Roman rhetorics of bad faith, insanity and superstition, and Christian polemical terms was applied to all non-orthodox in varying degrees, and the semantics of contamination, contagion and pollution were perfected to present their spread as a serious and dangerous development. In the vicious circle of cause and effect such characteristics resulted in the deepening of counter-measures.

Heresy, as the closest to orthodoxy, was made into a crime of public law, and persecuted for both affiliation and specific actions. Jews and pagans, due to their traditional anchoring, received more preferential treatment, but, nonetheless, endured significant restrictions in the ways they could exercise their beliefs. The middle-step of tolerance towards the latter two was meant as a temporary measure that as its main aim had their gradual extinction. Created in that way categories were closed and the only possible movement in-between them was a conversion to orthodoxy. To further enforce this. transgressors were severely punished, with the lowest status of apostates, that is those who consciously rejected the orthodox belief in any way.

The process of categorisation had multiple levels, all of which served several purposes. The more general categories flattened everything that was inside of them. Thus, individual followers of what had been seen as heretical belief were grouped into unified sects under the name of their founders. At that level the strategy of naming, and non-naming, granted further powers to law, building its esteem, positing it as the point of reference and allowing it to stomp on some and deprive others of authority. All heretics were joint with schismatics, astrologers and Manichaeans under the wider label of heresy, and equalised with regards to prescribing them to perfidy. The same applied to pagans, Jews and apostates respectively. The final level included a division between the orthodox and non-orthodox, which set the final aim straight—to get rid of the latter and build a unified empire consisting only of the former.

Neville Morley states that “the final test of any theory is not just whether it is persuasive, but whether it is productive, offering new ways of thinking about the ... world.”[194] This paper hopes to advance the understanding of the notions of orthodoxy and heresy, as well as the Theodosian Code itself, by challenging the established

---

[194]Morley (2004), p. 29.

assumptions shared by the general public and the scientific community. It is the first step in a bigger research project, striving to open a range of new possibilities.

The current endeavour could be further supported by the analysis of the Code's actual effects. Thus, the next step should include the comparison of the Theodosian Code with the subsequent Justinian Code, to see the differences and developments that took place over time concerning the notions of orthodoxy, heresy, and the non-orthodox in general, as well as the narration behind them. Also, if one takes into account the amount of simplification and flattening done by the Code, further research could try to establish which disputes were polarised by the Theodosian Code, that is, which options prevailed in binary oppositions, and which were completely discarded from the wider consciousness. The argumentative strategies of the Code could also be more closely compared with the polemical writings, to see which strategies were borrowed, and which were invented in the course of legislation.

The current theoretical framework could also be tested in other cases of radical disruptions in the existing religious landscape, for example, in the case of the Reformation. Further inquiry could test whether the same measures can be applied to the development of Lutheranism or Calvinism in their formational periods, when the notion of orthodoxy was reformulated. Another line of investigation could review the cases where practice, rather than belief, was reified. The new understanding of orthodoxy could also bring implications to the fields of law and religion. Although the political power of Christianity might have faded, law seems to retain its role not only in the secular, but surprisingly also in the religious sphere, which remains largely understudied.

References

Allport GW (1979) The nature of prejudice. Addison-Wesley Publishing Company, Reading, Massachusetts

Ando C (2000) Imperial ideology and provincial loyalty in the roman empire. Classics and contemporary thought. University of California Press, Berkeley, Los Angeles, London

Ando C (2006) Religion and Ius publicum. In: Ando C (ed) Religion and law in classical and Christian Rome. Franz Steiner Verlag, Stuttgart, pp 126–145

Barnard L (1995) The criminalisation of heresy in the later Roman Empire: a sociopolitical device? J Legal Hist 16(2):121–146

Bauer W (1971) Orthodoxy and heresy in earliest Christianity. Fortress Press, Philadelphia

Beck R (2006) The religion of the Mithras cult in the Roman Empire. Oxford University Press, Oxford

Bingham DJ (2006) Development and diversity in early Christianity. J Evangelical Theological Soc 49(1):45–66

Chadwick H (1959) The circle and the ellipse: rival concepts of authority in the early church. An inaugural lecture delivered before the University of Oxford. Clarendon Press, Oxford

Constas N (2003) Proclus of constantinople and the cult of the virgin in late antiquity: Homilies 1-5, texts and translations. Vigiliae Christianae: texts and studies of early Christian life and language. Brill, Leiden

DePalma Digeser E (2006) Religion, law and the Roman polity: the era of the great persecution. In: Ando C, Riipke J (eds) Religion and law in classical and Christian Rome. Franz Steiner Verlag, Stuttgart, pp 68–84
Ehler SZ, Morrall JB (1967) Church and state through the centuries: a collection of historic documents with commentaries. Biblo & Tannen Publishers, New York
Epiphanius of Salamis (2009) The Panarion, vol I (trans: Williams F). Brill, Leiden
Errington RM (1997) Christian accounts of the religious legislation of theodosius I. Klio 79(2):398–443
Errington RM (2006) In: Osborne R, Rhodes PJ, Talbert RJA (eds) Roman imperial policy from Julian to Theodosius. Studies in history of Greece and Rome. The University of North Carolina Press, Chapel Hill
Eusebius (1999) Life of Constantine (trans: Cameron A, Hall SG). Clarendon ancient history Series. Clarendon Press, Oxford
Flower R (2013) The insanity of the heretics must be restrained. Heresiology in the theodosian code. In: Kelly C (ed) Theodosius II: rethinking the Roman Empire in late antiquity. Cambridge University Press, Cambridge, pp 172–194
Fowden G (2001) Varieties of religious community. In: Bowersock GW, Brown P, Grabar O (eds) Interpreting late antiquity. Essays on the postclassical world. The Belknap Press of Harvard University Press, Cambridge, Massachusetts, London, England, pp 82–107
Geertz C (1983) Local knowledge: further essays in interpretative anthropology. Basic Books, New York
Gibbon E (2013) Chapter II. In: Bury J (ed) The history of the decline and fall of the Roman Empire: edited in seven volumes with introduction, notes, appendices, and index. Cambridge University Press, Cambridge, pp 28–58
Harries J (2004) Law and empire in late antiquity. Cambridge University Press, Cambridge
Harries J (2007) Roman law codes and the Roman legal tradition. In: Cairns JW, du Plessis PJ (eds) Beyond dogmatics: law and society in the Roman world. Edinburgh University Press, Edinburgh, pp 85–104
Hartog PA (2015) Orthodoxy and heresy in early Christian contexts. Reconsidering the Bauer Thesis. Pickwick Publications, Eugene, Oregon
Honoré T (1986) The making of the theodosian code. Zeitschrift der Savigny-Stiftung für Rechtsgeschichte: Romanistische Abteilung 103:133–222
Humfress C (2006) Cracking the "Codex": late Roman legal practice in context. Bull Inst Class Stud 49:241–254
Humfress C (2007) Orthodoxy and the courts in late antiquity. Oxford University Press, Oxford
Jasper D (2001) Transmission and reception of decretals and letters from Siricius (384-399) through Sixtus III (432-440). In: Jasper D, Fuhrmann H (eds) Papal letters in the early middle ages. The Catholic University of America Press, Washington, D.C., pp 7–41
Kahlos M (2007) Debate and dialogue: Christian and pagan cultures C. 360-430. Ashgate, Hampshire
Köstenberger AJ, Kruger MJ (2010) The heresy of orthodoxy. Crossway, Wheaton, Illinois
Lim R (2001) Christian triumph and controversy. In: Bowersock GW, Brown P, Grabar O (eds) Interpreting late antiquity. Essays on the postclassical world. The Belknap Press of Harvard University Press, Cambridge, Massachusetts, London, England, pp 196–218
Lyman RJ (2003) 2002 NAPS presidential address: Hellenism and Heresy. J Early Christ Stud 11(2):209–222
McMullen R (1964) Social mobility and the theodosian code. J Roman Stud 54(1 and 2):49–53
Mitnick EJ (2007) Law, cognition, and identity. La Law Rev 67(3):823–869
Morley N (2004) Theories, models and concepts in ancient history. Routledge, London and New York
Mousourakis G (2015) Roman law and the origins of the civil law tradition. Springer, New York
Nicene and post-nicene fathers, second series (1890) Christian Literature Publishing Co., Buffalo, NY. http://www.newadvent.org/fathers/26011.htm

Noethlichs KL (2006) Revolution from the top?<Orthodoxy> and the persecution of heretics in imperial legislation from Constantine to Justinian. In: Ando C, Riipke J (eds) Religion and law in classical and Christian Rome. Franz Steiner Verlag, Stuttgart, pp 115–125
Noethlichs KL (2015) The legal framework of religious identity in the Roman Empire. In: Rebillard É, Rüpke J (eds) Group identity and religious individuality in late antiquity. The Catholic University of America Press, Washington D.C., pp 13–27
Osborn EF (1989) Reason and the rule of faith in the second century AD. In: Williams R (ed) The making of orthodoxy. Essays in honour of Henry Chadwick. Cambridge University Press, Cambridge, pp 40–61
Ożóg M, Wójcik M (2014) Kodeks Teodozjusza. Księga Szesnasta (trans: Caba A). Synody I Kolekcje Praw. Wydawnictwo WAM, Kraków
Padovani A, Stein PG (2007) The Jurists' philosophy of law from Rome to the seventeenth century. A treatise of legal philosophy and general jurisprudence, 7 vols. Springer, Dordrecht
Pagels E (1979) The gnostic gospels. Weidenfeld and Nicholson, London
Paño MVE (2010) Heretical texts and maleficium in the codex theodosianus (Cth 16.5.34). In: Gordon Rl, Simón Fm (eds) Magical practice in the Latin West. Brill, Leiden, pp 105–138
Pearson BA (1990) Gnosticism, Judaism, and Egyptian Christianity. Fortress Press, Minneapolis
Pharr C (1969) The theodosian code and novels and the Sirmondian constitutions. Greenwood Press, New York
Roberts CH (1979) Manuscript, society and belief in Early Christian Egypt. The Schweich lectures of the British Academy. Oxford University Press, London
Robinson TA (1988) The Bauer thesis examined. The Edwin Mellen Press, Lewiston/Queenston
Robinson OF (2007) Penal practice and penal policy in ancient Rome. Routledge, London and New York
Sarat A, Simon J (2001) Beyond legal realism? Cultural analysis, cultural studies, and the situation of legal scholarship. Yale J Law Humanit 13(3):3–32
Scruton R (2007) Modern culture. Continuum, London and New York
Shepardson C (2014) Controlling contested places: late antique Antioch and the spatial politics of religious controversy. University of California Press, Berkeley
Sirks B (2013) Reform and legislation in the Roman Empire. Mélanges de l'École française de Rome - Antiquité 125(2):469–477
Sørensen J (2005) Religion in mind: a review article of the cognitive science of religion. Numen 52(4):465–494
Stachura M (2006a) Eunomian rights to draw testaments in the legislation of 389–399. Zeitschrift der Savigny-Stiftung für Rechtsgeschichte. Kanonistische Abteilung 92:45–62
Stachura M (2006b) Kodeks Teodozjusza - Nowo Odkrywane Zrodlo Historyczne. Przegląd Historyczny 97(3):311–331
Stark R, Bainbridge WS (1996) A theory of religion. Toronto studies in religion. Rutgers University Press, New Brunswick, New Jersey
Tuori K (2004) The Ius Respondendi and the freedom of Roman jurisprudence. Revue Internationale Des Droits de L'antiquité 51:295–337
Tuori K (2007) Legal pluralism and the Roman Empires. In: Cairns JW, du Plessis PJ (eds) Beyond dogmatics: law and society in the Roman world. Edinburgh University Press, Edinburgh, pp 39–52
Turner HEW (1954) The pattern of Christian truth. Bampton lectures. A. R. Mowbray & Co. Limited, London
Van Dam R (2002) Kingdom of snow: Roman rule and Greek culture in Cappadocia. University of Pennsylvania Press, Philadelphia
Wilken RL (1980) The Jews and Christian apologetics after Theodosius I Cunctos Populos. Harvard Theological Rev 73(3/4):451–471
Williams R (1989) Does it make sense to speak of pre-nicene orthodoxy? In: Williams R (ed) The making of orthodoxy. Essays in honour of Henry Chadwick. Cambridge University Press, Cambridge, pp 1–23

Freedom of Religion and the Invention of Tradition

Hugh McFaul

'Traditions' which appear or claim to be old are often quite recent in origin and sometimes invented.

(Hobsbawm 1983, 1).

Abstract This chapter will consider the significance of invented traditions to the relationship between law and religion. Drawing on the work of Eric Hobsbawm, it will explore the view that traditions can be manufactured and will seek to demonstrate how states can regulate and control minority religious groups by the construction of conceptions of traditional and non-traditional religion. Reference will be made to a number of recent cases heard before the European Court of Human Rights which show how the accommodation of religion can depend upon law and policy makers choosing to recognise certain beliefs and practices as *religious* beliefs and practices and, in certain contexts, this recognition is contingent upon religious groups acquiring legal personality. Achieving this recognition has proven to be problematic for some minority religious groups. This is particularly the case in ex-Soviet States where minority religions are sometimes perceived as non-traditional loci of foreign influence.

1 Introduction

This chapter will explore how tradition can inform our understandings of the relationship between law and religion. It will offer a critical perspective by arguing that notions of tradition have been used by states to limit the freedom of minority religions for political purposes. In particular it will argue that concepts of traditional religion can, in certain contexts, be manipulated or invented for political ends.

H. McFaul (✉)
The Open University, Milton Keynes, UK
e-mail: h.j.mcfaul@open.ac.uk

J. Giles et al. (eds.), *Law, Religion and Tradition*, Law and Religion in a Global Context 1, https://doi.org/10.1007/978-3-319-96749-3_6

To do this it will consider some examples from the significant number of cases that have come before the European Court of Human Rights (hereafter ECtHR) over recent years concerning the freedom of religion of minority religious groups. Many of these cases have, at their core, the issue of whether a group has been successful in meeting the criteria for registration as a religious organisation. The decision by states to confer or withhold the status of legal personality for minority religious groups has a direct impact on freedom of religion and demonstrates that states can be active in manufacturing notions of tradition, in particular what is classed as traditional religion within a society. Using Eric Hobsbawm's notion of invented traditions this chapter will seek to argue that conceptions of traditional and non-traditional religion can be actively constructed by the State to regulate and control minority religious groups.

The chapter will be presented in five parts; Hobsbawm's concept of invented traditions will be given a general introduction in Part I. Part II will offer some remarks on the concept of legal personality. Part III will outline the importance of the concept of legal personality for freedom of religion in the jurisprudence of the ECtHR. Part IV will show that achieving legal personality status has proven to be problematic for some minority religious groups, especially in ex-Soviet jurisdictions. Part V will conclude, utilising Hobsbawm's conception of invented traditions, that policies surrounding the conferral of legal personality can be a means by which the state can attempt to exert control over religious practice and, in so doing promote particular understandings of what counts as traditional religion.

2 The Invention of Tradition

Hobsbawm's influential essay on the invention of tradition formed the introduction to a collection of essays exploring examples of the impact of invented traditions in a number of historical contexts. In it, Hobsbawm suggests that traditions, although having the appearance of being timeless, can in fact, be recent in origin or invented.[1] He argues that:

> 'Invented tradition' is taken to mean a set of practices, normally governed by overtly or tacitly accepted rules and of a ritual or symbolic nature, which seek to inculcate certain values and norms of behaviour by repetition, which automatically implies continuity with the past. In fact, where possible, they normally attempt to establish continuity with a suitable historic past.[2]

An invented tradition can be distinguished from an authentic one by the fact there is an element of conscious construction, usually, but not always, by the state in their manufacture. Authentic traditions could therefore be said to evolve organically, without overt or conscious manipulation. One of the many examples of an invented tradition provided in his account is the deliberate choice of using a Gothic style, popular in the fifteenth century rather than the contemporary neoclassical style which

[1] Hobsbawm (1983), p. 1.

[2] Hobsbawm (1983), p. 3.

had republican associations, for the rebuilding of the UK parliament building in the mid nineteenth century; a decision which was repeated when the building was once again rebuilt to the same design after being destroyed during World War II.[3]

Thus a defining characteristic of an invented tradition is that there is an association with an historic past which is likely to be factitious. Hobsbawm posits three overlapping types of invented tradition:

> a) those establishing or symbolizing social cohesion or the membership of groups real or artificial communities, b) those establishing or legitimizing institutions, status or relations of authority, and c) those whose main purpose was socialisation, the inculcation of beliefs, value systems and conventions of behaviour.[4]

All three types of invented tradition are seen as using an association with an historic past 'as a legitimator of action and cement of group cohesion.'[5] The focus of this chapter will be particularly on the first and second of these types, as it will consider how the law acts to legitimize certain types of religious institutions and not others, and thereby regulate the membership of communities.

The concept of invented tradition is seen as being pertinent to historical scholarship in general but is of particular relevance to 'that comparatively recent historical innovation, the 'nation', with its associated phenomena: nationalism, the nation-state, national symbols, histories and the rest.'[6] Indeed, Hobsbawm warns against being misled by what he describes as a curious paradox that:

> modern nations and all their impedimenta generally claim to be the opposite of novel, namely rooted in the remotest antiquity, and the opposite of constructed, namely human communities so 'natural' as to require no definition other than self-assertion...[7]

So, just as Hobsbawm argues that, 'the national phenomenon cannot be adequately investigated without careful attention to the 'invention of tradition,'[8] likewise, it is the argument of this chapter that to adequately investigate phenomenon of tradition in the relationship between national laws and religion, it is necessary to consider the influence of invented traditions. Indeed Hobsbawm recognises that the study of invented traditions is one that is of concern to scholars in disciplines other than history,[9] and it is a reasonable assumption that scholars of law and religion can contribute to this field.

The remainder of the chapter will argue that, in seeking to buttress the recent historical innovation of the nation, the recent case law of the ECtHR illustrates that certain states, many of which have experienced the convulsions of a post-Soviet

---

[3]Hobsbawm (1983), pp. 1–2. The remainder of the volume for which Hobsbawm's essay forms the introduction explores a range of examples of invented traditions, including the British Monarchy, the invention of the Highland tradition in Scotland and case studies on Victorian India and Africa.

[4]Hobsbawm (1983), p. 9.

[5]Hobsbawm (1983), p. 12.

[6]Hobsbawm (1983), p. 13.

[7]Hobsbawm (1983), p. 14.

[8]See Footnote 7.

[9]See Footnote 7.

rebirth, have attempted to invent notions of traditional religion which control minority religious groups and create an association with a suitable historic past. A key mechanism by which this has been attempted is regulation of the conferral of legal personality on minority religious groups, and it is the concept of legal personality that will be the focus of part II.

3 Legal Personality

Legal personality is fundamental to any legal system.[10] The legal person is the subject of legal rights and duties and can, in principle, enforce rights in court, be held liable for breach of legal duties, be deemed capable of entering into a contract or owning property. Natural legal persons (human beings) are most obviously the objects around which legal rights and duties coalesce, so the legal person is largely synonymous with human personhood but is nevertheless conceptually distinct from it. The idea that personhood is conceptually distinct from human being is of course a distinction that is familiar in philosophy and theology.[11]

So from a legal perspective, the person is an abstraction, amounting to little more than a pragmatic fiction, the construction of which facilitates the coalescence of particular legal rights and duties, as Smith helpfully explains:

> To say that a subject has legal personality is to say that it is a party to legal relations without indicating in particular what the relations are. To say that one has title, is to say that one is a party to a particular class of legal relations, namely, those which go with the ownership of property. In either case, if one takes away all the rights, powers, privileges and immunities that shelter under the term, there is nothing left except the shelter which, thereafter, is but a word without a meaning.[12]

Legal rights and duties can in principle be allowed to coalesce around any entity, whether natural or artificial. Unsurprisingly human beings are generally given the status of natural legal personhood but it is well established that corporations can function as legal persons to serve the pragmatic purpose of groups of individuals engaged in a common endeavour.[13] This malleability is a key feature of legal personality and it has, for example, been put to extended use in modern capitalist societies

[10]For an extended discussion of the concept of legal personality see Smith (1928), Naffine (2010), Note (2001).

[11]For example, the idea that a person might not necessarily be a human being has long been present in Christian Theology where the doctrine of the trinity holds that God is Father, Son and Holy Spirit. Cardinal Newman, writing in the 19th Century, wrote that 'person' is the word: '... we venture to use in speaking of those three distinct and real modes in which it has pleased Almighty God to reveal to us His being' (cited in OED 2016).

[12]Smith (1928), p. 294.

[13]For example *Salomon v Salomon and Co* (1897) is the seminal case on corporate legal personality in UK law. It is interesting to note that the law relies on imagery of the body (corporeality, incorporation, corporation etc.) to conceptualise the abstraction of the legal person to artificial entities such as the company.

where it is a common for business organisations to attempt to create tax efficiencies by creating complex series of artificial corporate entities.

A concomitant feature of the malleability of the legal person is its indeterminacy. As will be explored in relation to the conferral of legal personality to minority religious groups in Parts III and IV below, the actual conferral of legal personality is often contested and can be revealing of changing societal attitudes to the status of particular individuals or groups within society. For example, legal systems were able to facilitate the existence of human slavery by denying slaves legal personality.[14] Likewise, the position of women in legal history illustrates that being human is not always sufficient to be the object of a full range of legal rights and duties; women were not originally considered to be legal persons in their own right by the common law.[15] More recently challenges to the conferral of legal personality have focused on attempts to break down the well-established legal divide between persons and animals.[16] In this way legal personality can be seen as a social construction which is revealing of wider social and political power structures.

Thus, as a matter of legal principle, the rights and duties which constitute legal personality can coalesce around any entity, whether a natural human person, a corporation or even non-human animal. Part III will show that in, some instances, legal personality is more readily conferred on religious organisations which fit pre-existing assumptions templates of what a religion should 'traditionally' look like. Further, in some instances, the decision to grant or withhold legal personality to particular religious groups illustrates the role of the state in the social construction of religion and is thus an example of a form of invented tradition, where the state, in order to protect and promote perceived national interests, seeks to consciously control concepts of traditional religion which can negatively impact the freedom of religion of minority groups.

---

[14] An example of the importance of legal personality in the emancipation of slaves can be seen in the English case of *Somerset v Stewart* (1772). For an extended treatment of how US courts have approached the issue of personhood and slavery see Note (2001).

[15] For example, in his 1765 text *Commentaries on the Laws of England*, William Blackstone argued that by marriage a husband and wife are one person in law and for the duration of the marriage the woman's independent legal existence is suspended and consolidated into that of her husband's. 'By marriage, the husband and wife are one person in law: that is, the very being or legal existence of the woman is suspended during the marriage, or at least is incorporated and consolidated into that of the husband: under whose wing, protection, and cover, she performs everything…' (Blackstone 1765, 442).

[16] Animals are generally seen as property and conceptually ineligible for the status of legal personality. However this has been subject to sustained legal challenge in the USA by the Non-Human Rights Project, a campaign group who have launched a series of cases seeking review of the lawfulness of the detention of a number of chimpanzees in New York State.

4 Legal Personality and Freedom of Religion Under the ECtHR

The preceding discussion has shown that legal personality is a fundamental and flexible legal concept which can be applied to abstract entities such as corporations as well as to human persons. Religious organisations are also able to take advantage of this legal form. The mechanisms for conferring the status of legal personality on the religious groups vary across Europe's national jurisdictions.[17] These include conferral of legal personality by the enactment of legislation, the conclusion of a covenant, registration, or through conclusion of co-operation agreements. If there is no specific legal mechanism for the conferral of legal personality on religious groups, the group will rely on the general law. If a religious group fails to meet a jurisdiction's requirements for the conferral of legal personality, or choose not to acquire it, they still benefit from the protection of freedom of religion under Article 9 European Convention on Human Rights (hereafter ECHR), often read in conjunction with the right to freedom of association under Article 11.

However, despite the fact that religious groups can claim the protection offered by the ECHR regardless of their domestic legal status, the acquisition of legal personality does generate clear legal advantages for religious communities under national law. These include the ability to collectively own property, perform state recognised marriages and gain access to state institutions for the purpose of providing pastoral care. Taking Poland as an example:

> The Constitution of Poland (Article 25.1) and the "Law on Guarantees of freedom of religion" of Poland provide that, in carrying out their functions, religious organizations may, among other activities: determine religious doctrine, dogma and rites; organize and publicly perform religious rites; lead the ministry of chaplains; govern themselves in accordance with their own rules (legal autonomy); establish, educate and employ clergy; acquire and dispose of movable and immovable property and manage it; produce, buy and sell objects of worship; use mass media; conduct educational activities; conduct charitable activities; create inter-church organizations at the state level; and belong to international religious organizations.[18]

The Organisation for Security and Co-operation in Europe/Office for Democratic Institutions and Human Rights (hereafter OSCE/ODHIR) have highlighted the importance of legal personality for religious organisation for the protection of freedom of religion. They argue that if the organisational life of a religious community is not protected then an individual's freedom to practice their religion is put at risk.

> The ability to establish a legal entity to act collectively in a field of mutual interest is one of the most important aspects of the freedom of association, without which that right would be deprived of any meaning. As regards the organization of a religious community, a refusal to recognize it as a legal entity has also been found to constitute an interference with the right

[17] Doe (2011) provides a detailed survey of the legal mechanisms for the conferral of legal personality on religious organisations.

[18] OSCE/ODHIR 2014 at [30].

> to freedom of religion under Article 9 of the ECHR as exercised by both the community itself and its individual members.[19]

It is clear that, by the standards of international human rights law, the collective freedom of a religious group is essential to the protection of religious freedom, and very often, the ability to access the status of legal personality of that group is fundamental to the exercise of that freedom. However, as was outlined in Part II, legal personality is a flexible concept and, in this context, its indeterminacy is compounded by the absence of an overarching definition of 'religion' in the jurisprudence of the ECtHR. Peroni argues the absence of a definition of 'religion' leaves open the possibility of inherent judicial bias in favour of manifestations of religion which are analogous to acceptable forms of religious belief and practice,

> any attempt to define the scope and content of the right to religious liberty will necessarily involve assumptions about the underlying nature of religion itself. The danger is that, in the process, some orthodoxies may be imposed while other dimensions of religion may be overlooked and denied legal protection.[20]

Part IV will show that in addition to the possibility of judicial assumptions that may favour religious orthodoxies, the state can be proactive in trying to manufacture notions of traditional religion, to the exclusion of groups presented as non-traditional.

5 The Regulation of Religious Groups in Post-soviet Europe

Placing administrative obstacles in the path of the legal recognition of religious groups has been recognised as undermining global access to freedom of religion. The 2012 UNCHR report on freedom of religion reports that such obstacles have a discriminatory impact on minority religions,[21] a concern that was echoed by the 2015 US State Department report on global religious freedom which stated that,

> Around the world, governments continued to tighten their regulatory grip on religious groups, and particularly on minority religious groups and religions which are viewed as not traditional to that specific country.[22]

The issue of legal personality for religious organisations has been the subject of several ECtHR rulings over recent years. The majority of these rulings have their origin in disputes regarding the registration of minority religions or new religious movements in ex-Soviet states which introduced or adapted rules regarding the registration of religious groups in the 1990s.[23] Registration of religious groups remains

---

[19] OSCE/ODHIR 2014 at [18].

[20] Peroni (2014), p. 236.

[21] See Bielefeldt (2012), US State Department (2015).

[22] US State Department (2015).

[23] ECtHR case law also provides some examples of how minority religions have encountered difficulties in negotiating domestic registration requirements in jurisdictions outside the ex Soviet sphere,

common in former Soviet states. For example, Latvia's Law on Religious Organisations of 7 September 1995, Romania's Law 489/2006 on the Freedom of Religion and the General Status of Denominations, and Moldova's Religious Denominations Act (Law no. 979-XII of 24 March 1992). There are other similar laws throughout the region. Space does not permit consideration of every case arising from registration issues but a few recent examples will be offered by way of illustration, with further examples given in the context of the wider discussion on Russia below.

Examples from Bulgaria include *Dimitrova v Bulgaria* (2015), where The Word of Life evangelical organisation was refused registration in 1994 under the Bulgarian Religions Act and was subject to restrictive measures ordered by the Sofia City Public Prosecutor's Office which had concluded that Word of Life was a harmful sect. Mrs Dimitrova hosted group meetings in her home which was searched and items were seized. Her claim for damages was dismissed on appeal. The ECtHR found a breach of Article 9 in conjunction with Article 13. A more recent Bulgarian example is *Metodiev and Ors v Bulgaria* (2017), where a breach of Article 9 and 11 was found for the refusal to register as a religious association the Ahmadiyya Muslim Community whose members were Ahmadi's (associated with Sunni Islam).

Hungary's recent registration law, Act no. CCVI of 2011, on the Right to Freedom of Conscience and Religion and the Legal Status of Churches ("The Churches Act"),[24] was the subject of proceedings before the ECtHR in *Magyar Keresztény Mennonita Egyház and Ors v Hungary* (2014). The Churches Act intended to recognise fourteen 'traditional faiths' without any requirement to register whereas any other religious groups would have to reregister but would also need to show that they had been operating in Hungary for a period of twenty years. The original legislation was struck down by Hungary's constitutional court in February 2013, after which new legislation was adopted in 2013. But the law still applied in that they had to apply to parliament for recognition as incorporated churches if they wished to take advantage of the fiscal advantages this status provided. In this case a number of religious groups complained to the ECtHR of a breach of Article 11, read in conjunction with Article 9. The applicants represented groups that had operated as registered religious organisations compliant with the 1990 Church Act, but not being included in the category of 14 traditional faiths, the applicants had been forced to re-register to access State funding. The court found a violation of Articles 9 and 11.[25]

The proliferation of ECtHR cases challenging the registration regimes for religious groups can perhaps be placed in the broader context of the post-Soviet expansion of the Council of Europe. As Evans points out, the ECtHR jurisprudence in relation to Art 9 was limited and 'looked for many decades as though it was going to be

including in Austria and Turkey. For which see *Jehovas Zeugen in Osterreich v. Austria* (2012) and *Religionsgemeinschaft der Zeugen Jehovas and Others v. Austria* (2008) and *Cumhuriyetçi Eğitim ve Kültür Merkezi Vakfi v Turkey* [2014] ECHR 1346.

[24]For a wider discussion on the Hungarian legislative framework see Venice Commission (2012).

[25]Note that the related judgment in *Magyar Keresztény Mennonita Egyház and Ors v Hungary (Just Satisfaction)* [2016] concerned the issue of just satisfaction of the claim.

effectively a dead letter.'[26] Indeed it was not until *Kokkinakis v Greece* (1994) that the court found a violation of Article 9. But the post-Soviet period led to a sharp increase in the number of Article 9 applications with 60 additional cases in the first decade of the new millennium compared to only 30 up to that point.[27] This increase is partly symptomatic of the transition that Eastern European states were making in consequence of becoming signatories to the ECHR. Sadurski argues this widened membership provides a diversity and heterogeneity within the constituency of the Council of Europe which is in clear contrast to the original Treaty signatories who were a 'club of largely like-minded West European countries which share[d] much of their legal and political culture and traditions.'[28] This expansion led to an increase in cases before the ECtHR from Eastern European jurisdictions relating to 'egregious violations of human rights.'[29] The result being that the ECtHR were required to respond to this more challenging expanded environment by playing a role more akin to that of a constitutional court; the ECtHR moved from being a 'fine-tuner' of national legal systems to a 'scrutiniser of failing legal and political systems.'[30]

This approach resulted in the use of 'pilot judgements' by the ECtHR where widespread and systemic violations were identified and the State ordered to take far reaching steps in redress.[31] This change of emphasis was underpinned by the Committee of Ministers of the Council of Europe which instructed the ECtHR to identify violations which result from 'an underlying systemic problem…in particular when it is likely to give rise to numerous applications, so as to assist states in finding the appropriate solution.'[32]

Sadurski argues that the ECtHR have used 'pilot judgements' to try to create alliances with domestic constitutional courts to offer their support in bringing pressure on the legislative and executive branches of a state to bring them in line with internationally agreed standards of human rights protections.[33] Evans argues that this type of alliance can be seen in the way in which the ECtHR supported the Moldovan domestic Supreme Court in *Biserica Adevarat Ortodoza din Moldova and Others v Moldova* (2007) finding against the Moldovan Government's refusal to register a religious group 'The True Orthodox Church of Moldova.'[34] Although Sadurski casts doubt on whether the political conditions within Russia, a state where many Article 9 challenges have originated, are sufficiently receptive to give proper effect to pilot judgements, a point which will be explored further below.[35]

---

[26]Evans (2010), p. 321.

[27]See Footnote 26.

[28]Sarduski (2009), p. 400.

[29]Sadurski (2009), p. 401.

[30]See Footnote 29.

[31]Sadurski (2009), p. 402.

[32]Resolution (2004) 3 of the Committee of Ministers.

[33]Sadurski (2009), pp. 420–421.

[34]See Footnote 26.

[35]Sadurski (2009), p. 429.

6 Freedom of Religion in Contemporary Russia

Russia has been the source of a significant number of cases regarding the registration of religious groups, examples of which will be discussed further here. To put these in context some brief comments will be offered on the background to contemporary relations between the Russian state and religious communities active in Russia.

The limited amount of religious toleration in pre Soviet Russia gave way to an openly hostile approach to religious communities after the revolution where the Soviet authorities divided religious communities into those who were supportive of the state and those who were a threat to it.[36] This conceptual approach retained currency in state approaches to religious minorities in post-Soviet Russia evidenced by a 'tendency to label adherents of non-traditional religions "sectarians" and harass them, as well as to identify the religious figures who were most loyal to the government, ultimately creating the foundation for the new regime's legitimacy by promoting the Russian Orthodox Church (ROC) as a symbol and pillar of state ideology.'[37]

This policy of promoting an acceptable conception of traditional religion manifested itself in restrictive legislation in 1997 in the form of the Federal Law on freedom of conscience and religious associations (no. 125-FZ of 26 September 1997—"the Religions Act").[38] This Act conceived religions to be either traditional, such as Islam, Judaism, Buddhism, Orthodox, or non-traditional. Provisions on establishment of a religious organization were changed such as, under Article 9, to restrict the founders to being Russian citizens and Article 11 provided a 15 year probation period for a religious organisation to operate within the jurisdiction in order to access the benefits of registration.[39]

The impact of this legislation on minority religions has been the subject of several judgments against Russia at the ECtHR.[40] For example, *Moscow Branch of the Salvation Army v. Russia* (2007) which concerned a Salvation Army group in Moscow. The Salvation Army had been present in Russia from 1913 but was dissolved in 1923 after being declared an anti-Soviet group. A group reformed in 1992 and as a result The Salvation Army resumed its activities in 1992 and was registered as a religious association. As a result of the 1997 Religions Act the group were required to re-register and ensure their articles of association complied with the current law by December 1999. The applicants attempted to do so in February 1999 but their application was refused and the Moscow authorities applied for the dissolution for the organisation. The ECtHR found that Russia was in breach of Article 11 read in light of Article 9 and reiterated the importance of the autonomy of religious groups in a democratic state:

---

[36] See Lunkin (2012).

[37] Lunkin (2012), pp. 157–8.

[38] See Durham and Homer (1998) for a detailed appraisal of this provision.

[39] See Lunkin (2012), p. 161.

[40] Note that there has been a softening of the 15 year requirement (Sibireva 2016) but recent legislative developments suggest that future Article 9 challenges are likely see BBC (2017).

> [T]he autonomous existence of religious communities is indispensable for pluralism in a democratic society and is thus an issue at the very heart of the protection which Article 9 affords. The State's duty of neutrality and impartiality, as defined in the Court's case-law, is incompatible with any power on the State's part to assess the legitimacy of religious beliefs.[41]

Jehovah's Witnesses of Moscow v. Russia (2010) is a similar case concerning a community of Jehovah's Witnesses in Russia which also resulted in a finding of a violation of Article 9 read with Article 11. In a strongly worded judgment the court found that a decision to dissolve the applicant community, revoke legal personality and to ban its future activities was disproportionate, indeed 'a blanket ban on the activities of a religious community belonging to a known Christian denomination is an extraordinary occurrence.'[42] The court identified that this was one of a number of instances following the enactment of the 1997 Religions Act where the Moscow authorities had neglected their duty of impartiality and neutrality by refusing the registration of religious groups, such as the Salvation Army and Scientologists which they described as 'non-traditional.'[43]

The pattern identified by the ECtHR in *Jehovah's Witnesses of Moscow v. Russia* (2010) was evidenced again in the case of *Church of Scientology of St Petersburg and Others v. Russia* (2014). Here the applicant Church was refused permission to register as a religious organisation under the Religions Act. In a withering judgment the ECtHR took pains to highlight the detrimental impact on religious minorities of the Religions Act:

> pursuant to Russia's Religions Act, a "religious group" without legal personality cannot possess or exercise the rights associated exclusively with the legal-entity status of a registered "religious organisation" – such as the rights to own or rent property, to maintain bank accounts, to ensure judicial protection of the community, to establish places of worship, to hold religious services in places accessible to the public, or to produce, obtain and distribute religious literature – which are essential for exercising the right to manifest one's religion … Thus, the restricted status afforded to "religious groups" under the Religions Act did not allow members of such a group to enjoy effectively their right to freedom of religion, rendering such a right illusory and theoretical rather than practical and effective, as required by the Convention.[44]

This is therefore one of significant line of cases where Russia has been found to be in violation of Article 9 due to its policy towards minority religious groups. The concluding section of this chapter will offer some remarks on how Hobsbawm's conception of invented tradition provides a useful perspective on this stream of ECtHR case law, and in doing so, illuminates our understanding of the relationship between law, religion and tradition.

---

[41] *Moscow Branch of the Salvation Army v. Russia* (2007) at [58].

[42] *Jehovah's Witnesses of Moscow v. Russia* (2010) at [155].

[43] Further cases concerning treatment of Jehovah's Witnesses in Russia seem likely to come before the ECtHR in coming years given recent policy developments. In July 2017 the Russian Supreme Court upheld the ban on Jehovah's Witnesses, confirming a ruling issued by an inferior court in April 2017 finding that they are an extremist organisation. See BBC (2017).

[44] *Church of Scientology of St Petersburg and Others v. Russia* (2014) at [38].

7 Inventing Traditional Religion

The discussion in Part IV has illustrated the difficulties that minority religions have encountered in achieving legal recognition, especially in ex-Soviet states. This difficulty has stemmed from the policy of domestic jurisdictions requiring religious groups to register in order to access the benefits that are associated with the status of legal personality, including the ability to hold property, engage with state institutions and enjoy the free exercise of the right of association for religious purposes. The ECtHR case law demonstrates that some ex-Soviet states have sought to create and enforce a distinction between 'traditional' and 'non-traditional' religions. This is clearly illustrated by recent legislation in Hungary and Russia which explicitly separates religious groups into these categories. This legislation demands that groups classed as non-traditional have the additional burden of registering as a religious group in order to enjoy the benefits that accrue from legal personality. The ECtHR case law also shows that domestic courts, especially in Russia, are more likely to refuse registration to religious groups that do not resemble acceptable forms of religiosity, as can be seen in the case law cited above in relation to Scientology, the Salvation Army and most recently in the active suppression of Jehovah's Witnesses.

The examples of unjustified refusals to register have been recognised by the ECtHR and the OSCE/ODIHR as a serious interference with the right to exercise freedom of religion, protected by Article 9 ECHR. The ECtHR has a developed jurisprudence which points to the importance of the conferral of legal personality to enable religious groups to have full access to the freedom of religion and association under Articles 9 and 11 of the ECHR.[45] Thus administrative obstacles to achieving this status which discriminate against minority religions conceived as non-traditional is a significant limitation on the freedom of religion.

How can this seam of ECtHR case law that has shown ex-Soviet jurisdictions to be so often in breach of Article 9 be explained? Given that not all European jurisdictions impose registration requirements on religious organisations it can appear puzzling as to what the purpose of these registrations requirements are, as Cranmer argues: 'Is its purpose to ensure legal certainty for those third parties who deal with such groups? Is it merely an obsessive pursuit of administrative tidiness? Or is there some more sinister motive?'[46]

One explanation that appears to have had currency in the period immediately after the accession of ex-Soviet states to the Council of Europe is that a period of adjustment was required for the new member states to align their legal systems with the normative framework provided by the European Convention and associated ECtHR jurisprudence. As discussed above this period led to the use of 'pilot judgements' by the ECtHR to provide robust guidance for how domestic authorities should comply

[45]This is an approach that has been firmly endorsed by the OSCE which asserts that 'obtaining legal personality status should be open to as many communities as possible, without excluding any community on the grounds that it is not a traditional or recognized religion or through excessively narrow interpretations or definitions of religion or belief.' (OSCE/ODHIR 2014 at [26]).

[46]Cranmer (2014).

with ECHR standards. Although this analysis might have held some force in the early part of the twenty first century, the ongoing violations of Article 9 and Article 11 experienced by minority or 'non-traditional' religious groups points to reasons other than the difficulties inherent in adjusting to the ECHR normative framework.

Hobsbawm's analysis of invented traditions provides a useful conceptual framework to approach this issue. As discussed in Part I of this chapter, Hobsbawm argues that modern nation states seek to present themselves as entirely natural manifestations of long established human communities that require no justification other than self-assertion.[47] This presentation is based on a conscious attempt to associate the state with suitable aspects of a distant past partly through the invention of tradition.

This analysis of the process by which new nations seek to consolidate political power and authority illuminates the way in which the nation states that emerged after the disintegration of the Soviet Union have actively sought to associate themselves with particular forms of 'traditional' religion while supressing other unsuitable or 'non-traditional' religions. Doing so can be viewed as an attempt to develop an association with acceptable forms of religious practice linked to an appropriate past. This has the effect of manufacturing a particular social consensus regarding what amounts to 'traditional' religion.

From both an historical and sociological perspective, the legislative distinction between traditional and non-traditional religious groups can be contested. Using Hobsbawm's terminology, it can be viewed as factitious. Fagan demonstrates that the religious history of Russia is far more diverse than this legislative distinction implies. The fact that most forms of religious expression were supressed during the officially atheist Soviet period and that the Salvation Army had a presence in Russia prior to the revolution is at odds with the presentation of minority religions being novel, invasive and destabilising loci of foreign influence. Likewise, the insights provided by sociologists of religion demonstrate that the binary and static categorisation of religious groups into 'traditional' and 'non-traditional' religious groups conceals the dynamic nature of religious practice.[48]

Applying Hobsbawm's analysis reveals the apparent intention behind the discriminatory treatment of minority religious groups is to construct a conception of the religious life of the nation which is consistent with and supportive of the political aims of the state. In the context of many ex-Soviet states, particularly Russia, this involves giving preferential treatment to the Orthodox Church seemingly as a means of cementing the authority of the current political regime, promoting group cohesion and buttressing the nation against perceived foreign influences.[49]

---

[47] Hobsbawm (1983), p. 14.

[48] Hammer and Rothstein argue that in this way religions resemble living organisms in that they change and develop over time. 'Established traditions also change, but do so at a pace that is so slow that their adherents manage very gradually to adapt, or even fail to notice any changes. An optical illusion thus sets time-honored religions in opposition to younger movements that can seem radically alien.' (Hammer and Rothstein 2012, p. 2).

[49] For a wider discussion on the symbiotic relationship between the Putin regime and the Russian Orthodox Church see Fagan (2013).

Thus Hobsbawm's analysis provides a useful conceptual framework to illuminate how the legislative and judicial apparatus has been used to actively shape conceptions of traditional religion for political purposes. In this way the case law cited above illustrating the marginalisation of minority religious groups in violation of the ECHR are, in Hobsbawm's terms, examples of the invention of tradition.

References

BBC (2017) Russia Jehovah's witnesses banned after they lose appeal. 17 July [Online]. Available at http://www.bbc.co.uk/news/world-europe-40635267. Accessed 9/08/2017

Bielefeldt H (2012) Report of the special Rapporteur on freedom of religion or belief, A/HRC/22/51 [Online]. Available at http://www.ohchr.org/Documents/Issues/Religion/A.HRC.22.51_English.pdf. Accessed 9/08/2017

Blackstone W (1765) In: Sharswood G (ed) Commentaries on the laws of England in four books. J.B. Lippincott Co., Philadelphia (this edition 1893) [online]. Available at http://oll.libertyfund.org/titles/2140. Accessed 30/09/2016

Council of Europe (2004) Resolution Res (2004) 3 of the Committee of Ministers on judgments revealing an underlying systemic problem. 12 May [Online]. Available at: https://search.coe.int/cm/Pages/result_details.aspx?ObjectId=09000016805dd190. Accessed 09/08/2017

Cranmer F (2014) Registering religious groups and Article 9 ECHR: scientology and Russia. In: Law & religion UK, 4 Oct [Online]. Available at http://www.lawandreligionuk.com/2014/10/04/registering-religious-groups-and-article-9-echr-scientology-and-russia/. Accessed 9/9/2017

Doe N (2011) Law and religion in Europe. OUP, Oxford

Durham W, Homer L (1998) Russia's 1997 law on freedom of conscience and religious associations: an analytical appraisal. Emory Int Law Rev 12(1):101–246

Evans C (2010) Individual and group religious freedom in the ECtHR: cracks in the intellectual architecture. J Law Relig 26(1):321–344

Fagan G (2013) Believing in Russia—religious policy after communism. Abingdon, Routledge

Hammer O, Rothstein M (2012) Introduction to new religious movements. In: Hammer O, Rothstein M (eds) The Cambridge companion to new religious movements. Cambridge University Press, Cambridge, pp 1–10

Hobsbawm E (1983) Introduction: inventing traditions. In: Hobsbawm E, Ranger T (eds) The invention of tradition. Cambridge University Press, Cambridge, pp 1–14 (reprinted Cambridge, Canto, 1995)

Lunkin R (2012) The status of and challenges to religious freedom in Russia. In: Hertzke A (ed) The future of religious freedom: global challenges. OUP, Oxford

Naffine N (2010) Author's introduction: the law of persons. Aust J Legal Philos 35:111–115

Note (2001) What we talk about when we talk about persons: the language of a legal fiction. Harvard Law Rev 114(6):1745–1768

OED (2016) 'Person' [Online]. Available at http://www.oed.com.libezproxy.open.ac.uk/view/Entry/141476?rskey=BsdqXD&result=1. Accessed 09/08/2017

OSCE/ODHIR (2014) Guidelines on the legal personality of religious or belief communities [Online]. Available at http://www.osce.org/odihr/39046?download=true. Accessed 09/08/2017

Peroni L (2014) Deconstructing "legal" religion in Strasbourg. Oxford J Law Relig 3(2):235–257

Sadurski W (2009) Partnering with Strasbourg: constitutionalisation of the ECtHR, the accession of Central and East European States to the Council of Europe, and the idea of pilot judgments. Human Rights Law Rev 9:397–453

Sibireva O (2016) Freedom of conscience in Russia: restrictions and challenges in 2015 [Online]. Available at http://www.sova-center.ru/en/religion/publications/2016/04/d34317/. Accessed 09/08/2016

Smith B (1928) Legal personality. Yale Law J 37(3):283–299
US State Department (2015) International Freedom of Religion Report [Online]. Available at https://www.state.gov/documents/organization/256199.pdf Accessed 3/09/2018
Venice Commission (2012) Act CCVI of 2011 on the right to freedom of conscience and religion and the legal status of churches, denominations and religious communities of Hungary, CDL-REF(2012)009-e [Online]. Available at http://www.venice.coe.int/webforms/documents/CDL-REF%282012%29009-e.aspx. Accessed 9/08/2017

Case Law

Biserica Adevarat Ortodoza din Moldova and Others v Moldova App no. 952/03 (ECtHR, 27 February 2007)
Church of Scientology of St Petersburg and Others v. Russia App no 47191/06 (ECtHR, 2 October 2014)
Cumhuriyetçi Eğitim ve Kültür Merkezi Vakfi v Turkey [2014] ECHR 1346
Dimitrova v Bulgaria [2015] ECHR 152
Jehovah's Witnesses of Moscow v. Russia (2010) 53 EHRR 4
Jehovas Zeugen in Osterreich v. Austria App no 27540/05 (ECtHR, 25 September 2012)
Kokkinakis v. Greece (1994) 17 EHRR 397
Magyar Keresztény Mennonita Egyház and Ors v Hungary (2014) ECHR 552
Magyar Keresztény Mennonita Egyház and Ors v Hungary (Just Satisfaction) [2016] ECHR 593
Metodiev and Ors v Bulgaria [2017] ECHR 568
Moscow Branch of the Salvation Army v. Russia (2007) 44 EHRR 912
Religionsgemeinschaft der Zeugen Jehovas and Others v. Austria (2008) 48 EHRR 424
Salomon v Salomon and Co (1897) AC 22
Somerset v Stewart (1772) 98 ER 499

Law and Religion in a Detraditionalized Europe

Zachary R. Calo

Abstract This essay employs the concept of tradition to analyze law and religion cases from the European Court of Human Rights. It argues that Europe is undergoing a detraditionalization process that has altered how religion informs individual and collective meaning. Law, in turn, gives shape to this process. From the perspective of tradition, recent decisions involving public religious symbols, Islamic headscarves, and conscience claims are revealed to have participated in this transformative social process.

1 Europe After Tradition

This essay employs the concepts of tradition and detraditionalization to examine recent European debates about law and religion. Particular attention is given to the jurisprudence of the European Court of Human Rights. The concern, however, is not simply with law and religion, but with how this jurisprudence reveals deeper impulses concerning the shape of European culture, the construction of social meaning, and, the experience of selfhood.

Although not coterminous, religion and tradition overlap in significant ways. Tradition, for purposes of this essay, is understood as the process by which a community understands itself and transmits that understanding across time. By extension, it concerns the ways in which individuals relate to collective forms of meaning. Religion is an essential component of tradition and for some, such as Christopher Dawson,

Z. R. Calo (✉)
Hamad bin Khalifa University, Doha, Qatar
e-mail: zacharycalo@gmail.com

Z. R. Calo
University of Notre Dame Australia, Sydney, Australia

Z. R. Calo
The Open University Law School, Milton Keynes, UK

J. Giles et al. (eds.), *Law, Religion and Tradition*, Law and Religion in a Global Context 1, https://doi.org/10.1007/978-3-319-96749-3_7

"A society which has lost its religion" will also lose tradition.[1] Commenting on Dawson, Rowan Williams similarly proposed that the declining role of religion in society imperils the possibility of traditions surviving. For Williams, a tradition is not a static form of being and believing, but an ongoing conversation within a framework of shared understanding. The loss of religious understanding as an animating social force accelerates the "end of history."[2] This end of history is not some cataclysmic civilizational collapse but rather the cessation of inquiry into human nature and human flourishing. With this end of history, the concern with such matters simply ceases to have a compelling hold on collective imagination. Without a grounding in a tradition or traditions, in other words, the capacity of a society to support a critical encounter with the deepest meanings of the human experience is hindered. Pope Benedict seems to have something similar in mind when he writes that Europe is losing its "history" and "roots," which he identifies as linked specifically to Christian identity.[3] What Benedict fears is that the loss of a religiously-grounded identity will destroy the coherence Europe as an ongoing experiment in collective inquiry and understanding. Without the resources of religious traditions and Christianity in particular, there will not be a sustained conversation about what values Europe should even embody. Removing the Christian dimension of European identity undermines Europe itself.

These ideas lead to the unexpected proposition that tradition is needed for social dynamism. While tradition is often seen as a conservative force that frustrates change and development, Williams and Benedict suggest that achieving a future requires the givenness of a past. To participate in a tradition is to live into in an ongoing reality that invites a dialogical encounter between the given and the not yet. Shared forms of understanding cannot evolve from a position of nowhere. Tradition, that is, places limits upon what persons can individually and collectively become. The future is not pure possibility. Persons are not complete masters of themselves. Personhood is rather achieved through an encounter with an authority outside the self. Tradition invites and indeed requires such conversation. Thus, far from being a roadblock to the emergence of new understanding, tradition is essential to progress. When Williams and Benedict speak of the end of history and the loss of memory, they are identifying the challenge of sustaining a dynamic social order without an anchor in tradition. The choice is not between tradition or progress, but tradition or chaos.

Lieven Boeve has produced particularly insightful writings on the relationship between religion and tradition in Europe. In his assessment, the current European situation is best characterized in terms of "detraditionalization." Boeve defines this concept as follows:

> Detraditionalization as a term hints at the socio-cultural interruption of traditions…which are no longer able to pass themselves from one generation to the next. The latter definitely applies to the Christian tradition in which the transmission process has been seriously hampered. Christianity no longer is the given and unquestioned horizon for individual and social

[1] Dawson (1933), 115.

[2] Williams (2008).

[3] Ratzinger and Pera (2007).

> identity.... On the contrary, because of the absence of such unquestioned and quasi-automatic transmission of tradition, identity is no longer given but has to be constructed.[4]

While Boeve introduces the concept primarily in reference to European Christianity, the concept could be applied more broadly to refer to other religious traditions and even non-religious traditions. Detraditionalization, though, is particularly useful in that it speaks not only to changing patterns of religious belief and observance but, more fundamentally, to the ways in which social meaning and moral order are created, sustained, and conveyed. Detraditionalization focuses on the disruption of Christianity's role as a culture-forming tradition that is able to inform conceptions of self and society.

When discussed in connection with religion, detraditionalization overlaps with the theory of secularization but also goes beyond it. A detraditionalized Europe is not simply a secular Europe unshackled in various ways from the impositions of religion.[5] To the extent that Europe has defined itself against something, it is not simply religion but normative traditions that give ongoing life to authoritative sources of meaning. The resulting social order is characterized by a void of thick meaning, a vacant space governed by no ideology, including secularism. Religion is perhaps the most insistant obstacle to the achievement of a detraditionalized reality, but it is not the only one. Detraditionalization thereby manifests itself not in a simple doctrinaire opposition to religion. What detraditionalization targets is religion as a cultural and life-forming force. It is a tradition that resists traditions.

Detraditionalization is an account of collective social change, but it most pointedly impacts the individual experience of being and becoming in the world. This quintessential human task of making the self is being fundamentally refashioned within Europe. In premodern societies, Charles Taylor observes, one could not image oneself outside of a fixed social order. The possibilities for self-creation were limited by the fact that "self-understanding was embedded in society."[6] While modernity breaks down these fixities, and opens space for new experiences of selfhood, detraditionalization pushes the process to its more totalizing completion. It frees the self to encounter a world that is a flattened moral plane defined by openness and possibility. Along these lines, Rowan Williams writes that a constitutive feature of modern Europe:

> is the belief that what is most uniquely human is a capacity for 'self-creation' – for the making of choices that will establish a secure place in the world and shape an identity that is not determined from outside, determined by social power that acknowledges no accountability or by doctrines and models that have no public evidence to support them.[7]

The "European enterprise," Williams adds, is defined by a belief that "the essence of the human task is *defining yourself*." The cultivation and realization of authentic

---

[4] Boeve (2005), 104–105.

[5] Boeve (2005), 107.

[6] Taylor (2004), 55–66.

[7] Williams (2008).

selfhood, in other words, becomes the quintessential experience of authenticity.[8] It is a project that has no end, but rather involves, in Russell Sandberg's apt characterization, the self "constantly being created and recreated, negotiated and renegotiated."[9] Detraditionalization is both a continuation and an acceleration of what begins with modernity. It is a way of speaking about the world that emerges when cultural vestiges of traditions are pushed away.

Law is central to detraditionalization. It shapes and reinforces detraditionalized space and mediates the experience between individual, community, and society therein. Because of the foundational role of religion in shaping tradition, law and religion debates are particularly useful for assessing this process.[10] In what follows, the essay considers how understandings of religious tradition have informed law and religion jurisprudence in recent judgments of the European Court of Human Rights. Three cases are considered: *SAS v. France* (2014), *Eweida v. United Kingdom* (2013), and *Lautsi v. Italy* (2011). Examining these law and religion cases from the perspective of tradition brings a new interpretive lens to this field of jurisprudence. It is not infrequently asserted that these cases reveal a contest between religious and secular values, and to some extent this is correct.[11] However, framing debate on these terms misses a critical dynamic, for what is occurring in law is not primarily a contest for the supremacy of one normative value system over another, but the emergence of a reality that moves beyond the categories of religious and secular. These cases concern different issues, and result in what might initially seem contrary decisions, but detraditionalization provides a framework for identifying a common process that is reshaping the moral account of self and society in Europe.

---

[8]Public life in turn, Williams adds, "organises the aspirations of individuals in such a way that they don't interfere with each other too dramatically." There are circumstances in which the aspirations of self-creation on the part of individual will conflict with those of another. In these instances, the violence of the law makes choices about how to carve into the ambitions of one for the sake of another. Williams (2008). Pope John Paul II makes a similar point in his 1995 encyclical letter *Evangelium Vitae*, in which he discusses "the promotion of the self…understood in terms of absolute autonomy." The concept of freedom, the Pope argued, has become linked to a form of anthropological individualism in which that prioritizes the project of become the maker and master of the self. *Evangelium Vitae*, Section 20.

[9]Sandberg (2015), 1.

[10]See Fokas (2015), 54–75.

[11]See, for instance, the provocative statements of former Anglican Bishop of Rochester Michael Nazir-Ali. Bishop joins row over right to wear the cross (2012).

2 Islam, Christianity, and the European Court of Human Rights

2.1 *SAS v. France*

SAS concerned the compatibility of a 2010 French law banning face coverings in public with the European Convention on Human Rights, including Article 9.[12] The law was generally understood to have targeted Muslim women who wore a full-face veil, and the applicant was a devout Muslim who wore the burka and niqab on certain occasions as an expression of religious faith.

Given that the law clearly interfered with the exercise of religion, the central question before the Strasbourg Court was whether the law could be justified under Article 9 as being "necessary in a democratic society in the interests of public safety, for the protection of public order, health or morals, or for the protection of the rights and freedoms of others." The French government maintained that the law was designed both to advance public safety and democratic values.

As stated in an explanatory memorandum accompanying the bill, "The defence of public order.... also makes it possible to proscribe conduct which directly runs counter to rules that are essential to the Republican social covenant, on which our society is founded The systematic concealment of the face in public places, contrary to the ideal of fraternity, also falls short of the minimum requirement of civility that is necessary for social interaction." Moreover, permitting the wearing of the full veil entailed a "breach of the dignity of the person" and a conspicuous denial of the equality between men and women.[13] Only a ban could preserve French political and social values from the symbolic and substance challenge posed by this practice.

In its judgment, the Court held the ban to be permissible under the European Convention insofar as it sought to establish conditions necessary to the sustentation of democratic values. Although exhibiting a certain hesitation, the Court concluded that it could "understand the view that individuals who are present in places open to all may not wish to see practices or attitudes developing there which would fundamentally call into question the possibility of open interpersonal relationships, which...forms an indispensable element of community life."[14] From this starting point, the Court found it acceptable to limit certain rights in order to create "a space of

---

[12]Article 9 provides: 1. Everyone has the right to freedom of thought, conscience and religion; this right includes freedom to change his religion or belief and freedom, either alone or in community with others and in public or private, to manifest his religion or belief, in worship, teaching, practice and observance; 2. Freedom to manifest one's religion or beliefs shall be subject only to such limitations as are prescribed by law and are necessary in a democratic society in the interests of public safety, for the protection of public order, health or morals, or for the protection of the rights and freedoms of others. The European Convention on Human Rights and its Five Protocols, Council of Europe, Nov. 4, 1950.

[13]*SAS v. France*, App. No. 43835/11, §25 ECHR 2014. The applicant, by contrast, characterized wearing the veil as an act of emancipation, self-assertion, and participation in society. *Id.* at §77.

[14]*Id.* at §122.

socialization which makes living together easier."[15] While the law impedes religious expression, it is an appropriate mechanism for upholding the values of pluralism, tolerance, and democracy.[16]

The Court addressed a number of other cases arising from bans on Muslim dress prior to *SAS*. This line of cases is notable in that the Court has consistently held that limitations on the wearing of Islamic dress by women are not violative of Article 9 rights.[17] By one measure, this judgment can be read as exhibiting a conventional reliance on the margin of appreciation, as in these prior cases. As the Court stated, regarding "Article 9 of the Convention, the State should thus, in principle, be afforded a wide margin of appreciation in deciding whether and to what extent a limitation of the right to manifest one's religion or beliefs is 'necessary'."[18] The Court added that, "It indeed falls within the powers of the State to secure the conditions whereby individuals can live together in their diversity," thus seeming to disclaim a deep role in analyzing the substantive legal issues at stake.[19] Both in its deference to domestic judgments, as well as its connecting bans on religious dress to the sustentation of pluralism, *SAS* does little to change existing jurisprudential patterns.

At the same time, this case presents facts that bring into relief certain impulses more occluded in the earlier cases. Even if this matter is located primarily in the line of cases about laique bans, it is not in the end only about face coverings and secularism, but Islam, European self-understanding, and the relationship between religion and tradition. In particular, what this case reveals is the extent to which law is being employed to advance a process of detraditionalization. *SAS* is particularly important because it expressly links the effacement of religious identity with the sustentation of liberal values. As such, the Court sanctions the use of law to separate a person from the substantive experience and expression of her tradition. In unmasking, the law is detraditionalizing. In fact, the Court impliedly adopts a binary framing of the situation in which two forms of tradition—religion and liberal freedom—stand in a posture or irreconcilable tension. Judges Nussberger and Jäderblom drew attention to this point in their dissent, noting that bans on the full-face veil are linked to "interpretations of its symbolic meaning."[20] The veil embodies values, and is constitutive of a tradition that is antithetical to a free society and a free self. In the Government's view, women who wore the veil were "effaced" from public life.[21] It is the role of the Court to

[15] See Footnote 14.

[16] *Id.* at §153.

[17] These cases include *Dahlab v. Switzerland*, App. No. 42393/98, ECHR 2001; *Leyla Sahin v. Turkey*, App. No. 44774/98, ECHR 2004; *Dogru v. France*, App. No. 27058/05, ECHR 2009. For a critical analysis of these cases see, Calo (2010), 261–280. More recently, the Court considered Belgian's ban on the full veil. See, *Belcacemi and Oussar v. Belgium*, App. No. 37798/13, ECHR 2017; *Dakir v. Belgium*, App. No. 4619/12, ECHR 2017.

[18] *SAS v. France*, App. No. 43835/11, §129 ECHR 2014.

[19] *Id.* at §141.

[20] *SAS v. France*, App. No. 43835/11 (dissenting opinion of Judges Nussberger and Jäderblom), §6 ECHR 2014.

[21] *SAS v. France*, App. No. 43835/11, §§77, 82, 85 ECHR 2014.

free these women from the burdens of their tradition, to make them members of the liberal public through a forcible unmasking.

It is notable that the Court does not expressly connect its defense of the ban with secular values. Indeed, the case is only superficially about secularism and religion. To read the Court's judgment as the imposition of doctrinaire laicism ignores the extent to which this case has the effect of undermining all ideology. The issue, as the Court frames it, is not a contest between the religious and the secular, but rather strong forms of religion that impose values onto free persons and the void of public life. The aim of living together on which the Court rests its decision is accomplished through denying persons their particularity. The public is a space in which persons must be literally unmasked from the weight of tradition through the liberation of law. Law frees so that women might create themselves.

This case also reveals the distinct ways in which Islam is informing and advancing the process of European detraditionalization. Headscarves and facial coverings serve a particularly important role by symbolizing forms of strong tradition against which the Court positions itself. Yet, this framing of Islam does not prompt the Court to advance a counter-tradition, be it Christian or secularist. While it has been argued that presence of Islam illuminates the extent to which European law and culture remain tethered to residual if eviscerated Christian presuppositions, *SAS* does not entail the reassertion of Christianity so much as resistance to a tradition that imbues thick moral meaning into public understanding. The problem with Islam is not that it threatens Christianity or secularism but a hallowed detraditionalized Europe.

A central feature of religious experience in a detraditionalized society is primacy of individual freedom and choice. As the Belgian government stated in its intervention, its government "had sought to defend a model of society in which the individual outweighed any philosophical, cultural or religious attachments."[22] It is in this respect that Islam has played a defining role in the detraditionalization process. The fully veiled woman, who herself represents Islam, carries the burden of tradition which the state must relieve. As Mark Hill notes, "it is the very concept of obligation (and, by extension, coercion) within Islam" that is viewed as inimical to liberal values.[23] Islam reminds Europe of the urgency and aims of detraditionalization.[24]

2.2 *Eweida and Others v. UK*

Eweida and Others v. UK, particularly the matters involving Lillian Ladele and Gary McFarlane, offers a useful companion to *SAS*.[25] Ladele and McFarlane were both

---

[22] *Id.* at §88.

[23] Hill (2016), 332.

[24] See Bhuta (2014), 9–35.

[25] The case of *Eweida and Others v. The United Kingdom* involved four consolidated cases. The analysis here focus on the disputes involving two of the claimants, Lillian Ladele and Gary McFarlane.

Christian claimants who objected on the grounds of religious conviction to performing professional activities involving homosexual couples. Ladele was employed as a registrar of births, deaths, and marriages in the London Borough of Islington. The Civil Partnership Act of 2004 provided for the legal registration of civil partnerships between two persons of the same sex and, in December 2005, Islington designated all existing registrars of births, deaths and marriages as civil partnership registrars. In accordance with her Christian convictions, Ms. Ladele believed same sex civil partnerships to be contrary to God's law and she refused to participate in their registration. She was informed that her refusal to do so could put her in breach of the employment code of conduct. In the ensuing litigation, the Court of Appeal concluded that Ms. Ladele's desire to have her religious views respected should not be allowed "to override Islington's concern to ensure that all its registrars manifest equal respect for the homosexual community as for the heterosexual community."[26]

McFarlane worked as a counsellor for Relate, a private organization that provides sex therapy and relationship counselling services. McFarlane confirmed to his employer that he had difficulty reconciling his Christian beliefs with working with same-sex couples.[27] McFarlane was eventually dismissed from his employment, after which he lodged a claim with the Employment Tribunal. In a 2009 judgment, the Tribunal found that McFarlane had not suffered direct discrimination because under the Employment Equality (Religion or Belief) Regulations 2003 he had not been dismissed because of his faith but because it was believed he would not comply with Relates' polices. Moreover, the Tribunal found that while these policies would put an individual who shared McFarlane's religious beliefs at a disadvantage, they served the legitimate aim of providing counselling services without respect to sexual orientation. The Employment Appeal Tribunal likewise rejected McFarlane's claim, noting that Relate was entitled to refuse to accommodate views counter to its fundamental principles.

The European Court dealt with these two matters was somewhat cursorily. Ladele had brought her complaint under Article 9 of the European Convention, taken in conjunction with Article 14. She maintained that she had been discriminated against on the grounds of religion and that the government had not demonstrated a reasonable relationship between its aims and the discriminatory practices.[28] The Court noted "the strength of her religious conviction" and also acknowledged that "it cannot be said that, when she entered into her contract of employment, [she] specifically waived her right to manifest her religious belief." At the same time, the Court concluded in finding against the claimant that, "the local authority's policy aimed to secure the rights of others" and "national authorities are given a wide margin of appreciation" in balancing competing Convention rights.[29]

---

[26]*Eweida and Others v. The United Kingdom*, Apps. Nos., 48420/10, 59842/10, 51671/10 and 36516/10, §§23-30 ECHR 2013.

[27]*Id.* at §§31–40.

[28]*Id.* at §§70–72.

[29]*Id.* at §106.

In assessing McFarlane's claim, the Court similarly acknowledged that his "objection was directly motivated by his orthodox Christian beliefs about marriage and sexual relationships" and that his refusal to undertake certain counselling activities was a manifestation of these beliefs.[30] McFarlane's position was that the margin of appreciation afforded to limitations on freedom of religion must advance the goal of protecting "true religious pluralism."[31] In determining whether the state had struck a fair balance with respect to competing rights, the Court noted that the applicant had knowledge of Relates' policies concerning sexual orientation prior to accepting employment. While this fact alone does not establish whether or not there has been interference with Article 9 rights, the Court found that, on balance, authorities had acted within their permissible margin of appreciation in refusing to find for McFarlane. The most important factor for the Court was that because the employer was implementing a non-discrimination policy, it should be granted a particularly "wide" margin of appreciation.[32]

As with *SAS*, these cases might be seen to evidence an antireligious or more specifically anti-Christian bias. This was the position of former Archbishop of Canterbury Lord Carey who argued that the cases in Eweida revealed that, "The secular human rights agenda has gone too far."[33] These decisions might also be seen as privileging legal claims of equality over those of religious freedom. Such arguments are not without basis, but they fail to diagnose the more elemental dynamics at work in this jurisprudence. The anti-Christian bias of which Carey spoke, or the privileging of equalitarianism over religious freedom, are symptoms of the detraditionalization process. Recognizing faith-based exemptions for Ladele and McFarlane would permit tradition to impose itself upon moral life. In the end, these cases are not narrowly about religious rights, but the normativity of tradition as it relates to individual and collective meaning within society.

If the effect of *SAS* was to liberate persons from the grip of tradition, Eweida liberated society from the encroachments of tradition. It did so by advancing an implicit account of religion as interiorized, individualized, and disconnected from community. Indeed, the fact that this case involved Christian claimants is significant in that European Christianity, unlike Islam, is understood to be already in large measure detraditionalized. By severing the connection between faith and action, and by pushing religion more fully into the private and noetic, the Court gives legal sanction to an already regnant arrangement. Yet the decision does more than define belief in these ways. It also limits the capacity of persons to participate fully in communities of inquiry and meaning. By reducing the claimant's religion to interior belief, these judgments isolate persons from embodied moral traditions. A tradition cannot exist apart from a community and the attendant institutions and practices through which tradition is enacted and sustained over time. This decision has the

[30] *Id.* at §108.

[31] *Id.* at §73.

[32] *Id.* at §109.

[33] Christians face judgement day in Strasbourg 'right to wear the cross' case (2013).

effect of cutting off persons from such a reality and limiting the capacity of traditions to carve moral meaning into the world.

It is not surprising that these disputes involved conflict between religious freedom and sexual rights. While religious freedom claims might come into conflict with any number of countervailing rights, sexual identity maintains a particularly central role in the anthropology of the detraditionalized society. Authentication of the sexual self has come to represent the essence of freedom that law should affirm and protect. It is the capstone of the project of self-creation that lies at the heart of a detraditionalized social space. Moreover, realization of the authentic sexual self is what becomes fully possible once the imprint of religious tradition is circumscribed. In this respect, religion and sexuality play key oppositional roles in the unfolding drama of detraditionalization. Their interplay also reveals the implicit teleology at the root of a detraditionalized order. Although this order is properly seen as one shorn of ends, defined instead by openness and possibility, there is also an implicit privileging of a certain kind of authenticity. Detraditionalization is not a neutral process.

2.3 *Lautsi v. Italy*

The much-discussed case of *Lautsi v. Italy* raises different issues from those in *SAS* and *Eweida*.[34] At first glance, this case would seem to fit awkwardly within a narrative of detraditionalization, as its holding permitted the retention of a form of public religiosity. Yet read differently, *Lautsi* does not reveal the weakness of detraditionalization so much as the extent to which it is already completed.

Lautsi concerned the permissibility of Italy displaying crucifixes in public schools. The applicant alleged that this practice was contrary to the principle of secularism according to which she wanted to raise her children.[35] In the Chamber judgment, the Court took that view that states must "refrain from imposing beliefs, even indirectly, in places where persons are dependent on it or in places where they are particularly vulnerable."[36] As applied to this case, the Court found that the "crucifix may easily be interpreted by pupils of all ages as a religious symbol" and that this might prove "emotionally disturbing" to children of a different faith or no faith.[37] As such, Italy had violated the right to freedom of religion under the European Convention.

In the subsequent Grand Chamber judgment, the Court reversed this decision and found in favor of Italy. The opinion gave particular attention to the Government's position "that the presence of crucifixes in State-school classrooms, being the result of Italy's historical development...gave it not only a religious connotation but also an identity-linked one, now corresponded to a tradition which they considered it important to perpetuate." In particular, the Government emphasized that the crucifix

---

[34] See, e.g., Temperman (2012).

[35] *Lautsi v. Italy*, App. No. 30814/06, §7, ECHR 2009.

[36] *Id.* at §48.

[37] *Id.* at §55.

was connected to the secular values of democracy and western civilization.[38] In light of these considerations, the Court took the view that the decision of "whether or not to perpetuate a tradition" lies within the margin of appreciation.[39]

It is tempting to read the Grand Chamber judgment not only as an endorsement of public religiosity, but as a statement on the importance of tradition and history as ongoing sources of meaning. After all, the language of tradition appears throughout the judgment. The Courts speaks, for instance, of putting crucifixes in classrooms as "a matter of preserving a centuries-old tradition."[40] The Court also referenced discussions of tradition in the submissions of third party interveners. A joint submission from French, German, and Italian nongovernmental organizations urged the Court to "leave a wide margin of appreciation to the States in this area because the organization of the relationship between state and religion varied from one country to another and...was deeply rooted in the history, tradition and culture of a country."[41] The concurring opinion of Judge Bonello added that, "[a] European Court should not be called upon to bankrupt centuries of European tradition."[42] Yet, these and other references to the enduring importance of tradition belie the extent to which the Court's decision sanctions an account of tradition that is not living and culture-forming, but a hollow historical vestige from which religious significance was already drained.

Even though the Grand Chamber judgment permitted Italy to continue displaying crucifixes in classrooms, this decision does not represent a challenge to detraditionalization. Rather, the Court's decision rests on defining the cross as lacking religious significance or projecting a predominantly religious message. While the Court describes the crucifix as "above all a religious symbol," it adds that "there is no evidence...that the display of the religious symbol on classroom walls may have an influence on pupils."[43] The reason for this conclusion seems to be that, although associated with Catholic Christianity, the crucifix has become a "passive symbol."[44] This language of "passive" is the same used by the United States Supreme Court in a case involving public displays of the Ten Commandments.[45] As with the Supreme Court, the European Court invokes this term to indicate that the symbol is divested of its original theological meaning. The crucifix, in other words, does not impose and project meaning into the public. It lacks power to impinge on the religious freedom of the claimant. It is an artifact of tradition that might be understood in a historical and cultural context, but does not hold a connection to a living tradition that seeks to actively shape public moral understanding. Passivity, in other words, speaks to the detraditionalized character of the crucifix.

---

[38] *Lautsi v. Italy* [GC], App. No. 30814/06, §67, ECHR 2011.
[39] *Id.* at §68.
[40] *Id.* at §36.
[41] *Id.* at §55.
[42] *Lautsi v. Italy* [GC] (concurring opinion of Judge Bonell), App. No. 30814/06, §1.2, ECHR 2011.
[43] *Lautsi v. Italy*, App. No. 30814/06, §66, ECHR 2009.
[44] *Id.* at §36.
[45] *Van Orden v. Perry*, 545 U.S. 677 (2005).

The passivity of the crucifix is what, in turn, allows the Court to endorse its continued presence in the classroom. While the Court's judgments in *SAS* and *Eweida* pushed back against forms of meaning that violated the norms of a detraditionalized order, such resistance was unnecessary in *Lautsi*. Even the Italian government's position in the case conceded that the "message of the cross was…a humanist message which could be read independently of its religious dimension and was composed of a set of principles and values forming the foundations of our democracies."[46] The Court does not need to detraditionalize the cross or impose meaning on it. The Court only has to reveal reality for what it has already become. The Court's understanding of the cross as already detraditionalized is made apparent in its somewhat pained attempt to distinguish the facts in *Lautsi* from those in *Dahlab v. Switzerland*, a case which the Court had upheld a prohibition on a Muslim primary school teacher wearing a headscarf in the classroom.[47] While the Court offers a number of observations about the unique situation in Italy, the essential difference ultimately concerns the perceived power of the headscarf to still project strong meaning in a way the crucifix does not.

Lautsi illuminates how detraditionalization works to cut society off from historical meaning. A detraditionalization crucifix is not as an ongoing source of meaning but a historical adornment of the past that has no bearing on the present. It undermines the dialectic by which traditions shape meaning in the world. Detraditionalization is thus not simply a forgetting of the past but an end to the possibility of conversation. In this respect, *Lautsi* is a particularly revealing of what Rowan Williams and Pope Benedict had in mind when speaking of Europe losing a sense of history. Although the Court talks about the historical and symbolic import of the crucifix, it does not imply that the symbol represents an ongoing tradition. The past is ossified and rendered morally nugatory. The crucifix is safe precisely because it does not—it cannot—impose meaning. It poses no challenge to the open social space unrestrained by the lingering presence of religion. Viewed in light of tradition, the categories of secularism and Christianity contribute little to an analysis of what is finally at issue in the case. Although the case attracted international attention and became a referendum on these competing systems of meaning, such a framework is largely inapposite. The process by which religion is being shaped by law is not primarily through a frontal engagement with secularism but a more subtle reworking of cultural meaning.

3 Religion and the Future of Tradition

Detraditionalization is not likely to be reversed, even as the void it opens remains a site of ongoing contestation. Still, the experience of detraditionalization has provoked counter-efforts to retraditionalize Europe by imposing a stable ordering narrative upon it. While these initiatives have taken many forms, they tend to identify in the past

---

[46] *Lautsi v. Italy*, App. No. 30814/06, §35, ECHR 2009.

[47] *Lautsi v. Italy* [GC], App. No. 30814/06, §73, ECHR 2011.

an account of Europe that offers resources for contemporary renewal. Resurrecting the idea of Christian Europe has proven particularly attractive in the current cultural climate. In certain forms, the idea of Christian Europe is a response to secularism, in others Islam. The two are often combined. For instance, one million Polish Catholics recently gathered along the country's borders to recite the rosary and pray, according to Krakow Archbishop Marek Jedraszewski, for "Europe to remain Europe." The Archbishop added that "we need to return to the Christian roots of European culture if we want Europe to remain Europe." While the official theme of "Rosary at the Borders" was to pray for Europe, it also took on an anti-immigrant and anti-Muslim tone. Christianity and Islam were defined as irreconcilable traditions, both living, but one native and one foreign, competing for the soul of Europe.[48]

Among the more compelling accounts of Christian Europe are those offered by Popes John Paul II and Benedict XV. Loeven Boeve summarizes the popes as arguing that "[o]nly a Europe that rediscovers its Christian roots can survive."[49] For John Paul and Benedict, a Europe without the Christian tradition is unstable and ultimately incoherent. There is no Europe apart from Christianity. As such, the public task of the Church is to reassert an account of Europe that finds its grounding in Christian belief and proclamation. It is "in the Christian tradition," John Paul II writes, that Europe's values are fully realized.[50] The Christian tradition makes possible the European tradition.

It is notable that John Paul and Benedict describe retraditionalization in terms of memory. For both popes, connection to a particular history gives meaning to the present. John Paul II, for instance, writes that "*the loss of Europe's Christian memory and heritage*" has "squandered a patrimony entrusted…by history."[51] Both also invoke the language of "roots" to describe the link between Christianity and Europe.[52] It is rootedness in Christianity that grounds the historic achievement and ongoing reality of European civilization.[53] Without Christianity, there is no Europe. From this perspective, retraditionalization is not a top-down project to be achieved through law, but one whose transformation must work from the bottom-up through culture. The task before the Church, as John Paul II and Benedict frame it, is to sustain the idea Europe being tethered to Christianity. The Church works within culture to sustain a civilizational narrative about what Europe is and should become. This understanding will of course have implications for law, but law exists downstream from culture.

---

[48]While Pope John Paul II and Pope Benedict XVI have developed the intellectual case for retraditionalization, this impulse equally finds a more populist expression. Approximately one million Polish Catholics recently gathered to pray the rosary along the country's borders. described the event as a prayer for "Europe to remain Europe." Polish Catholics Gather at Border for Vast Rosary Prayer Event (2017).

[49]Boeve (April 2007), 205.

[50]Pope John Paul II, *Ecclesia in Europa* (2003), §19.

[51]*Ecclesia in Europa*, §7.

[52]*Ecclesia in Europa*, §§7, 19, 25; See also, Ratzinger and Pera (2007).

[53]*Ecclesia in Europa*, §19.

It might be that religion provides the best, perhaps the only, significant challenger to detraditionalization. Yet this Catholic project, whatever its attractiveness, is not going to stem the tide of cultural erosion. There will not be a return to a Christian order. The counter-forces are deeper and more elusive than the popes seemingly acknowledge. The problem is not primarily a shift of people away from traditional Christian beliefs, as if a sociological uptick in self-identified Christians could sustain the work of retraditionalization as the popes frame it. The problem is rather with how belief is experienced and enacted. Dominant patterns of belief undermine the very resources and practices that support tradition.

The most critical factor is the growing individualization of religious life in which, as Boeve notes, Christians have "distanced themselves from the Churches."[54] Deinstitutionalization, in this respect, is a component part of detraditionalization. Deinstitutionalization might include a number of related phenomena, ranging from the diminished authority of institutions to the withdrawal of persons from participating in communal practices.[55] At base, deinstitutionalization results in the meaning-seeking and meaning-creating individual being the primary the source of authority. Collective forms of identity, embodied in institutions, give sustaining life to tradition. Without them, there cannot in any meaningful sense be tradition. Tradition ceases to exist when the individual is the source of meaning. The anthropology of detraditionalization, in which the individual is elevated above collective meaning, mitigates against any attempt to reconstitute tradition.

Law does not cause deinstitutionalization, but it affirms and reinforces the process. Given this state of affairs, it is unsurprising that institutions are increasingly a main site of contest within law and religion debate. Whereas the most pitched debates used to concern matters of individual religious freedom, the focus in Europe and elsewhere has shifted to institutions and such questions as the ministerial exception and religious autonomy. These debates often arise in connection with conflicts between religious freedom and neutral generally applicable laws, such as employment or antidiscrimination statutes. It is often assumed that these tensions have arisen as a result of new flashpoints involving such matters as sexuality. Yet the debate is not simply about conflicts between religious freedom and equalitarian norms, but also the distinctive importance of institutions. Institutions have become so central because they are the vehicle by which communities sustain and transmit tradition. It is through institutions that collective meaning is given embodied expression. In the collective, the individual is made part of something larger than the self and made subject to a source of authority outside of the self. As such, tradition-forming institutions are likely to find themselves more engaged in legal disputes and ever more legally vulnerable.[56]

---

[54] Boeve (2005), 104.

[55] The privatization of religion has been notably described by Grace Davie in terms of "believing without belonging." Davie (1990), 455–469.

[56] The European Court of Human Rights has addressed the issue of institutional religious freedom in a number of recent cases. On the whole, the Court has been generally protective of institutional religious freedom, though it has achieved this result more through a pragmatic balancing test than

In spite of these challenges, there is not a straight line that runs from detraditionalization to a legal assault on religious freedom. It is not infrequently asserted that there exists an anti-Christian bias working its way through law. George Carey, for instance, has criticized judges for allowing equalitarian claims to override individual religious freedom.[57] The trouble with such critiques is that they do not fully wrestle with the ways in which religious freedom is healthy and even expanding, particularly at the individual level.[58] This situation exists not in spite of, but because of, detraditionalization. After all, religion is an important means by which persons pursue meaning and define selfhood. Detraditionalization, by clearing away the obstacle of tradition, creates greater space within law for affirming such experiences. What is problematic within a detraditionalized environment is not religion as such, but forms of religion that interfere with the liberating impulse of detraditionalization. To put the matter simply, detraditionalization discriminates between types of religion. Just as former UK Prime Minister Tony Blair spoke of the "two faces of faith"—a framework that divides religion into good and bad forms—so too does detraditionalization draw lines between tolerably anodyne religion and world-forming religion.[59] It likewise distinguishes between individual forms of religion and collective forms of religion. There is a subtle violence to the encounter between religion and the dynamics of detraditionalization.

Detraditionalization manifests itself in ways that are not straightforward or predictable. The current legal environment is beset with complexities and contradictions. What detraditionalization does illuminate is a Europe increasingly defined by a legal impulse to push back against strong systems of meaning in individual, collective, and public forms. Yet, detraditionalization is not so much created by law but revealed through it. And while law is useful for examining the detraditionalization process, it might also be the case that law will become an increasingly marginal site of contestation.[60] Law pushes back against tradition and, in the process, relinquishes its authority as a source of tradition. Law might remain a guardian of detraditionalized social space, but legal wrangling with religion will be ever less important in defining the boundaries of this space.

---

assertion of a strong legal principle. *Obst v. Germany*, App No 425/03, ECHR 2010; *Schüth v. Germany*, App 1620/03, ECHR 2010; *Siebenhaar v. Germany*, App. No. 18136/02 (2011); *Fernández Martínez v. Spain*, App. No. 56030/07 (2012).

[57] George Carey: time to say that Christians have rights too (2012).

[58] See, Calo (2014).

[59] On Tony Blair's talk of the "two faces of faith," see Shakman Hurd (2015), Chap. 2.

[60] One notable expression of this is the attention given by Christian thinkers to offer new ways of exercising faith in a world that increasingly lacks legal and cultural crutches. Rather than examining ways of retraditionalization the social order, through law, politics, or even culture, some thinkers have moved to thinking instead about ways to create and maintain community in a detraditionalized society. Talk of the Benedict Option, faithful presence, and Christians as a "creative minority," to name just a few examples, all offer programs for defining and sustaining community in a post-Christian environment. Dreher (2017). On the concept of faithful presence, see Hunter (2010). For Pope Benedict's discussion of Christians as "creative minorities," see "Europe and Its Discontents," *First Things* (January 2006).

As detraditionalization progresses, an important question will be whether a new tradition or traditions can fill the resulting void? Whether, and in what form, a detraditionalized society can endure is a related matter with which Europe must now wrestle. Must something replace the traditions that have been pushed aside?[61] Above all, what can hold Europe together? Can human rights, for instance, provide a source of collective moral meaning to replace religion?[62] Will the presence of Islam hasten detraditionalization, as it provides more fuel for the process, or stall the process by forcing Europe to wrestle with constructive approaches to accommodation? Detraditionalization does not answer these questions but helps to diagnose the sources of the current crisis in meaning and its implications for law and religion.

References

European Court of Human Rights

Belcacemi and Oussar v. Belgium, App. No. 37798/13, ECHR 2017
Dahlab v. Switzerland, App. No. 42393/98, ECHR 2001
Dakir v. Belgium, App. No. 4619/12, ECHR 2017
Dogru v. France, App. No. 27058/05, ECHR 2009
Eweida and Others v. The United Kingdom, Apps. Nos., 48420/10, 59842/10, 51671/10 and 36516/10, ECHR 2013
Fernández Martínez v. Spain, App. No. 56030/07 (2012)
Lautsi v. Italy, App. No. 30814/06, ECHR 2009
Lautsi v. Italy [GC], App. No. 30814/06, ECHR 2011
Leyla Sahin v. Turkey, App. No. 44774/98, ECHR 2004
Obst v. Germany, App No 425/03, ECHR 2010
SAS v. France, App. No. 43835/11, ECHR 2014
Schüth v. Germany, App 1620/03, ECHR, 2010
Siebenhaar v. Germany, App. No. 18136/02, ECHR 2011

United States Supreme Court

Van Orden v. Perry, 545 U.S. 677 (2005)

[61] Boeve makes claim that, "Institutes cannot survive without common convications." Boeve (April 2007), 215.

[62] On the religious impulse within the human rights movement, see Hopgood (2006).

Books and Articles

Bhuta N (2014) Two concepts of religious freedom in the European Court of human rights. South Atlantic Q 113(1):9–35
Bishop joins row over right to wear the cross. The Telegraph (28 Apr 2012)
Boeve L (2005) Religion after detraditionalization: Christian faith in a post-secular Europe. Theological Q 123(70):99–122
Boeve L (Apr 2007) Europe in crisis: a question of belief or unbelief? Perspectives from the Vatican. Mod Theol 23(2):152–179
Calo ZR (2010) Pluralism, secularism, and the European Court of human rights. J Law Relig 26:261–280
Calo ZR (2014) Constructing the secular: law and religion jurisprudence in Europe and the United States. European University Institute Working Papers, available at http://cadmus.eui.eu/bitstream/handle/1814/32792/RSCAS_2014_94.pdf
Christians face judgement day in Strasbourg 'right to wear the cross' case. The Telegraph (12 Jan 2013)
Davie G (1990) Believing without belonging: is this the future of religion in Britain? Social Compass 37(4):455–469
Dawson C (1933) Religion and the life of civilisation. In: Enquiries into religion and culture. Sheed and Ward, New York
Dreher R (2017) The benedict option: a strategy for Christians in a post-Christian nation. Sentinel, New York
Fokas E (2015) Directions in religious pluralism in Europe: mobilizations in the shadow of European Court of human rights jurisprudence. Oxford J Law Relig 4:54–74
George Carey: time to say that Christians have rights too. The Telegraph (11 Feb 2012)
Hill M (2016) The changing landscape of law and religion in Europe. J Law Relig 31(3):321–335
Hopgood S (2006) Keepers of the flame: understanding amnesty international. Cornell University Press, Ithaca
Hunter JD (2010) To change the world: the irony, tragedy, and possibility of Christianity in the late modern world. Oxford, New York
John Paul II (1995) Evangelium Vitae
John Paul II (2003) Ecclesia in Europa
Polish catholics gather at border for vast rosary prayer event. New York Times (7 Oct 2017)
Pope Benedict XVI. Europe and its discontents. First Things (Jan 2006)
Ratzinger J, Pera M (2007) Without roots: the west, relativism, Christianity, Islam. Basic Books, New York
Sandberg R (2015) In Sandberg R (ed) "The Impossible Compromise" in religion and legal pluralism. Ashgate, Burlington, pp 1–20
Shakman Hurd E (2015) Beyond religious freedom: the new global politics of religion. Princeton University Press, Princeton
Taylor C (2004) Modern social imaginaries. Duke University Press, Durham
Temperman J (ed) (2012) The Lautsi papers: multidisciplinary reflections on religious symbols in the public school classroom. Martin Nijhoff, Leiden
Williams R (Jan 26, 2008) Europe, faith, and culture. Lecture, Liverpool Cathedral

Tradition as a Peacebuilding Tool

Jessica Giles

Abstract The concept of tradition, rather like that of secularism, has come to mean different things to different people in a variety of contexts. This Chapter explores an understanding of tradition as that group of rules or practices which sits alongside core governing texts of groups within civil society. It identifies tradition as that which facilitates the contextualisation of civil society groups over time. It then examines how tradition could be used as a tool for engendering peaceful civil society relations. To do this it first explains the rationale for identifying plural religious traditions as important for strong civil society building, including for the protection of fundamental rights and the socio-economic well-being of a nation. Tradition is then proposed as a means of countering the exclusion of plural religious voices from the public square arising both as a result of the secular narrative manifesting itself in extreme forms of *Laïcité* and as a result of forms of theocracy and confessionalism. The chapter does this by identifying the development of the concept of tradition, setting out dictionary definitions, definitions within the discipline of law and their interaction and links with definitions within the three Abrahamic faiths. The overarching thesis drawing these threads together is that the various methods of forming and using tradition by intermediate institutions of civil society could inform the creation of a platform as a dialogical basis to build consensus amongst individuals, institutions of civil society and governments. This envisages a plurality of religious voices not as a threat but rather as a richly diverse canvas upon which to paint the interactions of civic life and formulate the law that governs those interactions.

1 Introduction

Fragmentation of communities and societies has been occurring throughout history as various factors have led to the breakdown in peaceful relations between individuals, civil society groups and nation states. What has changed from time to time is the

---

J. Giles (✉)
The Open University, Milton Keynes, UK
e-mail: j.a.giles@open.ac.uk

J. Giles et al. (eds.), *Law, Religion and Tradition*, Law and Religion in a Global Context 1, https://doi.org/10.1007/978-3-319-96749-3_8

root causes of this breakdown. A recurring theme occurring in various guises is the polarization of views around the role of religion in civil society. Extreme modern forms of secularism manifesting in a laic model of government which ultimately exclude the expression of any form of religion from public life on the one hand contrast with forms of governance seeking to impose one particular and sometimes fundamentalist view of religion upon civil society. At both ends of the spectrum plural religious voices are excluded from public life.

This chapter explores why the inclusion of plural religious voices is important for the building and maintaining of peaceful civil society relations. It identifies tradition as a tool for creating a dialogical platform to facilitate this process.

The polyvalent character of tradition, whereby it consists of a number of different forms and purposes depending on context and usage, means that providing a single explanation is challenging. Attempting to synthesise the various definitions and methods of forming tradition to come up with a core definition by boiling the various interpretations down to their very essence or by comparing and contrasting definitions to identify unifying elements would fail to do justice to the sophisticated, nuanced and deeply thought-through approaches to the concept both within and external to the different faiths.

It is proposed that the very nature of various traditions, including religious traditions, provides a means of taking a multivalent approach to dialogue, enabling various routes to be identified in order to build consensus around the common good, law creation and adjudication. This directly contrasts with forms of bivalent reasoning which create stark contrasts between right and wrong leading to a need for correct and incorrect answers. It is argued instead that within these various understandings of tradition lies the key to a multivalent dialogical platform for engagement built on a nuanced consensus across institutions of civil society. Consequently, this study does not seek to identify one 'correct' definition of or method of forming tradition, but to use the various understandings to create a platform for dialogue and building consensus.

2 The Need for Plural Religious Traditions in the Public Square

The constitutional mechanism used for supporting religious pluralism in democratic constitutional structures is to build the right to freedom of religion into a bill of rights or to rely on forms of national or international law, including legislation protecting a spectrum of civil and political rights.[1] In essence this protects freedom of religion

[1]For example, Article 9 of the European Convention on Human Rights, incorporated into the law of England and Wales in the Human Rights Act 1998 and Article 18 of the International Covenant on Civil and Political Rights.

and belief as an individual right to manifest religious belief.[2] This is an important tool in the fostering of plural living together. Conversely a form of plural society is necessary in order for religious freedom to be enjoyed as a fundamental right. Rights frameworks are not and should be the only means of fostering and protecting plural living together, and while they provide the essential framework for it, the proposal in this chapter is that more needs to be done to create plural dialogue within civil society and to strengthen civil society groups, including religious ones. Plural religious voices expressed by faith traditions can be said to be important to peaceful civil society building on various grounds.

First, from a philosophical and theological perspective. Religious traditions themselves have much to contribute within their own philosophical theological literature on civil society building, human dignity, human flourishing and the common good.[3] This includes support for a plural society incorporating freedom of religion. Freedom of religion, both the *forum internum* (to believe) and *forum externum* (to practice), is regarded by many as essential to human dignity and human flourishing.[4] Freedom of religion can only be practiced within a plural society where religions are able to peacefully co-exist.[5] Building a platform for dialogue to include religions and in order for wider society and government to understand religious groups, is arguably not only vital for peaceful civil society relations but also is bound up with and important for the protection of human dignity and flourishing.

---

[2]Freedom of association is also protected as a fundamental right, however when they refer specifically to religion, rights frameworks protect it as an individual right.

[3]For example, Williams (2008, 2010) both as Master of Magdalene College, Cambridge and as the Archbishop of Canterbury, Metropolitan of the Province of Canterbury and Primate of All England (2002–2012) argues for religious integrity coupled with plural living together. Within the Christian reformed tradition theologians such as Abraham Kuyper, Herman Dooyeweerd, Nicholas Wolterstorff and Jonathan Chaplin explore Christian theological approaches to civil society; within the Roman Catholic tradition theologians such as Robert George and John Finnis; within Judaism authors such as Sacks and Walzer (ed) 2006. Although concerns have been raised as to whether or not democracy can flourish where Islam is the dominant faith: see Esmer (2013). However, Indonesia with its political philosophy of Pancasila would be an example of a Muslim majority country which promotes pluralism. In Indonesia there are six official religions. The political system operates on the basis of deliberative consensus emphasising representative democracy.

[4]The right to freedom of religion or belief is seen by Witte and others as the first or core fundamental right upon which the effective operation of rights frameworks depend (Witte 2007, 2). According to Witte, freedom of religion as a universal right, was established within nation states constitutional frameworks in Europe, and later in America, at least since the reformation. Some authors trace freedom of religion, as a right of the church to be free from state interference, back to the Magna Carta (Witte 2007; Griffith-Jones and Hill 2015, 3 ff). Witte in fact traces its origins even further back to the Edict of Milan 313.

[5]Bielefeldt, Ghanea and Wiener identify the importance of religious pluralism to support the right to freedom of religion and belief. They argue that pluralism goes beyond the anti-egalitarian politics of toleration and avoids the pitfalls of post traditional unification projects which fail to account for diversity (Bielefeldt et al. 2016), 6–7, 14–16. Following on from a rich Christian theological, as well as secular philosophical tradition, they discuss human dignity as the universal unifying factor, Bielefeldt et al. (2016), 16–21. Although this is not historically the only basis put forward as justification for freedom of religion or belief: see McIlroy (2013).

At an international level, rights frameworks incorporating freedom of thought, conscience and religion are based on the idea that they are universal. To find universal acceptance these rights frameworks need to find theoretical justification within faith traditions as well as secular philosophy. This is because in many states religion rather than the absence of religion is the norm. Rights frameworks are at danger of being perceived as underpinned by Western liberal democratic ideals or even forms of colonialism, divorced from the reality of religious daily living, understandings of human dignity and the common good and models of governance in place.[6] Consequently, further debate still needs to take place between religious and non-religious traditions. This is in order to find an acceptable basis for rights frameworks, potentially adopting multivalent forms of theological and philosophical reasoning accounting for differing underlying rationales. Ultimately either to find ways in which to contextualise rights implementation or to identify common ground for law creation and adjudication and to conceptualise a workable understanding of the common good.

It is proposed that a common understanding or conceptualization of the common good can be established within the various faiths in dialogue with institutions of civil society through the disparate traditions of those institutions—that by drawing upon the common practices and beliefs that create cohesion between members of civil society groups *intra se* it is possible to create the basis for dialogue between groups (*inter se*). This is because the tradition of a group is generally that which enables it to contextualize over time. Sacks argues that this avoids assimilation on the one hand and multiculturalism on the other but rather that this integrates diversity based on the concept of covenant built around the common good. It is based on cooperation rather than competition and individual self-interest (Sacks 2007, 23).

A second reason for the inclusion of a plurality of religious voices in the public square engaged in building consensus is based on a Weberian rationale. Religion can be deemed of importance to cohesive living together in society on a socio-economic basis.[7] According to the Pew Centre, over 84% of the 2010 global population registered an adherence to a faith and 55% registered adherence to one of the Abrahamic faiths.[8] Faith groups have an impact and influence in society in manifold ways. Grim and Grim (2016) at the Religious Freedom and Business Foundation argue that religion contributes nearly $1.2 trillion of socio-economic value to the US economy. Earlier research by Grim (2014), and Grim and Finke (2011), demonstrated a link

[6]For example, Dr. Mahathir Mohamad, former Prime Minister of Malaysia and Lee Kuan Yew, former Prime Minister of Singapore, advocates of Asian values, argue that human rights are culturally relative to Western societies. Although Devan Nair, former president of Singapore has argued for the universality of human rights. For academic debate on the issue see Inoguchi and Newman (1997), Khong (1997) and Sen (1997). For a discussion of the clash between the universalisms of Islam and human rights frameworks, see Cox (2013).

[7]Weber (1905) argues that religion creates a framework which shapes an individual's understanding. It thus affects their understanding of their interests and how they decide to act. Within this framework soteriology provides both relief from suffering and reassurance of meaning. Religion can thus provide an incentive for individuals to act less selfishly, in the interests of the common good.

[8]Pew Research Centre (2012). Of these .2% were Jews, 31.5% were Christians and 23.3% were Muslims. Consequently 55% adhered to the Abrahamic faiths. 16% were unaffiliated, 15% were Hindu, 7% Buddhists, 6% folk religionists and 1% other religions.

between those nation states where Government restrictions on religion and social hostilities involving religion are low and high levels of GDP growth. Conversely that where religious freedom is limited, levels of violent religious persecution and conflict tends to be high. This indicates that in order to facilitate the stability that occurs with increased levels of GDP growth, in particular in those states where civil society has broken down or where there is poverty which can also lead to rights abuses, increasing dialogue between faith traditions and empowering plural engagement of religious groups with other institutions of civil society and government could create a positive impetus towards change.

The Pluralism Project, established by Professor Diana Eck in the Divinity School at Harvard[9] and Eck (2009) in the Gifford Lectures, explore the positive impact of religious diversity in America. In particular how the communities and religious traditions of Asia and the Middle East have been woven into American life and culture. It explores thc challenges and opportunities of a commitment to pluralism. In the UK the *Living with Difference Report* of The Commission on Religion and Belief in British Public Life (2015) acknowledges the importance of hearing and engaging with different faith groups in public life, calling for an increased public dialogue and religious literacy in the public square.[10] Pluralism is supported as of practical benefit to society by faith groups themselves as well as NGOs and IGOs in the field.[11]

Plural social interaction can be said to be dependent on tradition. This is because within the three Abrahamic faiths, for example, tradition, that is those rules and practices that sit alongside core scriptures, plays a key role in providing the locus where rules for daily living are formulated. Tradition therefore directly affects the lives of believers and for many operates as a compass to orientate lived experiences and social interactions. Any consideration of cohesive living together within society, law creation and adjudication by implication consequently needs to take into account theological understandings of the concept of tradition. In this way meaningful social interaction and dialogue can take place.

Moves to work towards plural living together have to counter the strong push towards forms of secularism.[12] Vanoni and Ragone (2018) make a comparison between the strong laic form of secularism which seeks to drive the religious voice

[9]See in particular Pluralism Project @ 25 (2016).

[10]See also Casey (2016).

[11]This includes, for example, interreligious work of organisations such as KAICIID (founded by the Kingdom of Saudi Arabia, The Republic of Austria and the Kingdom of Spain, with a Board of Directors made up of representatives from major world religions): https://www.kaiciid.org; the Community of Sant'Egidio (officially recognised by the Catholic Church as a church public lay association): https://www.santegidio.org/pageID/30008/langID/en/THE-COMMUNITY.html; The Institute for Global Engagement (founded by the first US Ambassador at Large for Religious Freedom): https://globalengage.org; The Religious Freedom in Business Foundation: https://religiousfreedomandbusiness.org; The Faith and Belief Forum: http://www.3ff.org.uk; Global One 2015: https://globalone.org.uk/about-us/our-vision-mission/ (All accessed on 20 April 2018).

[12]Evidenced recently in the case of *Achbita and another v G4S Secure Solutions NV* (Case C-157/15) OJLR 2017 6(3): 622–623.

out of public life and, for example, the more moderate form of Italian *laicitá*. The later seeks, in some instances, to accommodate religion, albeit using weaker forms of justification, on the grounds of historical importance or cultural relevance.[13] Vanoni and Ragone point to the practical illogicality of the principle of neutrality and attempts to exclude religion altogether from public life.[14]

The third basis for inclusion of plural religious voices in civil society building is because a dialogical approach between religions, institutions of civil society and law makers, creating a plural public square, will have the effect of supporting the democratic legitimacy of the law-making and adjudication processes. This is because the lived reality of those within faith communities will consequently stand some chance of being reflected in law and law will find a broader basis of support. Vanoni and Ragone (2018) see attention to faith groups and their traditions as essential to the just resolution of religious freedom disputes. They include this approach in their proposals for a third way as a tool for judges when addressing legal issues which implicate religions.[15] In addition, religions are likely to feel less threatened and more likely to surrender those elements of their tradition established as mechanisms to protect core identity when under threat.[16] This will tend to increase the likelihood of accommodation of religion within civil society and by religion of civil society.

The fourth ground supporting engagement with religious traditions in civil society building is that this can facilitate the integration of minorities and immigrant communities. The argument of this chapter is that by using tradition as a platform for dialogue it is possible for civil society groups and states to retain their core identity and integrity while managing to find their own varied paths to work towards an agreed common good. The inclusion of the religious traditions of immigrant and refugee populations is particularly important in view of the fact that there are more than 65 million displaced persons across the globe.[17] Religion is likely to be the one constant that individuals are able to take with them as they flee their home. It is also likely to be that which could facilitate integration in host states. This is not only because of the emotional and spiritual support provided by a person's faith, but because faith groups tend to create supportive communities over and above that which can be offered by the state and can create welcoming environments for incoming immigrants and refugees.[18]

---

[13]For example see the Grand Chamber judgment of the European Court of Human Rights in *Lautsi v Italy* Application no 30814/04 [2011] ECHR 2412.

[14]This is echoed by Bielefeldt et al. (2016), 35–38.

[15]Further support can be found in the writing, for example of Newbigin (1989), Williams (2008) and Sacks (2007).

[16]The wearing of the veil within the Islamic tradition would be an example of this. Although contested, for some it represents a religious requirement and for others a cultural choice.

[17]UNHCR Refugee Agency (2017).

[18]Although in some cases religion can act as form of oppression, creating microcosms of communities from which refugees have fled: see Open Doors (2014). Such experience supports the pressing need to hear the religious voice of migrant communities in a dialogical manner so as to enable contextualisation within host communities.

Finding a means to envisage immigrant and refugee communities within the concept of the common good through dialogical approaches located in the traditions of immigrant communities addresses some of the concerns raised by Pin (2014, 419). Pin is troubled by the use by member states of rights frameworks to reinforce national identity in attempts to integrate migrants from plural backgrounds. Where there is a sense that civil society institutions and civil society itself can retain its core principles, but that a degree of mutual accommodation and contextualisation is required for communal peaceful coexistence to occur, states and existing civil society institutions can recognise and welcome the rich diversity that immigrant communities have historically brought and continue to bring. Seeing integration as a one-way process ignores the strength that incoming faith traditions bring as communities and individuals linked to a broader and potentially global network of faith. Seeking a dialogical approach arguably stands a greater chance of facilitating integration and contextualisation rather than seeking to impose legal and social frameworks alien to immigrant culture and tradition which is likely to have a ghettoizing effect.[19] As Pin writes:

> people, including newcomers, do not simply receive human rights: they also actively contribute to their conception and reconsideration, as religious and cultural traditions interact openly in shaping a common narrative of rights and duties. (Pin 2014, 437)

Dialogue with immigrant communities, which are in and of themselves an important part of the jigsaw puzzle that is involved in rebuilding broken host communities, could in fact enable Western democratic liberal models to understand how to communicate a more nuanced and contextualised idea of universalism of rights frameworks. These frameworks could consequently stand a chance of finding greater acceptance in non-Western nation states.

The fifth ground for considering religious traditions within a dialogical approach to consensus and peacebuilding is that globally religion can be said to be on the agenda in terms of foreign policy and international development, as states grapple with the breakdown of civil society and extreme poverty in the Middle East, Africa, parts of Asia and elsewhere.[20] The inclusion of religious freedom in external state policy requires a coherence with internal policies. Offering aid coupled with a requirement that a fragile state promote religious freedom is, as Annicchino and Ventura point out, only feasible where religious freedom is fostered in the home state (Annicchino 2014, 257–263).[21] A coherent approach to freedom of religion or belief requires a certain level of religious literacy and a willingness to incorporate various religious

[19]For example, see the Casey (2016).

[20]For example, in 2016 the European Union appointed a Special Envoy for Religious Freedom outside the EU, Dr. Ján Figeľ: https://ec.europa.eu/europeaid/special-envoy-jan-figel_en (date accessed 20 April 2018) and speaking at the opening of the European Academy of Religion, Italy 15 December 2016 https://www.youtube.com/watch?v=QE_-0tpmEfE and at the Institute for Cultural Diplomacy: Annual Conference on Cultural Diplomacy: 5 January 2017 https://www.youtube.com/watch?v=iimjLKoGk6g.

[21]See for further analysis Giles (2017).

traditions openly in civic life at home in order to use this fundamental right as a policy tool abroad.

Sixth, faith groups play an essential role in society as intermediate institutions. Using religious traditions to feed into a platform for plural dialogue increases the likelihood of their effectiveness in this role. The role of intermediate institutions is explored by Chaplin (2011) and Benson (2012). Chaplin, in his examination of the political philosophical theology of Dooyeweerd, identifies Dooyeweerd's concerns that there is a deep-rooted problem in ignoring plural living together. He analyses Dooyeweerd's theory that intermediate institutions, including faith bodies, act as a buffer within civil society between the universalizing tendency of the state and the individualism of members of civil society. He then goes on to explore how subsidiarity might be applied to refine this theory in order to fit contemporary society (Chaplin 2011, 14–16[22]). Scriven (2013) identifies that a political system needs to avoid undue concentrations of power while at the same time requiring a common vision of the common good to which society should aspire. Sacks (2007) describes this as "the home we build together". This then is the challenge for pluralism and the potential for normative institutional pluralism. Intermediate institutions of civil society can act to create a form of cohesion where no one group becomes too powerful so as to dominate others but where a sufficient vision of the common good enables peaceful coexistence. It is suggested that religious groups are able to use their traditions to work with other civil society institutions to facilitate strong plural living together between civil society institutions.

A seventh ground supporting the inclusion of the plural religious voice in civil society building is to counter the pervasive fear which is a reaction to forms of violent extremism and terrorism. This is to ensure that the vulnerability of some to radicalisation is not exacerbated by a lack of understanding of the various forms of religion and their practical outworkings. Also, to ensure that those members of the various faith groups who have nothing to do with violence and terror are not tarred with the same brush as those who do. Fostering plural living together based on a dialogue between religions and between those of no faith encourages religious literacy and understanding. It also could act as a tool to tackle the environment in which radicalisation can occur.

3 The Problematic Nature of Tradition

The use of tradition as a platform for institutions of civil society is not without potential for manipulation and misuse. Such misuse has been explored by Stopler in her work on equality rights. Stopler (2003) addresses the issue of entrenched or orthodox faith traditions underpinning the denial of basic rights and lacking widespread democratic consent in society, even within western liberal democratic traditions. She argues that despite being based on egalitarian principles western liberal democracies

[22]See also Benson (2010).

nevertheless support and even protect sex-discrimination on the basis of religious and cultural principles (Stopler 2003, 154ff.).

The problematic nature of tradition is also considered by McFaul (2018), Bakhshizadeh (2018) and Qureshi (2018). McFaul identifies how a state can invent or manipulate tradition so as to define which groups constitute a religion and to accord legal personality to those religions it deems worthy of recognition. Exploring Hobsbawm's concept of invented tradition and using Russia as an example, he identifies how a state is able to manipulate religious tradition in order to put forward one form of faith as the state religion and exclude specific groups from legal recognition.

In the context of Iran Bakshizadeh explores the problems that arise when religious and legal traditions become fixed so that the implementation of international norms becomes problematic. Qureshi explores a similar phenomena in relation to the blasphemy laws in Pakistan. He demonstrates how fundamentalist religious tradition combines with legal tradition to produce fixed blasphemy laws.

Ghanea (2017), Bakhshizadeh (2018) and Ravitch (2016, 2018), sound a note of optimism as they explore how faith traditions and national and international legal traditions can work together to improve rights protection. Ghanea proposes that the synergies between freedom of religion and women's rights be revitalised. Bakhshizadeh explores justification within Islamic tradition for the acceptance of international human rights norms to inform law reform in Iran. Ravitch considers four faith traditions, including Japanese Zen Buddhism, Roman Catholicism, American Episcopalian Christianity and American Conservative Judaism, and their approach to same-sex relations in order to explore how faith can inform social coexistence.

Calo (2018), considers a far more pervasive problem, namely de-traditionalization, that is the stripping away of cultural and social surrounds in order that individuals are liberated to seek personal authenticity. He identifies that the temptation here for religion is to seek to withdraw from, rather than engage with, a process of re-traditioning or at least with a living in diversity. This is a grassroots, as well as a legal and political, challenge and threatens the stability that is linked to the development of tradition over time, in the present and in the future. While it may not be possible to force dialogue upon civil society, facilitating dialogue by providing opportunities for it at whatever level members of society find acceptable would do something to counter this trend of de-traditionalization. Sacks makes a strong argument countering this focus on the self, in favour of a shared ethic which he terms a 'counter-fundamentalism of love' (Sacks 2005, in particular Chap. 4).

A dialogical approach set in a framework of normative institutional pluralism would work particularly well for groups which have established methods and forms of reasoning facilitating adaptation to cultural context.[23] This model needs further refinement to deal with the cultural phenomena identified both by Calo above and by Putnam and Campbell. Putnam and Campbell (2010) describe pluralism as a lived reality in society in the USA, pointing, however, to growing polarization and culture

[23] Strong support for a dialogical approach between faith traditions from within the Christian faith was put forward by Newbigin based on his theological training and lived experience as a missionary in India Newbigin (1989).

wars. They evidence a falling away from the effectiveness of intermediate institutions in facilitating plural living together. This is juxtaposed against an increase in personal interfaith ties, in particular through marriage and an acceptance of the interreligious in public life, echoing Calo's concerns over de-traditionalization. This is, according to Putnam and Campbell, despite a continuing strong link between religion and patriotism. They identify fluidity of religious belief as a mark of American society which mutes interreligious tensions because of strong interpersonal ties. Arguing that as long as these ties can sustain a common understanding of the public good, plural living together is likely to be sustained in the USA (Putnam and Campbell 2010).[24] The danger, however, of relying too heavily on individual, interpersonal ties is that the faith basis for these can more easily be eroded, in particular, without the presence of faith communities and without strong ties between intermediate institutions of civil society. It is these groups that provide the essential cohesion for society and a voice for religious concerns in public life. The individual voice is easily lost. The voice of a faith group is more easily heard.

In contrast to the USA, the United Kingdom sits somewhat uneasily between a constitutional settlement incorporating an established church supportive of a plural society bolstered by freedom of religion and belief on the one hand and increasing pressure from European rights jurisprudence seeking to enforce strong forms of *Laïcité*[25] and a public policy of 'neutrality' on the other. Ahdar and Leigh (2013) describe this as the British Kulturkampf. Recent evidence demonstrates that despite enjoying an established religion there are factors, including a general lack of religious literacy, which mitigate against a plural public square: see the Commission on Religion and Belief in British Public Life (2015).

An additional factor undermining positive understandings of tradition is the manner in which violent extremist groups have used religious tradition as justification for their own political or other ends. This has led both consciously and subconsciously to a public fear in particular of Islam but also of religion in general. If this fear is allowed to undermine the potential value of religions and their contribution to civil society it will exacerbate the pervasive effect of this fear, fragmenting society.[26]

For the reasons identified above it is argued that tradition can potentially provide a platform for dialogue between institutions of civil society in a manner which could lead to consensus building and cohesion both nationally and internationally. This will require thought as to how to engage with increasingly individualistic outlook and understandings of identity and religion which mitigate against cooperation and collaboration at an intermediate level. It will also require the use of mechanisms to protect against negative use of tradition by states and other actors.

Having explored the reasons for enquiring into the concept of religious tradition, this chapter will now examine various definitions of tradition to identify how tradition as a concept could provide a platform for dialogue between institutions of civil society.

---

[24]See in particular Chap. 1.

[25]See D'Costa et al. (2013) and Giles (2017).

[26]For further discussion on this see: Giles (2018).

4 Defining Tradition

The following section explores the definition of tradition in various loci including dictionary definitions, tradition within the law and within the Abrahamic Faiths. It does so to identify how elements from these traditions could be harnessed to create a multivalent dialogical platform to foster strong intermediate institutions and build consensus around the common good, law creation and adjudication. The ultimate aim being to create capacity for strong civil society building.

Dictionary definitions tend to recite and reinforce modern understandings of the concept of tradition, rooting this, in some cases, first in Judaism, then Christianity, followed by Islam. Taking Judaism as a starting point the Oxford English Dictionary (OED) (2002. 2017 update, 'Tradition')[27] defines tradition as:

> An ordinance of the Oral Law not in the Torah but held to have been delivered by God to Moses and transmitted orally from generation to generation; these ordinances considered collectively, constituting the Mishnah

De Lange (1986, 24) identifies eight different types of tradition within Judaism.[28] Tradition as a core concept within Judaism has its roots in the very early practices of Judaism whereby the *Torah* (the first five books of the law handed down by Moses) was supplemented by oral explanations of the rules for daily life which interpreted and built upon the Written *Torah*, these subsequently became known as the Oral *Torah*, the *Torah* then came to be interpreted to form a body of Jewish religious law named *halakhah*. It is *halakhah* that has the strongest resonance with the modern-day understandings of the concept of tradition. In Judaism the essence of the word tradition, *masoret*, is passing something on.

The linguistic roots of the word "tradition" are also found in the Latin verb *tradere*, 'to hand down' or 'to bequeath'; in Greek *Paradosis*. The OED, further explores its use within the Abrahamic faiths:

> The action or an act of imparting or transmitting something; something that is imparted or transmitted.
>
> A belief, statement, custom etc., handed down by non-written means (esp. word of mouth, or practice) from generation to generation; such beliefs, etc., considered collectively.
>
> In early use often used critically, e.g. with reference to Jewish practices and Catholic teachings.

In so far as it relates to theological use of that term the OED reads:

> Doctrine, or a particular doctrine, which is not stated in scripture but which is believed to have comparable authority, having been transmitted orally or by other non-written means.

---

[27] OXFORD ENGLISH DICTIONARY definition of "Tradition". By permission of Oxford University Press.

[28] De Lange identifies Tradition as all those materials encompassed with the interpretation of the *Torah*, the tradition of Worship, biblical tradition, legal tradition, ethical tradition, mystical tradition and theological tradition, eschatological tradition. One might also add to this the philosophical tradition and Kabbalah.

And for the Christian Church the OED describes it as:

> Doctrine, or a particular doctrine, which, though not explicit in the Bible, is believed to derive from the oral teaching of Christ of the Apostles and to be divinely revealed. Also: the transmission of such doctrine. In later use (in Roman Catholic and Orthodox usage) often with capital initial, or modified by *holy*, *sacred*, etc.

And for Islam:

> An account of a saying or act of Muhammad not recorded in the Qur'an but believed to have been initially transmitted orally and subsequently written down; these accounts considered collectively, especially those constituting the collection accepted as authoritative in Sunni Islam but not in Shia Islam.

This aspect of tradition is further defined to include the idea that it is a practice or custom that is generally accepted and has been established for a period of time. It is located within a society, faith or social group and is considered collectively.

It is a term that is also used within art, literature and music to establish persons or groups of persons followed by others.

Downie's definition in *The Oxford Companion to Philosophy*[29] is telling in that it portrays a divergence from the sophisticated manner in which religious groups identify and refine tradition over time, it does appear, nevertheless, to portray current popular and political understandings of tradition:

> Customary sets of belief, or ways of behaving of uncertain origin, which are accepted by those belonging to the tradition as persuasive or even authoritative and which are transmitted by unreflective example and imitation.
>
> [...] The nature of traditions is such that they cannot (logically) be willed; rather they have grown up. Traditions exist in all areas of life – literature, religion, legal institutions, and so on – the term is of particular interest in political philosophy. For those political philosophers hostile to the idea of tradition it is perceived as representing entrenched privileges holding back political and social progress, and it is to be contrasted with a vision of human beings controlling their own destinies with rational decisions and asserting rationally based rights. This latter was the position of revolutionary political thinkers such as Rousseau, Tom Paine, and Richard Price. Their position was opposed by thinkers such as Edmund Burke, who had less faith in reason. For traditionalists like Burke social life is kept going not mainly by rational decision-making but by feeling, habit, emotional attachments and conventions.

It is the assumption by Downie that the origin of a tradition is uncertain and the transmission or transformation of tradition over time is unreflective that is perhaps least accurate when examined in the light of the manner in which some faiths have carefully ascertained and developed their tradition over time. Faith traditions tended to identify early faith leaders capable of creating and passing on authoritative teachings and establish systems that would ensure the authenticity of the tradition as it developed.

Similarly, if one considers tradition within the scope of the law, in particular for countries with common law systems, precedent, which forms a constituent part of legal tradition, will have been developed carefully and thoughtfully over centuries.

---

[29]Downie (2005), 1760–1761 (by permission of Oxford University Press).

Also within politics and law creation through parliamentary processes, tradition will have been thought through and applied for a reason, even if that reason is not evident to those applying it in the modern day.[30]

Scott and Marshall in *The Oxford Dictionary of Sociology* have another interesting definition of the concept, they perceive tradition as:

> A set of social practices which seek to celebrate and inculcate certain behavioural norms and values, implying continuity with a real or imagined past, and usually associated with widely accepted rituals or other forms of symbolic behaviour. Research has established that many traditions which are popularly perceived to be of long standing are in fact relatively recent inventions. Examples include the distinct Highland culture (of kilts, tartan, and bagpipes) of Scotland, a late 18th- and early 19th-century creation; the lifetime employment system in Japan, which was created in the 1920s to bolster a strategy of economic modernization; and the supposedly indigenous political and economic traditions of many African societies (which were in fact invented by colonial authorities in order to make the necessary connections between local and imperial political, social, and legal systems). Some fascinating case-studies along these lines are reported in Eric Hobsbawm and Terence Ranger (eds.), *The Invention of Tradition* (1983).[31]

The concept of tradition has synergies with but is distinction from various other terms, such as doctrine and culture. This is particularly so when considered in the light of a faith tradition. Some of these terms are encompassed within the concept of tradition, others overlap with it. Doctrine,[32] for example, will have grown up within and be encompassed by the tradition of a given faith. Culture[33] may either be considered part of or synonymous with a particular tradition or may legally be set apart from it. This occurs, for example, where in the legal sense religious practices might be protected—for example by equality legislation or the right to freedom of religion or belief—whereas cultural practices might not. However, this distinction can also be blurred where, for example, the wearing of the veil is regarded legally as an exercise of religious freedom[34] even though within Islam it might be regarded as a cultural rather than a religious requirement (Wagner et al. 2012). Alternatively, a well-known religious symbol such as the crucifix can benefit from protection as a cultural and historic symbol in a classroom pursuant to the right to freedom of

---

[30]The use of constitutional conventions within Parliament in the UK is an example of political tradition developed over time based on conduct rather than rules or legal norms. For example the Salisbury Convention—this states that the House of Lords will not oppose legislation from the House of Commons that was part of its election manifesto.

[31]Scott and Marshall (2009), 238 (by permission of Oxford University Press).

[32]Teaching on a particular subject matter which is regarded as true concerning that subject matter.

[33]Ideas, customs or social behavior.

[34]This is so within the UK: for example, see *R v D (R)* [2013] EW Misc 13 (CC); in the jurisprudence of the European Court of Human Rights: for example, see *Ebrahimian v France* [2015] ECHR 1041; and in the jurisprudence of the Court of Justice of the European Union: for example, see the *Achbita* case and *Bougnaoui and another v Micropole SA* (Case C-188/15) 2017 OJLR 6(3): 620–622. Although in many of these legal cases the wearing of a veil was limited in the interest of the enjoyment by others of other rights, the court acknowledged that the wearing of the veil was an exercise of religious freedom in the first place but that this right to religious freedom was legitimately limited. This avoided any lengthy legal disputes as to whether the veil was an expression of religious freedom or a cultural requirement.

thought, conscience and religion under Article 9 of the European Convention on Human Rights. In the *Lautsi* case, for example, the Grand Chamber of the European Court of Human Rights ruled that a crucifix in the classroom did not amount to a process of indoctrination and did not infringe the Article 2 of Protocol 1 ECHR rights of a parent, rather that the crucifix was of cultural and historical importance within Italian society.[35] Similarly, Christmas crib scenes may be displayed in public buildings in France where their importance is primarily of cultural rather than religious significance. The requirement is that they are within the festive nature of Christmas.[36]

It is at this point that the distinction between religious practices and culture becomes important both in order that an individual seeking to manifest their religious belief might be protected and in order that the correct justification for the exercise of religious freedom might be found. It is here that we see a modern example of the phenomena identified by Bobrowicz (2018) of law shaping and informing religion. Bobrowicz explores this in the context of the Roman Theodosian code, identifying its influence on the shaping of orthodoxy. An overt modern-day example of this would be the application of the political philosophy of Pancasila in Indonesia[37] where the state recognizes freedom of religion in respect of six faiths (Islam, Christianity (Protestantism and Catholicism—counted as two religions), Hinduism, Buddhism and Confucisanism and sets out the scope of the doctrine and permissible practice of those religions: see Decision No 140/Puu-VII/2009.[38]

While there are some discrepancies between dictionary definitions, most notably as to the care or otherwise that is taken to ascertain the content of tradition, it is at this stage possible to outline the main threads that have been woven. Tradition thus includes the notion of passing on and adding to; it is that which supplements a core body of rules, and can become authoritative texts. It is that which facilitates and cements relationship (with a deity) and creates cohesion within a community. It enables a community to survive as a minority group within civil society and can be regarded as divine law. It is normative and binding compared to that which has historical significance but which is not normative and binding. It can also be described as rules governing daily life. Already it is possible to discern how tradition might be used to facilitate dialogue between groups. This is because of its use as a tool for facilitating cohesion and relationship. It both protects identity and importantly

[35]*Lautsi and others v Italy* (2012) 54 EHRR 3.

[36]Thebault (2017).

[37]Pancasila is based on five principles: belief in the One and Only God; a just and civilized humanity; a unified Indonesia; democracy, led by representatives of the people and; social justice for all Indonesians.

[38]Decisions No 140/PUU-VII/2009: Constitutional Court, Republic of Indonesia, 19 April 2010. 2012 OJLR 1(1): 527–528. In that case the court ruled that the Indonesian Blasphemy Law, Law 5/1969, by allowing the state to ban a group that was considered to have deviated from the teachings of a religion, did not infringe the right to freedom of religion enshrined in the Indonesian constitution. This was because the blasphemy law was seen as a legitimate interference with that right in the interests of public order and religious values. The Blasphemy Law was upheld as necessary to maintain social harmony and prevent religious deviancy.

is open to development over time. It contains within itself a method for formulating rules governing conduct often based around a moral code. Having outlined the various dictionary definitions of "tradition" this chapter will now move on to consider tradition as a concept within the discipline of law.

5 Tradition and Law

'Law' is applied within the context of this chapter as a body of rules made by a government or group of governments, governing the interaction of individuals with each other and with the state, and the interaction between nation states. It will contain mechanisms for enforcement. In a national context and sometimes in an international context it will carry sanctions for infringement. National and international law can be created by national parliaments or representatives of nation states. 'Religious law', is that body of rules applicable to members of a religious group governing individual behaviour mandated by their religion as well as the interaction between members of that group and between individuals and the state. It can be created by religious groups for members of that group or by a state. A system of adjudication will be in place to resolve disputes concerning the law and a framework of moral and/or theoretical reasoning will underlie law creation and adjudication in terms of the formulation of norms and the process by which law comes into being, as well as the manner in which disputes are resolved. Enforcement will depend on the authority and power of the law-maker and the extent of the control it seeks to assert over those subject to the law.

The concept of tradition engages with the discipline of law at various points. First, when a society, and in particular a government, establishes norms in order to formulate law. A tradition will have been developed whereby ethical reasoning is applied to establish the moral basis for law. Tradition will also dictate which groups within society or individuals are heard in the debate around law creation. Second, in the process whereby moral principles are applied to the formulation of law. A tradition will have developed around how the law is created, this would include sources used and manner in which they are used and interpreted together with the process by which the rule is formulated, written down and ultimately accorded the status of law. In a common law system this will involve both Parliament and the courts.[39] Third, tradition is also evident in the adjudication of disputes. This

[39]The legal aspects of tradition also take into account judicial reasoning and interpretative tools. Where courts apply a literal interpretation to statutory interpretation this involves adhering to that which Parliament made evident by the words it used, where the courts apply the mischief rule or a purposive approach this facilitates a more responsive and adaptive approach to statutory interpretation. The literal rule is akin to orthodoxy—sticking with the rules as they were created, the mischief and purposive approaches provide scope to adapt the rules either within what might be considered tradition or taking it outside established ways of thinking or reasoning. Where the gap between established rules and newly created rules is too great it is at this point that tradition—in the sense of an ongoing and continuous body of law—might be said to be broken. For an exploration

involves rules on interpretation of legal instruments and rules on judicial reasoning and precedent (*stare decisis*). The common law, in particular, entails the concept of previous generations of jurists passing on their wisdom to future generations on the basis of some form of precedent or established reasons. Fourth, tradition will have influenced a particular constitutional settlement in place within a nation state or an intergovernmental or supranational legal system operating between states. That tradition will govern not only the constitutional structure, but the mechanisms put in place to ensure that structure operates effectively. This is because written law cannot govern the minutiae of the operation of government and its relations with its citizens. There will be a need for the exercise of discretion and the operation of certain practices. The United Kingdom, with its 'unwritten' constitution, is an example of a constitutional settlement which is particularly dependent on tradition and where the constitutional tradition and in particular the role of judges within that tradition is currently the subject of lively debate.[40]

In the view of some jurists, rabbis, theologians and academics the concept and use of tradition in relation to law creation and adjudication has, since the enlightenment and for some since the European reformation, been changing.[41] There has been a move away from faith and their traditions as a basis for national and international law creation and adjudication. Over time there have been moves within the faiths to counter this with orthodoxy and to revert to a time when tradition was first fixed, before cultural adaptations occurred. This has particularly been seen within Islam with the expansion of neo-fundamentalism in the form of the Muslim Brotherhood. For reasons outlined at the beginning of this chapter there is a need to reassess where we are and reconsider what we mean by tradition, how we operate in the light of tradition and how this might impact upon governance, moral reasoning, law creation and legal adjudication. Authors such as David are already starting to blaze this trail, drawing attention to the rich Jewish and Islamic traditions that have potential to feed into current legal debates (David 2014). Similarly, the Christian tradition has seen authors such as Cochran and Calo (2017), McIlroy (2009), Chaplin (2011), Reed (2013), Sagovsky (2008) and Strickland (1999) engage theology to re-invigorate the voice of the various faiths in governance, law creation and adjudication. Feeding into this debate is the need to understand the manner in which the faiths adopt and develop tradition and how this might inform national and international legal thinking. Before delving into the three Abrahamic faiths to discover how tradition is developed within these faiths, it is first necessary to explore the concept of tradition within the law in a little more detail. This will provide a backdrop for the proposal that tradition as a concept, in particular within the different faiths, can interact with governance, law creation and adjudication to provide a means of building consensus within society and protect individual identity and fundamental rights whilst also fostering strong intermediate institutions.

---

of Jewish legal reasoning in the context of halakhic tradition see David (2014), 11 ff. David looks, inter alia, at legal discretion and legal reasoning in a comparative Jewish/Islamic context.

[40]Etkins (2018).

[41]See McConnell (2016) and Witte (2007).

Ravitch (2018), Bobrowicz (2018), McFaul (2018), Qureshi (2018), Bakhshizadeh (2018) and Vanoni and Ragone (2018) all argue that links between law and faith traditions do not or should not necessarily form one-way traffic either by law imposing norms on faith traditions or faith traditions imposing norms on law creation and adjudication. The dialogical approach between faith traditions, between these traditions and other institutions of civil society and between these intermediate institutions and the state anticipates both contextualization of faith traditions as well as accommodation of religion within civic life.

5.1 Glenn and Chthonic Legal Tradition

Glenn in his study on legal traditions identifies a point where law and tradition were synonymous. He commences from a point even earlier than that identified within the dictionary definitions already outlined, exploring first the concept of chthonic legal traditions. Glenn defines chthonic legal tradition as follows:

> To describe a legal tradition as chthonic is thus to attempt to describe a tradition by criteria internal to itself, as opposed to imposed criteria. It is an attempt to see the tradition from within, in spite of all problems of language and perception, and to see it from a time prior to the emergence of colonial language. 'Indigenous' or 'aboriginal' traditions are what they are because they have been chthonic, for hundreds of thousands of years, though they also, inevitably bear new designations since the colonial encounter of the last few hundred. (Glenn 2014, 62)

Glenn further explains that:

> There was no point of origin of chthonic legal tradition. There was no recorded revelation; no dramatic rupture from other traditions; no single, literally unforgettable achievement. A chthonic legal tradition simply emerged, as experience grew and orality and memory did their work. Since all people of the earth are descended from people who were chthonic, all other traditions have emerged in contrast to chthonic tradition. It is the oldest of traditions; its chain of tradition is as long as the history of humanity. (Glenn 2014, 62)

Chthonic legal tradition can be summarised as rules emerging from the practice of a community over time, being passed down over time. Glenn's concept of chthonic legal tradition could perhaps be best described as pre-legal or pre-formal legal rules, it is closest to the definition of tradition that emerges from the study of the concept in this chapter as a body of rules which sits alongside core texts governing a group, except that with chthonic tradition the rules governing the group are all contained in tradition and there is no formal core text. It identifies a form of coexistence based on that which exists outside formal written law or rules. It is the essence of the dialogical platform proposed in this chapter. In his book *Legal Traditions of the World* Glenn goes on to use the word tradition in a broader manner than is adopted in this chapter (Glenn 2014). Thus, he examines Talmudic, Civil law, Islamic, Common law, Hindu and Confucian legal traditions in order to consider in his final chapter whether there is potential for reconciling legal traditions to facilitate sustainable diversity in law.

When using the term 'tradition' in this context Glenn is using it to encompass the whole of a legal tradition: both its core and additional elements. His study of legal tradition is useful for the present project in that he proposes that it is possible for legal traditions to work together but still sustain diversity. The study undertaken in this chapter differs from Glenn's work in that it identifies 'tradition' with that element of the 'law' or norms, customs and practice of a group which supplements the written law or core principles and is more akin to Chthonic legal tradition. This contrasts with what Glenn would describe as modern legal tradition which encompasses a whole type of legal system, whether religious or national and judicial and includes core legal rules (such as legislation) and supplemental rules. In this chapter tradition is defined to encompass that which supplements the core tenets or principles of the group to which is applies. This is an important distinction because it is proposed in this chapter that 'tradition' can enable a faith or institution within society to contextualise themselves, because of its flexible nature, while facilitating core integrity.

While Glenn's concept of tradition is broader than that discussed here, his arguments supporting sustainable diversity in law provide the theoretical mechanism whereby the more limited concept of tradition outlined in this chapter might be used as a tool to build consensus. This could support increased religious freedom and diversity in civil society by using multivalent reasoning, as discussed by Glenn, as a tool for building consensus around the common good.

5.2 *The Tradition Project*

The concept of tradition and its links to the law has been taken up recently by the Tradition Project at St John's University New York. Launched in Autumn 2016, it took an interdisciplinary and innovative approach to defining tradition for the 21st Century. Movsesian,[42] the project leader, identifies the starting point by defining tradition as 'a broad understanding of what the received wisdom of the past continues to offer contemporary law and culture'.[43]

McConnell, in his keynote lecture, considers the concept of tradition as it is applied by him to common law reasoning within the United States. He highlights a distinct move away from the operation of the common law as tradition. He sees tradition as the legal rules whose authority derives from longstanding practice. He contrasts this with rules and mores imposed by command from some kind of sovereign and expert. He highlights the idea that traditions also have the characteristic that they are not frozen in time but are evolving. He notes that they are there and of value precisely because they survive the test of time as a living force that animates and informs the

[42]Frederick A Whitney Professor, St John's Law School and Director of the Centre for Law and Religion.

[43]References to the Tradition Project have links provided on the Tradition Project web page at: http://www.stjohns.edu/about/news/2016-10-27/center-law-and-religion-s-tradition-project-convenes-new-york date accessed May 2017.

present. He regards the bearing of fruit on the basis of a tradition as a condition of the passing of it on to future generations. Interestingly he comments on the fact that tradition has a social coordination role, which 'participates in democratic consent'. His view is that because of this democratising element it is the most effectual source of law.

He also goes on to distinguish tradition from the notion that 'old is good', linking tradition to Darwinian logic on the basis that traditions survive because they accomplish something. He suggests that there will be mutations of a given tradition and if they produce fruit they will become the rule.[44]

According to McConnell, the conceptualization of tradition within the field of legal reasoning and its practical effect has transformed since the 19th Century. Previously judges adjudicated on the basis that they did not create law but 'discovered' the law, they considered society and asked themselves what were the rules, norms and practices that a reasonable person in society would expect. They were operating a concept of tradition and working within it. *Stare decisis* required a considerable body of judicial opinion to support a decided point of law. This meant that judges had to decide a case before them on a string of existing case law. The common law and the operation of the doctrine of *stare decisis* has since the 19th Century, in his view, taken a more positivist approach to adjudication so that the judges of the time establish law. One 5:4 decision in the Supreme Court is now capable of creating precedent. Thus, McConnell argues, *stare decisis* becomes a type of positive law and does not sit so easily within the concept of tradition.

This development towards a form of positivism in judicial interpretation has resonances with the current debate between Finnis, senior judges and legal academics across common law jurisdictions on the Judicial Power Project.[45] This project debates the legitimate role of the common law judge. Finnis directs his attention to 'groupthink', the idea that members of a group decide in accordance with group norms and seek uniformity and group unity.[46] This in turn picks up on a debate raised by Griffiths in *The Politics of the Judiciary* where Griffiths pointed to the similar educational and cultural backgrounds of the judiciary which he claimed led to the specific way in which cases were decided (Griffiths 1997). Lee in *Judging Judges* critically analyzes Dworkin's theory of adjudication,[47] and, recognizing the complexity of judging, discusses the need to take account not only of the past but to contextualize judicial decision making in the present and look towards the future (Lee 1988/89). As Lee explains inevitability some cases, because of the issues raised and their context, leave a justifiable feeling of discomfort (Lee 2003). Lee's work is perhaps closest to the notion of common law as tradition as defined in this chapter since, rather than envisioning the judicial role as existing soley in the present and taking a restrictive

[44]Presumably when a government decides to legislate this then creates a formal rule, which, although based on tradition, steps outside the definition of tradition as identified thus far.

[45]http://judicialpowerproject.org.uk (date accessed August 2018)

[46]Irving (1973).

[47]Namely that judges weigh and apply competing rights in all cases, law consequently embraces moral and political as well as strictly legal rights.

approach to judicial rules of statutory interpretation, it accounts for development over time with a view to past, present and future.

Law creation and adjudication is thus familiar with and dependent upon tradition. The move away from reliance on tradition towards a more positivist approach evident in some legal systems could be counteracted by the creation of a dialogical plural platform which through multivalent reasoning is able to build consensus to inform law creation and adjudication. This would support Vanoni and Ragone's (2018) thesis for a third way to inform adjudication, providing a strong mechanism for doing so.

An interesting approach is taken by Elaine Mak in her comparative analysis of the changing practices of western highest courts where she explores instances of common law judges taking note of decisions from outside their own jurisdiction (Mak 2013). This informs the current study since it demonstrates the existence of a practice of synthesizing of different traditions, albeit within the overarching umbrella of common law jurisdictions. In this process one legal tradition voluntarily accepts reasoning from another legal tradition where there is no or limited resources within its own case law. If one understands common law to be the development of tradition as that which supplements statutory formal rules, this provides an existing example of one (common law) tradition working as a platform for dialogue with another (common law) tradition to resolve a dispute which potentially has wide ramifications on the constitutional settlement within a state. An example of this is the case of *R v D (R)* 2014 OJLR 3(1), 176 in the Crown Court at Blackfriars, London, where the court reasoning relied heavily on the Canadian Supreme Court case of *R v NS* 2014 OJLR 3(1), 175 when deciding whether a defendant should be required to take off a niqab in court when giving evidence. This also occurs on a regular basis where national courts follow the judicial decisions of the Court of Justice of the European Union or the European Court of Human Rights. Pin identifies one European Court of Human Rights case were the Grand Chamber compared the law of England and Wales with law in Australia, New Zealand, South Africa, Canada, Hong Kong and the USA (Pin 2014, 431).[48] This plural approach to legal tradition works either because both jurisdictions have sufficiently similar frameworks for the development of tradition or because an overarching formal legal framework is in place requiring the taking account of another legal tradition. This plural approach to legal adjudication has been addressed by Fry (2014) who suggests that joining the religious voice to implementation of international law in particular would inject a measure of regionalism and pluralism in the debate such that tensions between universalism and localism might be alleviated and global social stability improved. This involves courts not only taking account of other legal traditions but of faith traditions as well.

The danger of using a plural approach to legal tradition which ignores the voice of religion is evidenced most recently in the *Achbita* and *Bougnaoui* cases[49] in the Court of Justice of the European Union. In the *Achbita* case the CJEU gave precedence to the right to conduct a business pursuant to Article 16 of the Charter of Funda-

---

[48] *Al Khawaja and Tahery v The United Kingdom* App nos 26766/05 and 22228/06, [2011] ECHR 2127.

[49] Giles (2017) and CJEU judgments in the cases: 2017 OJLR 6(3): 620–622.

mental Rights of the European Union over the right to freedom of religion pursuant to Article 10 and as a protected characteristic pursuant to the Anti-discrimination Directive, Council Directive 2000/78/EC of 27 November 2000 establishing a general framework for equal treatment in employment and occupation (OJ 2000 L 303, p 16). The opinion of Advocate General Kokott in *Achbita*, in contrast to that of Advocate General Sharpston in *Bougnaoui*, demonstrated a willingness to ignore the importance of the religious voice in the public square. Ultimately the judgments reflected the neo-functional drive towards economic integration over and above priorities set for human flourishing and well-being within pre-existing international and national fundamental rights instruments. The dangers of this approach which allows religious interests to be too easily outweighed have been identified, *inter alia*, by myself (2017, 2018) and Weiler (2017).

The CJEU is a prime example of judicial law-making creating a unique and recently developed legal tradition built from existing traditions of its members states and the European Court of Human Rights. This process has been perceived as a hotly contested topic since the publication of his thesis by Rasmussen *On Law and Policy in the European Court of Justice* and the replies by Cappelletti "Is the European Court of Justice Running Wild?" and by Weiler "The Court of Justice on Trial" (Rasmussen 1986; Cappelletti 1987; Weiler 1987). More recently this debate has calmed down such that Beck has been able to identify what could be described as the legal tradition of the Court of Justice of the European Union (Beck 2012). This is arguably a prime example of syncretism, the coming together of the legal traditions of the various member states to create a supranational court with a body of judges trained within the legal systems of their own member states ruling by consensus. In contrast, the practice and jurisprudence of the European Court of Human Rights with its application of the margin of appreciation demonstrates a greater ability to accommodate diversity and consequently takes a stronger plural approach. In and of itself this makes for an interesting exercise in multivalent reasoning leading to a majority judgment where the dissenting voices can be heard. The CJEU, on the other hand, gives a single judgment representing the views of the entire court. Finnis might well legitimately raise the accusation of groupthink here, in particular in relation to the operation of the CJEU. The plural voices are subdued or lost in the ultimate judgment, the overarching aim being the unification project that is the European Union and the need for uniformity throughout the Union to create conditions for economic integration.

Religious tradition, as defined within this chapter, can, in this context, arguably provide a stabilising framework for judicial decision making and play a legitimizing role for the development of legal tradition or precedent by providing a basis for the acceptable bounds of judicial decision making on the basis of multivalent reasoning accounting for the past, present and future. Consequently, it could provide a means to resolve the concerns as to the politicization or otherwise of the judiciary. It could also provide a means for retaining a plurality of voices while still ensuring sufficient consensus necessary for decision making and the resolution of disputes. More importantly it could facilitate the voicing of dissenting opinion essential to counter groupthink mentality. Ultimately it could also act to prevent the erosion of fundamental rights protection.

Echoing the Finnis/Lee debate in the United Kingdom, Dreher, in the United States, in his commentary on the inaugural speech and Tradition Project conference, equates tradition to an icon, referring to Pelikan who saw tradition as "a mark of an authentic and living tradition which points us beyond itself" noting that on this view, tradition finds it roots in transcendence.[50] Arguing that the Enlightenment's claims of universal rights grounded in reason did not see itself as depending on tradition, for Pelikan this makes it very difficult to hold on to supposedly universal truths without having grounded them in the tradition that produced them. It is argued in this chapter that in order to find acceptance as universal norms, rights frameworks and enforcement mechanisms need to find a basis in multi-faith theological philosophy as well as in secular philosophy. As a result, the legal reasoning underpinning their development and adjudication will require the acceptance of multivalent rather than bivalent forms of reasoning in order to account for difference.

Moreland supports the need to enable religious tradition to inform law creation and adjudication, identifying the link between tradition and (legal) reasoning:

> The better view, I think, is to appreciate that rationality (including legal reasoning) is inescapably embedded in a tradition, even when the "tradition" is an emancipation from tradition itself. American Christianity has a long tradition of rejecting certain forms of tradition (not least Catholicism) and placing an emphasis on "thinking for oneself" (Nathan Hatch and John McGreevy). This, in turn, has shaped in historically complex ways how the American religious, political, and legal traditions interact.

He suggests that Newman's treatment of tradition and argument might help tackle differences and points out that achieving clarity about the traditions (even if one of emancipation from tradition) would be of great value to legal argument.[51]

In summary, tradition in its modern and legal contexts appears to have retained some sense of the value of rules and practices existing outside formal legal rules, and belongs to society being moulded over time to produce that which is most valued or valuable to civil society. However, since the 19th Century, the influence of this conceptualization has been eroded by an increasingly positivist view of law such that tradition and the operation of law have become somewhat separated, potentially to the detraction of the adjudication of disputes and the creation of law. For some this results in the loss of what is seen as a democratic form of law making and adjudication, while for others it can provide a break from fundamental, orthodox and oppressive forms of religion which might otherwise deny basic fundamental rights. It is the argument of this chapter that given the high percentage of those who adhere to faith within any given society it is necessary to find a way of building consensus with various faiths in order to contextualise, and to move forward to gain increased rights and equality

---

[50] https://www.theamericanconservative.com/dreher/tradition-law/ (Date accessed May 2017) and http://www.theamericanconservative.com/dreher/the-tradition-conference/ (Date accessed May 2017).

[51] http://mirrorofjustice.blogs.com/mirrorofjustice/2016/10/tradition-and-reason.html (Date accessed May 2017).

protection, whilst ensuring faith groups have a voice in law creation and adjudication. It is argued that tradition as developed within the various faiths provides such a basis for moving forward because this provides a *loci* for contextualising any given faith while enabling any particular faith to retain the integrity of its scriptural principles. Tradition can become a bridge between modern civic life and religious communal living ensuring a two-way dialogical process whereby law is equally able within acceptable limits to accommodate religion. In order to establish how this might be undertaken, tradition as a concept with the three Abrahamic faiths will be explored in order to identify what they might bring to the dialogical platform.[52]

6 Tradition Within the Abrahamic Faiths

The theological concepts of tradition have been crafted from and constituted within not only texts and oral forms but within artforms and communal practice. David Burrell identifies this as the 'pluriform richness of religious traditions', an understanding of which he regards as a pre-requisite of any comparative theological exercise (Burrell 2011, 2).

The analysis of religious tradition in this chapter is a descriptive definitional one: it does not seek to move into the substantive comparative realm at this stage. Consequently, it will consider how the concept of tradition has developed and been applied within the three Abrahamic faiths focusing on texts and practices within those faiths. It will not compare the theological content of each tradition in any depth. The body of tradition within a faith will often contain the tools for ethical reasoning and for contextualizing scripture in the light of historical developments and the civil society within which a given faith community might find itself. Burrell warns, in this regard, against the temptation to seek to preference one tradition above another for the purposes of comparative theology. He explains:

> The three traditions grouped under 'Abrahamic faiths' have a special difficulty relating to each other, given the unalterable order of their chronological appearance. Indeed, given their close association, it would be surprising if the successor tradition did not consider itself to be superior to, or even claim to replace its predecessor [...] Yet Foucault's strategy of intellectual 'archaeology' will offer the antidote needed to restore this imbalance, reminding us how easily we will fail to construe a succeeding generation if we neglect to identify the lineaments of predecessors in its very structure. (Burrell 2011, 2)

Burrell's warnings identifying Foucault's academic tools for 'archaeological' engagement[53] are apposite for the current study of the concept of tradition and its relevance within constitution framing, law creation and adjudication today. They also

[52]The three Abrahamic faiths have been chosen for this study because it was necessary to place a limit on the length of this chapter.

[53]In the sense that this encourages a non-reductive and non-totalising examination of history, but rather examines differences, forms of mutation and transitions and looks for relations between them: Kendall and Wickham (1999), 24.

sit well within the framework of legal reasoning of the common law tradition. With this is mind let us start to dig.

6.1 Some Initial Definitional Thoughts

As a broad generalization, the three Abrahamic faiths distinguish between scripture on the one hand and teachings or rulings about Scripture that are considered authoritative on the other. There can in addition be further material or practices that may or may not be regarded as tradition. The authoritative teachings about Scripture have often been established long ago—this body of teaching is considered within the Christian tradition, post-reformation and using counter-reformation terminology, to be Tradition with a capital 'T'. This distinguishes it from those religious practices (tradition with a lower case 't') which gave rise to the complaints which acted as the tinder box for the European reformation epitomised by Luther's *Ninety-Five Theses* of 1517.

Within each faith there are practices pertaining to religious and personal observance of the faith. These can be considered as tradition with a lower case 't' within the Christian faith, whereas they are more likely to be considered Tradition (with a capital 'T') within Judaism and Islam. This is because Judaism and Islam tend to be more prescriptive concerning rules for daily living. Consequently, this distinction between Tradition and tradition is not as clear cut as may at first appear; but it does provide a means of distinguishing that which is regarded as authoritative for believers of a particular faith (as part of scripture or Tradition) and that which is practiced by the faith community outside of authoritative teachings (tradition or in some cases cultural practices). An example of tradition within the Christian faith would be the wearing of a crucifix on a chain around the neck or as a pin on clothing. This is not required by scripture or Tradition, but many Christians will wear such symbols. This chapter will henceforward refer to Tradition with a capital 'T' in respect of authoritative teachings which supplement scripture.

It should be born in mind that these faiths have interacted with both theological and secular philosophical frameworks. Thus, over time variable understandings of what constitutes Tradition and tradition have developed. An example of this would be the differences evident between Orthodox Judaism on the one hand and Reform and Reconstructionist Judaism on the other. For Orthodox Jews *halakhah* (authoritative rules) incorporates the divine law as laid out in the *Torah*, rabbinical laws, rabbinical decrees and customs combined. For Reformed or Reconstructionist Jews, modern views of how the *Torah* and rabbinic law developed imply that Jewish law is no longer normative today but that interpretation of the *Torah, Talmud* and other Jewish works is a matter of personal interpretation (traditionalist wing). Liberal and classical wings of Reformed Judaism regard most Jewish religious rituals as no longer necessary. Tradition within this context holds a different meaning and has a very different effect on the religious and personal lives of members of the faith. It also has consequential effects on believers' worldviews when it comes to living within and contributing to any given civil society.

It is this ability of religious groups to hold together despite often contradictory differences that Glenn (2014, Chap. 10) identifies as multivalent thought. This is a contribution that faiths can make to a public discourse around the common good and law creation and adjudication. There is every reason to anticipate that this type of reasoning could be applied to multi-faith existence within societies encompassing a complexity of norms governing diverse social institutions. The following section explores whether within faith Traditions there lies a key to providing additional mechanisms to create a platform for dialogue and cohesive living.

6.2 Judaism and Tradition

De Lange explains that Judaism cannot be described as a religion in the manner in which Christianity or Islam might be so described. It is rather a way of life. According to de Lange it cannot be reduced to a system of beliefs and although it can be defined sociologically by its institutions, worship and ritual observance, these expressions of Judaism can change from place to place (de Lange 1986, 5). For de Lange Judaism is best defined in the history of the Jews, that is through a historical approach (de Lange 1986, 7).

Judaism is consequently the attachment to the historical development of the Jewish people, commencing with the establishment of the covenantal relationship between God and the Children of Israel. Its core text is the *Torah*. Jews believe that God promised Abram that his offspring would become a great nation. The covenantal relationship sets out that as God loves his Children, so His Children should love and worship God and care for one another and His world as He does. It is through the observance of *halakhah*, Jewish religious law, that Jewish people live out this covenantal relationship and engage in everyday personal experiences of God.

De Lange writes:

> Judaism is a profoundly traditional religion, in the sense that each generation instinctively looks for guidance to the past, and is reluctant to overthrow received values and patterns of behavior. It is also a religion in which the idea of Tradition has always played a vitally important part. (de Lange 1986, 23)

One reason for this is the lack of creedal basis, another is the lack of a central religious authority. When challenged with new ideas Jews are therefore required to look back into their Tradition since there is no canon of faith or human authority to which to address questions. Jewish Tradition tends to be far more undefined and less formulaic than other faith Traditions and this facilitates flexibility. Judaism uses the word *kabbalah* to describe the process of receiving Tradition.

For the Jews the *Torah* provides rules for living.[54] The concept of Tradition within the meaning of *Torah* refers to that which has been passed on—firstly in the oral *Torah*, then in the Gaonic period in the *Talmud*. Between 882–942 A.D. Gaon Saadya authored the first systematic expositions of Jewish beliefs in Iraq. De Lange explains that from this point on the theory of Tradition was rationally justified and for Saadya became one of the three pillars of Judaism along with revelation and reason. Further, that having reached this point Judaism then adopted the reverence prevalent in the Middle Ages towards antiquity such that it was not until Abraham Geiger (1810–74) and others took up ideas of progress within Judaism that Reform Judaism developed and Tradition was adopted as a tool for contextualizing or at least reforming Judaism (de Lange 1986, 28). Subsequently the concept of Tradition was adopted by modernisers and traditionalist alike with considerable disagreement over its content.

The *Talmud* consisted of records of rabbinic discussions on matters of law and practice. Alongside this the ancient rabbis also developed the *Midrash*. This is a body of reflections and expositions on biblical topics. Each of the named authorities created a link in the chain of Tradition. Materials were authored between the second century CE and completed during the 12th century. Together the *Talmud* and the *Midrash* provide discussions and commentary forming the basis of a Tradition which supplements the *Torah*.

In addition to the *Talmud* and *Midrash*, the term *Halakhah* encompasses Jewish traditional religious law. This outlines the way in which Jews should conduct themselves. It is an interpretation of the Written and Oral *Torah*, comprising the 613 *mitzvot* (commandments based on the *Torah*), *Talmudic*[55] and rabbinic law and the customs and Traditions in the *Shulchan Aruch* (Code of Jewish Law). *Halakhah* includes a body of rabbinical opinions, legislation, customs, recommendations and behaviors passed down and subject to a specific type of legal reasoning.[56]

David makes a sophisticated link between the concept of Tradition and the problem of knowing and remembering. Outlining the heteronomous perception of memory, he explores the idea that memory is not only an epistemological question, but a theological challenge. This becomes highly relevant to consideration of the development of Tradition where the ancient original content tends to have been passed down orally, from memory, before being formally written down (2014, 106).[57] Traditionally, memory was about the relationship between Israel and their God, whereas Hellenic thought based on Platonic and Aristotelian thought perceived memory as

---

[54] *Torah* can be used to mean the written and oral law which includes Jewish scripture as a whole and includes all authoritative Jewish religious teachings throughout history.

[55] The initial consolidation of rabbinic literature. *Aggadah*, which means 'the telling', is a body of rabbinic exegetical, narrative, philosophical, mystical and other 'non-legal' texts. Authors of *halakhah* drew upon and incorporated the *Aggadah* into the *Talmud* and *Midrash*. *Midrash* is the genre of rabbinic literature which included early interpretations and commentaries on the Written and Oral *Torah*.

[56] For a detailed account of legal reasoning applicable to *halakhah* see David (2014), 11 ff.

[57] This question is not about the authority of the sources, that is the authority of those who passed the tradition down but how their remembering might have affected the tradition they did in fact pass down.

that which connects subject and reality or subject and true knowledge about reality. David's view is that the point at which the two met produced a conceptualisation of memory as inner writing upon or within the heart. He points out that the construct of inner writing is also used within Christianity (David 2014, 97).[58] For the Rabbis memory was encompassed in the duty to remember the *Torah*, the oral covenant of memory, resulting, after the destruction of the Temple, in the study of the *Torah* as of highest importance in mediating relations between God and humankind. Tradition thus becomes an important tool of relationship not just of law. It is this understanding of Tradition as a relational tool that can potentially form the core basis within Judaism for contributing to a dialogical relationship with those outside the faith, as well as those within it. Coupled with the potential for multivalent reasoning already existing within Judaism (David 2014, 45ff and 83 ff) Judaism thus will prove to be a strong partner on the dialogical platform for discourse across various groups in civil society. Judaism, in addition, according to Last Stone (2006) is concerned with establishing bonds of social solidarity between diverse members of society. Jewish tradition thus contributes a conception of the individual as heteronomous, not autonomous, and located in community. This is particularly evident in the work of Sacks (2005, 2007).

An additional unifying factor potentially undergirding a dialogical platform based on Tradition is the similarities found across religious Traditions rather than within them. Classical Judaism, for example, gives rise to a similar approach to *halakhah* when compared with Ratzinger's Catholic theological approach to Tradition. Ratzinger regards Tradition and Scripture as authoritative and Tradition as capable of ongoing interpretation and development. This has parallels in Classical Judaism, which regards *halakhah* as authoritative but capable of interpretation in the light of current day circumstances. The startling difference between the two faiths lies in the absence of a hierarchy of authority within Judaism and its presence within Catholicism. The similarities may, nevertheless, provide sufficient ground for meaningful discourse to take place between faiths. Glenn points out that each Tradition is able to hold together disparate strands within itself. This may provide scope for the different faith Traditions to work together despite their differences.

6.3 *The Christian Conceptualisation of Tradition*

The Cambridge Dictionary of Christian Theology summarises Tradition within the Christian faith as:

> a body of authoritative beliefs, teachings, or practices that, in the faith of believers, conveys the gospel message of Jesus Christ. (Thiel 2011, "Tradition")

It is first referred to in Paul's letter to the Corinthians:

[58] 2 Cor 3:2-3, 6 NRSV.

> For I handed on [*paredoka*] to you as of first importance what I in return had received: that Christ died for our sins in accordance with the scriptures, and that he was buried, and that he was raised on the third day in accordance with the scriptures, and that he appeared to Cephas, then to the twelve.[59]

Tradition, as first understood by the Christian Church, encompassed a set of beliefs contained in teachings, a doctrine, outlining the saving death and resurrection of Jesus Christ. This was expressed in the form of a Creed, namely a shared statement containing core tenets of the faith expressed in a fixed formula. It was also understood as a process of 'traditioning' (Thiel 2011, "Tradition"):

> that unfolds in acts of believing, confessing, enacting, and receiving the faith from person to person and from generation to generation.

It flourished in the daily practice of Christians. Until the canon of scripture was fixed and the Conciliar creeds established, it stood in juxtaposition against Christological heresy. This role for Tradition could prove of vital importance in modern times where the need for religious literacy and correct understanding of core scriptural and other texts has a vital role to play in combatting violent extremism and countering terrorism. For example, scriptural reasoning is used by Dr. Fatima Akilu who runs the deradicalization program for the Nigerian Government, working with victims and members of Boko Haram.[60]

After the Canon of scripture had been agreed in the third century AD, disagreements arose concerning the interpretation of scripture, which were resolved by adjudication by bishops meeting in councils. Creedal teaching emerged from this.[61] These Conciliar creeds were treated as inspired by the Holy Spirit and authoritative. In addition to the creeds the Church developed Tradition around liturgical practices, the veneration of martyrs and ecclesial structures. The writings of certain ancient patristic authors such as Augustine, John of Damascus and Dionysius the Areopagite were also included within tradition.[62] Later papal decretals were also included. When Martin Luther spoke out in Germany in the 16th century against Catholic traditions and customs, including indulgences, identifying them as abuses of faith, a clearer distinction between Scripture as distinct from Tradition started to emerge.

During the counter-reformation Roman theologians worked with the Scripture/Tradition dualism and countered Lutheran reformation theology with treatises devoted to explaining and justifying Tradition.[63] Chemnitz (1566–75) importantly

---

[59] 1 Cor. 15:3-5 NRSV.

[60] The Telegraph. 16 April 2018. Meet the former NHS psychologist trying to get inside the mind of Boko Haram. https://www.telegraph.co.uk/news/worldnews/africaandindianocean/nigeria/11644162/Meet-the-former-NHS-psychologist-trying-to-get-inside-the-mind-of-Boko-Haram.html.

[61] Councils took place in Nicaea, Constantinople, Ephesus and Chalcedon.

[62] In the early to high Middle Ages questions arose concerning the authority of the scriptural commentaries of the Early Church fathers and of the Conciliar creeds compared to scripture: Hugh of St Victor (1091–41), St Bonaventure (1221–74) and William of Ockham (1288–1348). Henry of Ghent (1217–93) foresaw the issue which was to redefine the concept of tradition and that sparked the European reformation, namely what happens when ideas that are matters of private judgment and custom are raised to the level of tradition (Rowland 2013, "Tradition").

[63] For example Driedo J. 1533. *De ecclesiasticis scripturis et dognmatibus*.

distinguished between 'Tradition' as the deposit of faith and 'tradition' as pious practices. Cano in 1563 in *De locis theologicis* developed the concept of Tradition as containing doctrine. Candler explains Tradition thus: 'Becomes a thing to be interpreted rather than the act of interpretation itself.' (Rowland 2013, Tradition).

According to Rowland (2013) parallel treatment of revelation by Francisco Suárez as information about God rather than a disclosure of God himself meant that revelation was no longer perceived as a revelation of the soul as it has been in the writings of Aquinas (1225–74). These two interpretations fed into a rationalist metaphysics, which in turn influenced the conceptualization of Tradition. The Catholic Church in the light of counter-reformation theology and in order to protect its Tradition, established the Magisterium. This was the shared teaching authority of the pope and bishops. The teachings were presented in papal encyclicals and both issued under the dogma of papal infallibility. The Magisterium insisted in 1965 on the mutual co-inherence of Scripture and Tradition.[64]

The modern theology of Tradition was established in the 19th century as theologians sought to situate the gospel and Tradition not only within history but also within contemporary society. The reformed theologian Schleiermacher developed a theory of doctrinal development. This described how Christian doctrine was reshaped over time by Christian communities.[65] This was subsequently embraced by Catholic theologians, at the University of Tübingen.[66] At the same time High Church Anglicans in Oxford developed the work of Hooker (1554–1600).[67] Hooker retained a role for Tradition and reason and after him Newman (1801–90) (who later converted to Catholicism) affirmed the need for a sacred hierarchy to act as the final organ of authority to resolve doctrinal disputes. Newman wrote a highly influential theology of Tradition in the 19th Century identifying Tradition as guided by the Holy Spirit enabling the Christian community over time to identify the essence of its understanding of divine revelation so as to formulate doctrine. He regarded historical crises as pivotal in the development of Tradition. He established seven criteria by which it would be possible to distinguish true developments of Tradition from corruptions of it, these are summarized by Rowland (2013, 169–208) as:

1. Preservation of type. That is where there is growth but the end product is the same as the original.
2. Continuity of principles.
3. Power to assimilate alien matter to the original idea. If it is difficult to assimilate an idea this is likely to indicate corruption.

[64] *Dogmatic Constitution on Divine Revelation* (1965) of Vatican Council II. DV 2.9.

[65] Schleiermacher (1830).

[66] Rowland (2013), Tradition. Rowland cites as examples: Drey (1777–1853), Möhler (1796–1838) and Johannes von Kuhn. The emphasis here was on living truth rather than transmission of old ideas, with the Holy Spirit active in human life. It was participation in the Trinity rather than adoption of a higher moral teaching that facilitated the engagement with and development of tradition.

[67] McGrade (2013).

4. Logical Sequence. The level at which the development can be said to be a logical issue of its original reflects the extent to which it can be regarded as genuine or true.
5. Anticipation of its Future. Early and recurring indications of tendencies which come to be fully realized indicate that the subsequent development is in accordance with the early idea.
6. A conservative action upon its past. There is a corroboration and illustrations of a previous body of thought.
7. Chronic vigour. Corruption will be transitory in nature.

Arguably, as Moreland suggests, the provision of a framework for the development of Tradition along the lines of Newman's principles could have relevance today by providing a structure to limit unchecked transformations of the law in the hands of unelected judges. This approach might appear restrictive for those who have an expansive view of the constitutional role of judges and the operation of judicial precedent, particularly in the field of rights protection.[68] Such a framework could also enable institutions within society to safely retain integrity based on their founding principles, while developing a joint Tradition as a platform for dialogue in a clear and careful manner in order to facilitate contextualization of themselves within any given society by working with governments, and other civil society institutions.[69] Coupled with Judaism's relational approach and ability to use multivalent reasoning it is already possible to identify the contribution which faith groups could make to a strong dialogical platform. It would accommodate faith groups within society, which tend to take a more deliberative and gradual approach towards change and increase the chances of building consensus between extremes on either side. While it is important to undertake reform, it is similarly important that reforms take those subject to the law with them.

According to Rowland, following on from Newman, Alasdair Macintyre (1929–) put forward the notion that Traditions are found not only in books and lectures but can be transmitted through social practice. He recognized that thinking took place in a given context or structure within which there would be first, an understanding of truth which ordered particular truths; second, a conception of a range of senses within which statements were required to be judged true or false or to be construed; third, a conception of a number of different genres through which statements could be classified—for example historical, literal or dramatic and; fourth, a contrast between use of genres in situations where truth was at stake and those where standards of rhetorical effectiveness alone were relevant.

---

[68] Authors such as Möller (2012).

[69] An example of this within the Christian faith is demonstrated in the theological approach to Tradition of Cullmann and Ratzinger. Although from different theological positions, Ratzinger (Roman Catholic) and the Swiss Lutheran theologian Cullmann (1954), who made a study of the word *Paradosis* (Tradition) in the New Testament, both argue that Christ stands behind the transmission of Tradition, working in it, being its content and its author. Rowland's view is that while not accepting the concept of a Magisterium or Church hierarchy continuing the work of the Apostles throughout all time, Cullmann brought the two sides more closely together on the role and concepts of scripture and Tradition (Rowland 2013; Tradition).

Along with Gadamer, MacIntyre was therefore placing Tradition not merely within its historical context but within the context of particular languages and situations. Similarly, in the hands of these more recent scholars Tradition is seen as capable of acting as a means of contextualizing religious beliefs not only through established means but additionally through social practice. It is this understanding of Tradition's role that could enable a dialogical platform to provide a locus for the debates around same-sex and equality rights, facilitating a deeper understanding and ability for opposing sides to accommodate each other.

More recently Christian theologies of Tradition have taken issue with the established understanding that Tradition represents a universal truth and that there exists an unbroken continuity throughout history. According to Rowland these theologies stood against French Traditionalists who preserved the Christian heritage as an impersonal process resulting in fixity, demonstrating unwillingness to engage with intellectual questioning. In contrast to this the Flemish Dominican Schillebeeckx (1914–2009) sought to relate Catholic Tradition to trends in contemporary culture and intellectual life. Similarly, Liberation theologians have identified Tradition with the bolstering of empowered majorities and called for fresh understandings in the light of the experience of excluded groups. According to Theil (2011) post-modern theologies aim to expand the concept of Tradition and regard Christian communities as 'contested spaces' shaped by their rituals, texts and histories, rather than continuous agreement. This provides a thinner conceptualization of Tradition, loosing the thicker concept based on continuous agreement. The Catholic Tradition's response is to seek to redefine its understanding of continuity.

Differences now exist between those who see Tradition as constituting resources within itself for its own self-perpetuation and those who perceive it as open to elements external to the Tradition itself and as culturally situated.[70] Rowland (2013) explains that there remains within Christian theology a debate on the nature of Tradition itself. The divide between Scripture and Tradition has narrowed but that between Tradition and history and universality has arisen, whilst debates occur around the place of hermeneutics and the application of linguistic philosophy.

The debate around cultural situation and self-perpetuation of Tradition is particularly relevant to the issue of whether Tradition can be used to facilitate contextualization of religion so as to create dialogue, build consensus and inform law creation and adjudication. This is because law (in the sense of national, supranational or international law) necessarily adapts over time to accommodate the changing nature of the society within which it locates itself both nationally and globally. If a faith Tradition becomes fixed the dialogue between faith and law becomes more difficult as does the dialogue between different faith traditions. If, on the other hand, Tradition is perceived as giving faith the ability to contextualize, it then becomes possible to envisage it as a tool for dialogue or bridge between faith and law. If one then looks to liberation and feminist theologies as they inform Tradition, it is possible, for example, to find within faith Traditions the ability to open up further dialogue

[70]Resonances can be identified here both within Orthodox Judaism where there is a more fixed approach to tradition.

around some of the more pressing issues arising in fundamental rights dialogue most specifically equality issues and women's rights.

In terms of its relevance to law creation and adjudication, the manner in which Tradition has been developed over time and the various theological approaches to it are reflected in legal systems and approaches to adjudication. Common law systems, for example, will be most familiar with Ratzinger's approach to interpreting existing Tradition in the light of circumstance. Positivists will be more comfortable perhaps with post-modern theologies that adopt a thinner version of Tradition, moving away from a concept of continuous agreement. Liberation theology would call for legal tradition to encompass the needs of excluded groups. This could, for example, support legislation and adjudication in favour of minority rights.

This exploration of the concept of Tradition within the Christian faith has proposed that the Christian concept of Tradition could contribute to a dialogical platform. As developed by Newman and refined by MacIntyre, Tradition holds the potential for a framework upon which to test the authentic development of Tradition over time within given contexts and create a bridge between religious groups and the cultures in which they find themselves. Its use as a tool for contextualisation and as an instrument to mitigate against counter-terrorism and extremism have been identified as particularly important implications of Tradition with the Christian faith. The challenge would be to find sufficient commonality or consensus amongst the different approaches to Tradition within the Christian faith in order to inform a dialogical platform. It is arguable that the rich diversity and history of the development of Tradition provides a valuable resource. Further that the building of consensus incorporating this rich diversity would be well worth the effort required to do so.

6.4 Islam and Tradition

Islam professes that there is only one incomparable God (Allah) and that Muhammad is the last messenger of God. For Muslims God is merciful, all-powerful and unique. God is revealed in scriptures, natural signs and a line of prophets (including Adam, Noah, Abraham, Moses and Jesus (although Muslims reject the doctrine of the Trinity and the divinity of Jesus)). Muhammad is the last, final authoritative prophet.

For Islam the Qur'an is the primary scriptural text. It is taken, in Arabic, to be the word of God in its purest form given by Muhammad (570-8 June 623 CE). It is read together with the teachings, example, sayings and tales (the *Sunnah*, composed of accounts called *hadith*) of and about Muhammad. In addition, Islamic law is found in *qiyas* (analogical reasoning for Sunni Islam) or *aql* (dialectical reasoning for Shia Islam) and *ijma* (consensus among jurists).

There are various schools of jurisprudence today within Islam. Sunni Islam encompasses the Hanafi, Maliki, Shafi'I, Hanbali and Ẓāhirī schools of law. Sunni Shari'a today is based on the schools of law, the canonization of the *hadith*, the development of specific dogmatics and political developments (Radtke 2010, 46). Religious practices include the five pillars of Islam: the creed, this is the recitation of faith (*shahada*); daily prayers said five times a day (*salat*); alms giving (*zakat*); fasting during Ramadan (*sawm*) and; pilgrimage to Mecca at least once in a lifetime (*hajj*). Islam teaches resurrection of the dead, a final tribulation and eternal division of the righteous and the wicked. Shi'a Islam is divided into three major sects: Fivers. Seveners and Twelvers.

Islamic law does not distinguish between church and state and scholars are both jurists and theologians. *Shari'ah* is Islamic law setting out a set of duties incumbent upon a Muslim. The study of Islamic law is called *Fiqh* (Islamic jurisprudence). *Usul al-fiqh* is the legal theory underlying Islamic law. This is used to preserve the original religion. Historically religion and state were one and the same—the Islamic community of Medina did not distinguish between the two (Busse 2010).[71]

Just as the Christian and Jewish faiths developed various strands of orthodoxy or fundamentalism, so Islam developed into two main groups with a spectrum of faith communities in-between. Sunni and Shi'a Islam. The ultra-conservative reform branch of Sunni Islam is known as the Salafi movement and developed in Arabia in the first half of the 18th Century (although some claim that they are part of the Wahhabi movement). Those who adhere to Sunni Islam make up the majority of Muslims at between 75 and 90%. Sufism developed early on within Sunni Islam as a form of mysticism, opening the way for all Muslims to rise to higher forms of religious knowledge.

The Arabic word *sunna* is translated as 'tradition' or 'custom'. A *sunni* refers to someone who follows tradition. Depending on how 'tradition' is defined within the context of the Muslim faith either a Sunni or a Shi'a Muslim can be considered a *sunni*—that is someone who follows tradition (Radtke 2010, 36).

Within Sunni Islam it was the *ulamas* (scholars or learned ones) who were regarded as the guardians of Islamic doctrine and it fell to them to interpret Scripture and existing Tradition and to transmit it. They continue to influence society and politics today. Their influence extends to dogma, religious practices and law.

There has been no equivalent within Islam to the Christian reformations. However there have been moves to reassert pure Islam against 'depraved' forms of development of the faith. According to Peters (2010, 70) this happened in the 18th and 19th centuries when reassertion of purity was linked to political movements. These movements were fundamentalist in as much as they adhered to strict scripturalism and rejected scriptural criticism. They went even further and sought the unity of Islam against plural trends within the faith and sought to resist external influence regarding all believers as equal before God. Wahhabism was one such movement founded in the mid-eighteenth century.

From the later part of the 18th Century onwards Islam developed in the context of Western expansion. Military, legislative, administrative and education reforms were

---

[71] Jews, Christians, Hindus and Zoroastrians were to some degree tolerated (Busse 2010, 9–10). This strain of Islam developed into Islamic fundamentalism and Wahhabsim—a pure Islam purged of any developments arising during the centuries after the establishment of Islam. This can be found in particular today in Saudi Arabia. A League of the Islamic World (*Rabitat al-'alam al-islami*) was founded in the later half of the 20th Century to propagate Islam in non-Islamic countries, building mosques and spreading the message of Islam throughout the world.

made in line with Western ideas. A key concern for Muslim communities became the requirement to protect their cultural identity and their faith Tradition, particularly in the face of Western prejudice. According to Peters (2010, 85, 103), Islam and Islamic Tradition became part of an individual's cultural identity as much as a religious belief, in an attempt to counter Westernisation. Towards the end of the 19th century religious change led to political and social reform. Many Western values were employed to develop a form of Islam acceptable to Europeans. Three pioneers of reform were Si Saiyid Ahmad Khan, Jamal al-Din al-Afghani and Muhammad 'Abduh. Key to their reforms were the lack of desire to create a purely Islamic state, declaring Islam and modern civilization congruent, adopting a number of universal values including democracy, tolerance, intellectual freedom and progress. There was an acceptance of separation of religion and politics. In contrast modern neo-fundamentalists attack Western ideals on the basis, *inter alia*, that they are responsible for individualism and social chaos.

Islamic Tradition, like Judaism and Christianity, has assumed different forms according to the place where it sits on the spectrum of belief. What might be described as the 'core' Tradition of Islam can be found in the *hadith*. Unlike Christian Tradition, it was fixed centuries ago within both Sunni and Shia Islam. Neo-conservative and fundamentalist groups within Islam rely on this original Islamic Tradition. Other forms of Islam accept the core Tradition but have contextualized the out-workings of their faith over time. Of all three religions the Islamic Tradition, with its reliance on a line of warrantors as a guarantee of authenticity of *hadith*, has the most fixed form of Tradition across the spectrum of belief and is heavily reliant on Tradition to enable it to adapt and survive in contexts where it is a minority religion. Where it can perhaps helpfully contribute to interfaith dialogue and links between law creation and religion lies in its methodological approaches. Because of the more direct links between the Islamic faith and legal and political systems, Tradition in Islam has developed similar methods of law creation and adjudication to those that would be recognized in the West.

The perceived fixed nature of Islam, which has sought to protect Muslim identity over time, together with the challenge Islam poses to laws on equality and women's rights has created something of a barrier to dialogue within Western liberal democracies. There is, however, evidence among the Imamate that attitudes are changing. On the other hand, outside of the Western liberal democratic tradition, Islam has found the individualism engendered by rights frameworks and the permissiveness of modern Western life a challenge. Using Tradition as a tool for contextualisation either within a nation state or within a global community of nation states could potentially prove a safe way forward in order to facilitate a dialogue around issues of fundamental concern within the Islamic faith in a manner which accords the faith Tradition respect and facilitates integrity whilst seeking to build consensus around basic norms for national or global communal living together. An example of this can be seen in the work of Bakhshizadeh (2018) as she considers different interpretations of Islamic Tradition and how this impacts on equality rights and the traditional role accorded to women under law in Iranian society.

7 Tradition as a Platform for Multivalent Dialogue

This chapter has sought to justify the inclusion of religious tradition as one of a plurality of voices within civil society that can contribute to strong intermediate institutions which foster the protection of fundamental rights frameworks, build consensus around the basis for the common good, and ultimately support peaceful relations in society. It has focused on the definition of Tradition as a concept, exploring its development in various guises and *loci* including dictionaries of the English language, philosophy and sociology. It has looked at the concept in law and within the three Abrahamic faiths. This exercise was undertaken to establish how tradition is developed and used within the institution or group to which it belongs and understand how this might lead to building a multivalent dialogical platform for institutions to engage with each other to create a strong plural civil society. What has been proposed is that despite, or rather because of, its various guises Tradition can be used as a platform to facilitate dialogue aimed at building sufficient consensus for peaceful living together but still capable of protecting individual identity.

Heeding Calo's (2018) warnings concerning current trends towards de-traditionalisation leading to increasing fragmentation of civil society, our archaeological excavations have revealed that the faith Traditions in particular have embedded within them the ability to hold together various strands or understandings of Tradition such that these might provide insights into a multivalent method of entering into dialogue (Glenn 2014, Chap. 10). In particular, Judaism provides an understanding of the concept which can facilitate relationship and community building as well as the contextualisation of itself over time. Christianity contains mechanisms for contextualisation and cultural adaptation and an approach to Tradition which in modern times protects authenticity and could assist in countering forms of extremism. In Newman's model, it provides a framework for safely developing Tradition while seeking to protect core identity. It too, along Judaism and Islam, brings a strong sense of the importance of community building. Islam contains tools of legal reasoning and law creation which facilitates a multivalent approach to decision making. This could facilitate communal living together in a national and international context, countering the more severe effects of the secular dialogue evidenced in extreme forms of *Laïcité*, as well as forms of theocracy and confessionalism. It would also address the democratic deficit and fracturing of social cohesion that arises when the body of faith Traditions are ignored by those governing and by law creators and adjudicators. It is proposed that the very process of building and engaging with this plural dialogical platform would reinvigorate not only strong religious intermediate civil society institutions, but the role of civil society institutions overall. Ultimately creating a strong peaceful civil society in which the plural religious voice is heard.

References

Ahdar R, Leigh I (2013) Religious freedom in the liberal state. Oxford University Press, Oxford
Annicchino P (2014) Coherence (and constistency) or organised hypocrisy? Religious freedom in the law of the European Union. In: Foblets MC, Alidadi K, Nielsen JS, Yanasmayan Z (eds) Belief, law and politics, what future for a secular Europe? Ashgate, Farnham
Bakhshizadeh M (2018) An analysis of the possibility of fulfilling gender equality within the legal system of the Islamic Republic of Iran. In: Giles J, Pin A, Ravitch F (eds) Law, religion and tradition. Springer International Publishing AG, Switzerland
Beck G (2012) The legal reasoning of the court of justice of the EU. Hart Publishing Ltd., Oxford
Benson IT (2010) Living together with disagreement: pluralism, the secular, and the fair treatment of beliefs in Canada today. The ronning centre forums II. A presentation by Iain T Benson with a response by Alex Fielding. The Chester Ronning Centre for the Study of Religion and Public Life, Camrose, Alberta
Benson IT (2012) Living together with disagreement: pluralism, the secular and the fair treatment of beliefs in law today. Connor Court Publishing, Ballan, Australia
Bielefeldt H, Nazila G, Wiener M (2016) Freedom of religion or belief. An international law commentary. Oxford University Press, Oxford
Bobrowicz R (2018) The inverted relationship: constitutive theory of law and the enforcement of orthodoxy in the book XVI of the theodosian code. In: Giles J, Pin A, Ravitch F (eds) Law, religion and tradition. Springer International Publishing AG, Switzerland
Burrell DB (2011) Towards a Jewish-Christian-Muslim theology. Wiley, Chichester, West Sussex
Busse H (2010) The world of Islam a brief historical survey. In: Ende W, Steinbach U (eds) Islam in the world today. Cornell University Press, New York
Calo Z (2018) Law, religion and the detraditionalization of Europe. In: Giles J, Pin A, Ravitch F (eds) Law, religion and tradition. Springer International Publishing AG, Switzerland
Cappelletti Mauro (1987) Is the European court of justice "running wild"? Eur Law Rev 12:3
Casey L (2016) The Casey review: a review into opportunity and integration. Department for Communities and Local Government. Ref: ISBN 978-1-4098-4953-7. https://www.gov.uk/government/uploads/system/uploads/attachment_data/file/575973/The_Casey_Review_Report.pdf. Date accessed 28 Aug 2017
Chaplin J (2011) Herman Dooyeweerd. Christian Philosopher of state and civil society. University of Notre Dame Press, Notre Dame, Indiana
Chemnitz M 1566–75 (1875) Examen Concilii Tridentini (translation from Latin to German). Examen Concilii Tridentini: d.h. Prüfung des Concils von Trient Verlag von L. Volkening, St. Louis, Mo
Cochran Robert, Calo Zachary (2017) Agape, justice and law: how might Christian love shape law? Cambridge University Press, Cambridge
Commission on Religion and Belief in British Public Life (2015) Living with difference. Community, diversity and the common good. The Woolf Institute, Cambridge
Cox N (2013) The clash of unprovable universalisms—International human rights and Islamic law. Oxford J Law Relig 2(2):307–329
Cullman O (1954) Tradition. Zwingli-Verlag, Zürich
David JE (2014) Jurisprudence and theology in late ancient and medieval Jewish thought. Springer, Switzerland
D'Costa G, Evans M, Modood T, Rivers J (eds) (2013) Religion in a liberal state. Cambridge University Press, Cambridge
de Lange N (1986) Judaism. Oxford University Press, Oxford
Downie RS (2005) Tradition, 2nd edn. In: Honderich T (ed) The Oxford companion to philosophy. Oxford University press, Oxford. pp 1760–1761
Eck D (2009) The age of pluralism. The Gifford lectures. Edinburgh University, Edinburgh, Scotland. https://www.giffordlectures.org/lectures/age-pluralism. Date accessed 20 Apr 2018

Esmer Y (2013) Democracy, civil society and Islam. In: de Hart J, Dekker P, Halmat L (eds) Religion and civil society in Europe. Springer, Dordrecht
Etkins R (ed) (2018) Judicial power and the balance of our constitution. Two lectures by John Finnis. Judicial power project. Policy exchange. http://judicialpowerproject.org.uk/wp-content/uploads/2018/01/Judicial-Power-and-the-Balance-of-Our-Constitution.pdf
Fry JD (2014) Pluralism, religion, and the moral fairness of international law. Oxford J Law Relig 3(3):393–418
Ghanea N (2017) Women and religious freedom. Synergies and opportunities. US Commission on International Religious Freedom. https://www.uscirf.gov/sites/default/files/WomenandReligiousFreedom.pdf. Date accessed 1 Mar 2018
Giles J (2017) A hope for coherent and permissive religious freedom policy: the *Bougnaoui* and *Achbita* cases. PILARS CC1. http://law-school.open.ac.uk/sites/law-school.open.ac.uk/files/files/PILARs-CC-1-2017-Bougnaoui.pdf
Giles J (2018) Neutrality in the business sphere, an encroachment on rights protection and state sovereignty? Oxford J Law Relig 7(2)
Glenn PH (2014) Legal traditions of the world, sustainable diversity in law, 5th edn. Oxford University Press, Oxford
Griffiths J (1997) The politics of the judiciary, 4th edn. Fontana, London
Griffith-Jones R, Hill QCM (2015) Magna Carta, religion and the rule of law. Cambridge University Press, Cambridge
Grim BJ (2014) Is religious freedom good for business? A conceptual and empirical analysis. Interdisc J Res Relig 10:article 4
Grim BJ, Finke R (2011) The price of freedom denied. Religious persecution and conflict in the twenty-first century. Cambridge University Press, Cambridge
Grim BJ, Grim ME (2016) The socio-economic contribution of religion to American Society: an empirical analysis. Interdisc J Res Relig 12:article 3
Inoguchi T, Newman E (1997) "Asian values" and democracy in Asia. First Shizuoka Asia-Pacfici Forum, Jamamatsu, Shizuoka, Japan. http://www.unu.edu/unupress/asian-values.html. Date accessed 23 Feb 2018
Irving LJ (1973) Groupthink. Yale Alumni Magazine, pp 16–19
Kendall G, Wickham G (1999) Using Foucault's methods. Sage Publications, London
Khong CO (1997) Asian values: the debate revisited. First Shizuoka Asia-Pacfici Forum, Jamamatsu, Shizuoka, Japan. http://www.unu.edu/unupress/asian-values.html. Date accessed 23 Feb 2018
Last Stone S (2006) Judaism and civil society. In: Walzer M (ed) Law, politics and morality in Judaism. Princeton University Press, Princeton
Lee S (1988/89) Judging judges. Faber and Faber Ltd, London
Lee S (2003) Uneasy ethics. Pimlico, London
Mak E (2013) Judicial decision-making in a globalised world. A comparative analysis of the changing practices of Western Highest Courts. Hart Publishing, Oxford
McConnell M (2016) keynote lecture for the tradition project. St John's University, New York. http://www.stjohns.edu/about/news/2016-10-27/center-law-and-religion-s-tradition-project-convenes-new-york. Date accessed May 2017
McFaul H (2018) The recent, and sometimes invented, origins of some 'longstanding' traditions. In: Giles J, Pin A, Ravitch F (eds) Law, religion and tradition. Springer International Publishing AG., Switzerland
McGrade S (2013) Richard Hooker. Of the laws of ecclesiastical polity. The Clarendon Press, Oxford. Reprint Nashotah House Press, Nashotah, WI
McIlroy D (2009) A trinitarian theology of law: in conversation with Jürgen Moltmann, O'Donovan and Thomas Aquinas. Wipf and Stock Publishers, Eugene, Oregon
McIlroy D (2013) Locke and rawls on religious toleration and public reason. Oxford J Law Relig 1(2):1–24
Möller K (2012) The global model of constitutional rights. Oxford University Press, Oxford
Newbigin L (1989) The gospel in a pluralist society. SPCK, London

Open Doors Germany (2014) Religiously motivated attacks on Christian refugees in Germany. Open Doors (OD), Germany. https://www.opendoorsuk.org/about/how-we-help/advocacy/Open-Doors-Germany-Refugee-Report-2016
Oxford English Dictionary (2002, 2017 update). Oxford University Press, Oxford. http://www.oed.com.libezproxy.open.ac.uk/view/Entry/204302?rskey=4DoMLM&result=1#footerWrapper
Peters R (2010) Revivalist movements in Islam from the eighteenth to twentieth century and the role of Islam in modern history. Anticolonialism and nationalism. In: Ende W, Steinbach U (eds) Islam in the world today. Cornell University Press, Ithaca and London
Pew Research Centre (2012) The global religious landscape. Demographic study, Washington. Pew Research Center's Forum on Religion & Public Life. Date accessed 20 Apr 2018. http://www.pewforum.org/2012/12/18/global-religious-landscape-exec/
Pin A (2014) Religion, national identities, and the universality of human rights. Oxford J Law Relig 3(3):419–439
Pluralism Project @ 25 (2016) Pluralism and the practice of peacebuilding. Harvard Divinity School, Cambridge, Massachusetts. https://www.youtube.com/watch?v=a6JEhWD1jgk. Date accessed 7 Feb 2018
Putnam RD, Campbell DE (2010) American grace. How religion divides and unites us. Simon & Schuster, New York
Qureshi MA (2018) The Blasphemy laws of Pakistan: experimenting with history and tradition. In: Giles J, Pin A, Ravitch F (eds) Law, religion and tradition. Springer International Publishing AG, New York
Radtke B (2010) In: Ende W, Steinbach U (eds) "Sunni Islam" in Islam in the world today. Cornell University Press, New York
Rasumssen H (1986) On law and policy in the European Court of Justice. Martinus Nijhoff Publishers, Dordrecht
Ravitch F (2016) Freedom's edge: religious freedom, sexual freedom and the future of America. Cambridge University Press, New York
Ravitch F (2018) Tradition's edge: interactions between religious tradition and sexual freedom. In: Giles J, Pin A, Ravitch F (eds) Law, religion and tradition. Springer International Publishing AG, Switzerland
Reed E (2013) A theology of international law. Bloomsbury T&T Clark, London, Oxford
Rowland T (2013) Tradition. In: Adams N, Pattison G, Ward G (eds) The Oxford handbook of theology and modern European thought. Oxford University Press, Oxford
Sacks J (2005) To heal a fractured world. The ethics of responsibility. Continuum, UK, London
Sacks J (2007) The home we build together. Recreating society. Continuum, UK, London
Sagovsky N (2008) Christian tradition and the practice of justice. Society for Promoting Christian Knowledge, London
Schleiermacher F (1830) Brief outline of theology as a field of study, 2nd edn. Wipf and Stock Publishers, Eugene, Oregon
Scott J, Marshall G (2009) The Oxford dictionary of sociology, 3rd rev edn (last updated 31 Dec 2012). Oxford University Press, Oxford
Scriven J (2013) Belief and the nation. Wilberforce Publications, London
Sen A (1997) Human rights and Asian values. The New Republic, 14–21 July. https://www.scribd.com/document/245530276/Human-Rights-and-Asian-Values-pdf. Date accessed 23 Feb 2018
Stopler G (2003) Countenancing the oppression of women: how liberals tolerate religious and cultural practices that discriminate against women. Colum J Gender Law 12:154
Strickland WG (ed) (1999) Five views on law and gospel. Zondervan, Michigan
Thebault D (2017) Whoever said that the Nativity scene was religious. Oxford J Law Relig 6(3):399
Thiel JE (2011) Tradition. In: McFarland IA, Fergusson DAS, Kilby K et al (eds) The Cambridge dictionary of christian theology. Cambridge University Press, Cambridge
UNHCR Refugee Agency (2017) Forced displacement worldwide at its highest in decades. http://www.unhcr.org/uk/news/stories/2017/6/5941561f4/forced-displacement-worldwide-its-highest-decades.html

Vanoni LP, Ragone G (2018) From the secularisation theory to the pluralistic approach: reconciling religious traditions and modernity in Italian case-law. In: Giles J, Pin A, Ravitch F (eds) Law, religion and tradition. Springer International Publishing AG, Switzerland
Wagner W, Sen R, Permanadeli R, Howarth CS (2012) The veil and Muslim women's identity: cultural pressures and resistance to stereotyping. Cult Psychol 18(4):521–541
Walzer M (ed) (2006) Law, politics and morality in judaism. Princeton University Press, Princeton
Weber M (1905) The protestant work ethic and the spirit of capitalism (revised 1920 edition). Oxford University Press, Oxford
Weiler J (1987) The court of justice on trial. Common Market Law Rev 24:55
Weiler J (2017) Je Suis Achbita. Eur J Int Law 28(4), editorial
Williams R (2008) Islam, Christianity and Pluralism: The Zaki Badawi memorial lecture, Lambeth Palace, London, 26 April 2007. Islam Christ Muslim Relat 19(3):339–347
Williams R (2010) The finality of Christ in a plural society. https://www.youtube.com/watch?v=0VyMtQsOlKI. Date accessed 7 Feb 2018, http://aoc2013.brix.fatbeehive.com/articles.php/585/the-finality-of-christ-in-a-pluralist-world (date accessed August 2018)
Witte J (2007) The reformation of rights: law, religion and human rights in early modern calvinism. Cambridge University Press, Cambridge

FSC
www.fsc.org
MIX
Papier | Fördert
gute Waldnutzung
FSC® C083411

Kolibri 360 GmbH
Ferdinand-Jühlke-Straße 7
99095 Erfurt, Deutschland
produktsicherheit@kolibri360.de